THE ATLANTIC CRITICAL STUDIES

CHARLES DICKENS'

Hard Times

THE ATLANTIC CRITICAL STUDIES

CHARLES DICKENS'
Hard Times

Pulakesh Ghosh

ATLANTIC
PUBLISHERS & DISTRIBUTORS (P) LTD

Published by
ATLANTIC
PUBLISHERS & DISTRIBUTORS (P) LTD
7/22, Ansari Road, Darya Ganj, New Delhi-110002
Phones : +91-11-40775252, 23273880, 23275880, 23280451
Fax : +91-11-23285873
Web : www.atlanticbooks.com
E-mail : orders@atlanticbooks.com

Branch Office
5, Nallathambi Street, Wallajah Road, Chennai-600002
Phones : +91-44-64611085, 32413319
E-mail : chennai@atlanticbooks.com

Printed in India at Nice Printing Press, A-33/3A, Site-IV, Industrial Area, Sahibabad, Ghaziabad, U.P.

To

Prof. Rama Kundu

Who taught us how to read a novel

General Preface

The Atlantic Critical Studies are study-aids modeled on the study-aids available in England and America, among other places, and are primarily meant for the students of English literature in Indian universities.

However, in consideration of the local conditions and the various constraints under which our students have to study—non-availability of relevant critical books, dearth of foreign and Indian journals, inaccessibility to good, well-equipped libraries, just to mention a few of them—the models have been considerably improved upon, both qualitatively and quantitatively.

Thus, while these Studies are meant to be comprehensive and self-sufficient, the distinguished scholars who have prepared these study materials, have taken special care to combine lucidity and profundity in their treatment of the texts.

The select bibliography at the end is meant not only to acknowledge the sources used but also to help a student in the pursuit of further studies if he/she wants to.

Atlantic Publishers & Distributors believes in quality and excellence. These studies will only reconfirm it.

MOHIT K. RAY
Chief Editor [English Literature]
Atlantic Publishers & Distributors (P) Ltd.,
New Delhi

Contents

1

Introduction: Charles Dickens

> Whatever the word "great" means, Dickens was what it means. Even the fastidious and unhappy who cannot read his books without a continuous critical exasperation, would use the word of him without stopping to think. They feel that Dickens is a great writer even if he is not a good writer. He is treated as a classic; that is, as a king who may now be deserted, but who cannot now be dethroned. The atmosphere of this word clings to him; and the curious thing is that we cannot get it to cling to any of the men of our own generation. "Great" is the first adjective which the most supercilious modern critic would apply to Dickens. And "great" is the last adjective the most supercilious critic would apply to himself. (Chesterton 10-11)

The profoundest of the Dickens critics, Mr. George Gissing, remarks in his criticism on Dickens that the world in which Dickens grew up was a hard and cruel world. He notes its gross feeding, its fierce sports, its fighting and foul humour, and all this he summarizes in the words "hard and cruel". The quintessential difference between the beginning of the nineteenth century and the end of it is a difference simple but huge. If the first period was full of evil things, it was full of hope also. If the second period was even full of good things, it was occupied in asking what was the good of good things. Joy itself became joyless; and the fighting of Cobbett was happier than the feasting of Walter Pater. The men of Cobbett's time were industrious enough to brook and inflict brutality; but they were also sturdy enough to alter it. This "hard and cruel" age was, after all, the age of reform. The gibbet stood up black above them; but it was black against the dawn. This dawn, against which the gibbet and all the old cruelties stood out so black and clear, was the developing idea of the liberalism of the French Revolution. It was a clear and a happy philosophy, and only against such philosophies do evils appear evident at all. If the optimist is a better reformer than the pessimist, the man who believes life to be excellent is the man who alters it most.

It may be said that at the end of the nineteenth century the pessimists could hardly curse even the blackest thing as they could hardly see it against its black and eternal backdrop. Nothing was bad, as everything was bad. Life in prison was infamous—like life anywhere else. The fires of persecution were vile—like the stars. "We perpetually find this paradox of a contented discontent. Dr. Johnson takes too sad a view of humanity, but he is also too satisfied a Conservative. Rousseau takes too rosy a view of humanity, but he causes a revolution. Swift is angry, but a Tory. Shelley is happy, and a rebel. Dickens, the optimist, satirizes the Fleet, and the Fleet is gone. Gissing, the pessimist, satirizes Suburbia, and Suburbia remains" (Chesterton 13). This atmosphere was the atmosphere of the Revolution the principal concern of which was the concern of human equality, and one of the factual and fast consequences of the idea that all men are equal is soon to produce very great men.

"I am a fond father", Dickens says, "to every child of my fancy." No man encouraged his characters so much as Dickens. The ungovernable sense of life which goes along with the old Dickens sense of liberty gives the experience of the best of the revolution. The first of all democratic doctrines is that all men are interesting; although some of his people appear dull people the bores in his books are brighter than the wits in other books. To attempt to imagine Dickens and his life it is a must to imagine the old atmosphere of a democratic optimism—a confidence in common men. When the world first awoke from the mere enchantment of Dickens, from the direct tyranny of his temperament, there was, of course, a reaction. At the head of it appeared the Realists, with their documents, like Miss Flite. They proclaimed that the scenes and types in Dickens were wholly implausible; they were not "like life" and on this rather paradoxical ground Dickens' novels cannot be dubbed literature. The realist for a time prevailed. A more symbolic school of criticism soon followed. Men saw that it was necessary to give a much deeper and more delicate meaning to the expression "like life". Streets are not life, cities and civilizations are not life, faces even and voices are not life itself. Life is within, and no man has seen it at any time. But "Dickens is "like life" in the truer sense, in the sense that he is akin to the living principle in us and in the universe; he is like life, at least in this detail, that he is alive. His art is like life, because, like life, it cares for nothing outside itself, and goes on its way rejoicing" (Chesterton 20). Dickens's art is like life because, like life, it is irresponsible, because, like life, it is incredible.

Dickens has profited as little from the fall of the realists as from their triumph; there has been a revolution, there has been a counter revolution, there has been no restoration. While the Realists were yet living, the art of Dickens was justified by Aubrey Beardsley. But men like Aubrey Beardsley were allowed to be fantastic, because the mood which they overstrained and overstated was a mood which their period perceived. The impossibilities of Dickens seem much more impossible than they really are, because they are already attuned to the opposite impossibilities of Maeterlinck. For every mood there is an appropriate impossibility fitted to the frame of mind. Every train of thought may end in any ecstasy, and all roads lead to Elfland. But few walk far enough along the street of Dickens to find the place where the cockney villas grow so comic that they become poetical.

The whole story of Dickens's life moves like a Canterbury pilgrimage along the great roads of Kent. He was born at Landport, in Portsea, on February 7, 1812. His father, John Dickens, was a clerk in the Navy Pay-office, and was temporarily on duty in the neighbourhood. After Dickens's birth, the family moved for a short period to Norfolk Street, Bloomsbury, and then for a long period to Chatham, which thus became the real home, and for all serious purposes, the native place of Dickens. He was born and grew up in a paradise of small prosperity. He fell into the family during one of its well off periods, and he never in those early days of life thought of himself as anything but as a comfortable middle-class child, the son of a comfortable middle-class father. His father seemed, most probably, a hearty and kindly character, a little florid of speech, a little careless of duty in some details, notably in the detail of education. His neglect of Dickens's mental training in later and more trying times was a sort of unconscious selfishness which remained a little acrimoniously in Dickens' mind through life.

Dickens's father found it more amusing to be an audience than to be an instructor; and instead of giving the child intellectual pleasure, called upon him, almost before he was out of petticoats, to provide it. "Some of the earliest glimpses we have of Charles Dickens show him to us perched on some chair or table singing comic songs in an atmosphere of perpetual applause. So, almost as soon as he can toddle, he steps into the glare of the footlights. He never stepped out of it until he died. He was a good man, as men go in this bewildering world of ours, brave, transparent, tender-hearted, scrupulously independent and honourable; he was not a man whose weaknesses should be spoken of without some delicacy and doubt. But there did mingle with his merits all his life this theatrical quality, this atmosphere of being shown off—a sort of hilarious self-consciousness. His literary life was a triumphal procession; he died drunken with glory" (Chesterton 27).

Dickens had all his life the faults of the little boy who is kept up too late at night. The boy in such a case exhibits a psychological paradox; he is a little too irritable because he is a little too happy. Dickens was always a little too irritable because he was a little too happy. Like the over-wrought child in society, he was splendidly sociable, and yet suddenly quarrelsome. In all the practical relations of his life he was what the child is in the last hours of an evening. He was thrown back perpetually upon the pleasures of the intelligence, and they started burning in his head like a pent and painful furnace. In his own peculiarly lively way he has described how he crawled up into an unconsidered garret, and there found, in a dusty heap, the undying literature of England. The books he mentions chiefly are *Humphrey Clinker* and *Tom Jones*. When he opened those two books in the garret he caught hold of the only past with which he is at all connected, the great comic writers of England of whom he was fated to be the last.

Dickens' happy boyhood got a thunder-bolt when his lordly father was a bankrupt, and in the Marshalsea prison. So long as John Dickens was in easy days of family life, he seemed an easy man, a little long and luxuriant in his phrases, a little careless in his business routine. He seemed only a wordy man, who lived on bread and beef like his neighbours; but as bread and beef were taken away from him, it was found that he lived on words. His mother was passionately proclaiming herself the principal of a girl's school, a girl's school to which nobody would go. And he himself, the conqueror of the world and the prospective purchaser of Gads-hill, passed some distracted and bewildering days in pawning the household necessities to Fagins in foul shops. He had been hurriedly flung into the factory by James Lamert, a relation of his mother's. It was a blacking factory. He found himself in the great dreary factory, pasting the same kinds of labels on to the same kinds of blacking-bottles from morning till night. The coarseness of the whole thing—the work, the rooms, the boys, the language—was a sort of bestial nightmare to young Dickens, excessively intellectualized, and at this time, excessively egotistical. All day he worked on insufficient food at the factory. The external oppression, the material circumstances by which he was surrounded caused his internal depression. It afterwards appeared in his works as Murdstone and Grinby's in *David Copperfield*. He scarcely spoke of it then, and he scarcely spoke of it afterwards. While in the fullness of his fame, Forster once told him that a man had spoken of knowing him. On hearing the name, he somewhat curtly acknowledged it, and spoke of having seen the man once. Forster innocently answered that the man said he had seen Dickens many times in a factory by Hungerford Market. Dickens was suddenly struck with a long and extraordinary silence. Then he invited Forster, as his best friend, to a particular interview, and told him the whole story for the first and the last time. He told the world some part of the matter in the account of Murdstone and Grinby's in *David Copperfield*. He never spoke of the whole experience except once or twice, and he never spoke of it otherwise than as a man might speak of hell. Dickens, in *David Copperfield*, called his father Wilkins Micawber. In his personal circle he called him the Prodigal Father.

At night Dickens came back disconsolately to a lodging-house kept by an old lady who appeared afterwards as Mrs. Pipchin. Once a week only he saw anybody for whom he cared a straw; that was when he went to the Marshalsea prison, and that gave his juvenile pride, half manly and half snobbish, bitter annoyance of another kind. Physically he was always very weak and never very well. Once he was struck down in the middle of his work with sudden bodily pain. The boy who worked next to him, a coarse and heavy lad named Bob Fagin who was averse to Dickens suddenly showed that enduring sanity of compassion which Dickens had shown many times in the characters of the common and unclean. Fagin made a bed for sick Dickens out of the straw in the workroom, and filled empty blacking bottles with hot water all day. When the evening came, and Dickens was somewhat recovered, Bob Fagin insisted on escorting the boy home to his father. "The situation was as poignant as a sort of tragic farce. Fagin in his wooden-headed chivalry would have died in order to take Dickens to his family; Dickens in his bitter gentility would have died rather than let Fagin know that his family were in the Marshalsea. So these two young idiots tramped the tedious streets, both stubborn, both suffering for an idea. The advantage certainly was with Fagin, who was suffering for a Christian compassion, while Dickens was suffering for a pagan pride. At last Dickens flung off his friend with desperate farewell and thanks, and dashed up the steps of a strange house on the Surrey side. He knocked and rang as Bob Fagin, his benefactor and his incubus, disappeared round the corner. And when the servant came to open the door, he asked, apparently with gravity, whether Mr. Robert Fagin lived there. It is a strange touch. The immortal Dickens woke in him for an instant in that last wild joke of that weary evening. Next morning, however, he was again well enough to make himself ill again, and the wheels of the great factory went on. They manufactured a number of bottles of Warren's Blacking, and in the course of the process they manufactured also the greatest optimist of the nineteenth century" (Chesterton 35-36).

Dickens who dropped down groaning at his work, who was hungry four or five times a week, whose best feelings and worst feelings were alike flayed alive, was the man on whom some comfortable critics have unhasitatingly complained that his view of life was too rosy to be anything but unreal. It is true that he was a dreamy child, thinking mostly of his own dreary prospects. But he saw and remembered much of the streets and squares he passed. Indeed he went the right way to work unconsciously to do so. There are details in Dickens' descriptions—a window, or a railing, or the keyhole of a door —which he endows with vibrant force of life. The things seem more real than things really are. Indeed, that degree of realism does not exist in reality; it is the unbearable realism of a dream. And this kind of realism can only be gained by walking dreamily in a place; it cannot be gained by walking observantly. The little Dickens Dickensized London.

Dickens was in the habit of visiting his father at the Marshalsea every week. The talks between the two must have been a comedy at once more cruel and more delicate than Dickens ever described. Ostensibly the cause of Charles's ultimate liberation was a quarrel between his father and Lamert, the head of the factory. His mother, with a touch of strange harshness, was for patching up the quarrel and sending him back. Perhaps, with the fierce feminine responsibility, she felt that the first necessity was to keep the family out of debt. But old John Dickens put his foot down here. The boy was miserable; the boy was clever; the boy should go to school. He went to the Wellington House Academy, Mornington Place. It was a fantastic experience for Dickens to go from the world to a school, instead of going from school to the world. Dickens, we may say, had his boyhood after his youth. He had seen life at its coarsest before he began his training for it, and knew the worst words in the English language probably before the best. He retained this odd chronology in his semi-autobiographical account of the adventures of David Copperfield, who went into the business of Murdstone and Grinby's before he went to the school kept by Dr. Strong. David Copperfield, also, went to be carefully prepared for a world that he had seen already.

Somebody once asked old John Dickens where his son Charles was educated. "Well, really", said John Dickens, in his spacious way, "he may be said—ah—to have educated himself." After leaving school, Dickens found employment as a clerk to Mr. Blackmore, a solicitor, as one of those inconspicuous under-clerks whom he afterwards turned to many grotesque uses. Here, no doubt, he met Lowten and Swiveller, Chuckster and Wobbler, in so far as such sacred creatures ever had embodiments on this lower earth. But, it is typical of him that he had no fancy at all to remain a solicitor's clerk. The resolution to rise which had glowed in him even as a dawdling boy, when he gazed at Gads-hill, which had been darkened but not quite destroyed by his fall into the factory routine, which had been released again by his return to normal boyhood and the boundaries of school, was not likely to content itself now with the copying out of agreements. He set to work, without any advice or help, to learn to be a reporter. He worked all day at law, and all night at shorthand. It is an art which can only be effected by time, and he had to effect it by overtime. But learning the thing under every disadvantage, without a teacher, without the possibility of concentration or complete mental force, without ordinary human sleep, he made himself one of the most rapid reporters then alive. There is a curious contrast between the casualness of the mental training to which his parents and others subjected him and the savage seriousness of the training to which he subjected himself.

Dickens was only nineteen when he began to report in the House of Commons. Dickens succeeded in becoming a shorthand writer; succeeded in becoming a reporter; succeeded ultimately in becoming a highly effective journalist. He was appointed a reporter of the speeches in Parliament, first by *The True Son*, then by *The Mirror of Parliament*, and last by *The Morning Chronicle*. He went into the reporter's gallery full of the triumphant Radicalism which was then the rising tide of the world. His restless nature found more pleasure in the wandering side of journalism. He went about wildly in post-chaises to report political meetings for the *Morning Chronicle*. All this time the creative part of his mind had been in a stir or even a fever. While still a small boy he had written for his own amusement some sketches of queer people he had met; notably, one of his uncle's barber, whose principal hobby was pointing out what Napoleon ought to have done in the matter of military tactics. He had a notebook full of such sketches. He had sketches not only of persons, but of places, which were to him almost more personal than persons. In the December of 1833 he published one of these fragments in the *Old Monthly Magazine*. This was followed by nine others in the same paper, and when the paper (which was a romantically Radical venture, run by a veteran soldier of Bolivar) itself collapsed, Dickens continued the series in the *Evening Chronicle*, an off-shoot of the morning paper of the same name. These were the pieces afterwards published and known as the *Sketches by Boz*; and with them Dickens enters literature. Dickens adopted the pseudonym, Boz. The *Sketches*, apart from splendid splashes of humour here and there, might not manifestations of the man of genius, yet it did make his fame. His contemporaries could see a new spirit in it. The *Sketches by Boz* stand out very symbolically in the life of Dickens. They constitute in a manner the dedication of him to his especial task; the sympathetic and yet exaggerated painting of the poorer middle-class. He was to make men feel that this dull middle-class was actually a kind of elf-land.

Dickens was married on April 2, 1836. Forster remarks that a few days before the announcement of their marriage in the *Times*, the same paper contained another announcement that on the 31st would be published the first number of a work called *The Posthumous Papers of the Pickwick Club*. It is the beginning of his career. *Pickwick*, indeed, "is not a good novel; but it is not a bad novel, for it is not a novel at all.... This is not a novel, for all novels have an end; and "Pickwick", properly speaking, has no end..." (Chesterton 65). As it happens, the book ends after Mr. Pickwick has taken a house in the neighbourhood of Dulwich. But he did not stop there. Mr. Pickwick was still having the same high adventures on the same high roads. He broke out, that he took again the road of the high adventures; we know that if we take it ourselves in any acre of England, we may come suddenly upon him in a lane.

As the world advances through history towards its present epoch, it becomes more specialist, less democratic, and folklore turns gradually into fiction. For ages after our characters have dressed up in the clothes of mortals they betray the blood of the gods. Even the phraseology is full of relics of this. When a modern novel is devoted to the bewilderments of a weak young clerk who cannot decide which woman he wants to marry, or which new religion he believes in, we still give this knock kneed cad the name of "the hero"—the name which is the crown of Achilles. The popular preference for a story with "a happy ending" is not, or at least was not, a mere sweet-stuff optimism; it is the remains of the old idea of the triumph of the dragon-slayer, the ultimate apotheosis of the man beloved of heaven.

Dickens answered with the same ingenious self-justification as in the other cases—that surely it often happened that a man met us first arrayed in his more grotesque qualities, and that fuller acquaintance unfolded his more serious merits. This, of course, is quite true; but any honest admirer of *Pickwick* will feel that it is not an answer. For the fault in *Pickwick* (if it be a fault) is a change not in the hero but in the whole atmosphere. The point is not that Pickwick turns into a different kind of man; it is that *The Pickwick Papers* turns into a different kind of book. And however artistic both parts may be, this combination must, in strict art, be called inartistic.

Pickwick is a romance of adventure, and Samuel Pickwick is the romantic adventurer. But the strange and stirring discovery which Dickens made was this—that having chosen a fat old man of the middle classes as a good thing of which to make a butt, he found that a fat old man of middle classes is the very best thing of which to make a romantic adventurer. *Pickwick* is supremely original in that it is the adventures of an old man. It is a fairy tale in which the victor is not the youngest of three brothers, but one of the oldest of their uncles. The result is both noble and new and true. There is nothing which so much needs simplicity as adventure. And there is no one who so much possesses simplicity as an honest and elderly man of business. For romance he is better than a troop of young troubadours; for the swaggering young fellow anticipates his adventures, just as he anticipates his income. Hence both the adventures and the income, when he comes up to them, are not there. But a man in late middle-age has grown used to the plain necessities, and his first-holiday is a second youth.

Samuel Pickwick in his youth was probably an insufferable young coxcomb. He knew then, or thought he knew, all about the confidence trick of swindlers like Jingle. He knew then, or thought he knew, all about the amatory designs of sly ladies like Mrs. Bardell. But years and real life relieved him of this idle and evil knowledge. He has had the high good luck in losing the follies of youth to lose the wisdom of youth also. Dickens has caught, in a manner at once wild and convincing, this queer innocence of the afternoon of life. The round, moon-like face, the round, moon-like spectacles of Samuel Pickwick move through the tale as emblems of a certain spherical simplicity. They are fixed in that grave surprise that may be seen in babies; that grave surprise which is the only real happiness that is possible to man. Pickwick's round face is like a round and honourable mirror, in which are reflected all the fantasies of earthly existence; for surprise is, strictly speaking, the only kind of reflection. All this grew gradually on Dickens. It is odd to recall to our minds the original plan, the plan of the Nimrod Club, and the author who was to be wholly occupied in playing practical jokes on his characters. He had chosen that corpulent old simpleton as a person peculiarly fitted to fall down trap-doors, to shoot over butter slides, to struggle with apple-pie beds, to be tipped out of carts and dipped into horse-ponds. But Dickens, and Dickens only, discovered as he went on how fitted the fat old man was to rescue ladies, to defy tyrants, to dance, to leap, to experiment with life, to be a *deus ex machina* and even a knight errant. Dickens made this discovery. Dickens went into the Pickwick Club to scoff, and Dickens remained to pray.

If Dickens was a great event in English literature, he was a great event in English history also. If he had not his place with Fielding and Thackeray, he would still have his place with Wat Tyler and Wilkes; for the man led a mob. A man reading the Dickens novel wished that it might never end. Men read a Dickens story six times because they knew it so well. The Dickens novel was popular, not because it was an unreal world, but because it was a real world; a world in which the soul could live. In reaching the period of the publication of *Pickwick,* we reach this sudden apotheosis of Dickens. Henceforward he filled the literary world in a way hard to imagine. The man in the street has more memories of Dickens, whom he has not read, than of Marie Corelli, whom he has. There is nothing in any way parallel to this omnipresence and vitality in the great comic characters of Boz. If Dickens brought in a man merely to carry a letter, he had time for a touch or two, and made him a giant. Dickens not only conquered the world, he conquered it with minor characters. In dealing with Dickens, we are dealing with a man whose public success was a marvel and almost a monstrosity.

Dickens did not write what the people wanted. Dickens wanted what the people wanted. And with this was connected that other fact which must never be forgotten, that Dickens and his school had a hilarious faith in democracy and thought of the service of it as a sacred priesthood. Hence, there was this vital point in his popularism, that there was no condescension in it. He approached the people like a deity and poured out his riches and his blood. This is what makes the immortal bond between him and the masses of men. He had not merely produced something they could understand, but he took it seriously, and toiled and agonized to produce it. His power, then, lay in the fact that he expressed with an energy and brilliancy quite uncommon the things close to the common mind. But the common mind means the mind of all the artists and heroes; or else it would not be common. Plato had the common mind; Dante had the common mind; or that mind was not common.

In order of artistic value, next after his humour, comes his horror. And both his humour and his horror are of a kind strictly to be called human; that is, they belong to the basic part of us, below the lowest roots of our variety. His horror for instance is a healthy churchyard horror, a fear of the grotesque defamation called death; and this every man has, even if he also has the more delicate and depraved fears that come of an evil spiritual outlook.

Pickwick is coherently comic and consistently rambling. If his natural turn for terrors was kept down in *Pickwick,* his natural turn for joy and laughter is kept down in *Oliver Twist.* In *Oliver Twist* the smoke of the thieves' kitchen hangs over the whole tale, and the shadow of Fagin falls everywhere. The little lamp-lit rooms of Mr. Brownlow and Rose Maylie are to all appearance purposely kept subordinate, a mere foil to the foul darkness without. *Oliver Twist* had begun in Bentley's *Miscellany*, which Dickens edited in 1837. It was interrupted by a blow that for the moment broke the author's spirit and seemed to have broken his heart. His wife's sister, Mary Hogarth, died suddenly. To Dickens his wife's family seems to have been like his own; his affections were heavily committed to the sisters, and of this one he was peculiarly fond. He took up the work of *Oliver Twist* again later in the year, and finished it at the end of 1838. His work was incessant and almost bewildering. In 1838, he had already brought out the first number of *Nicholas Nickleby*. But the whole world was roaring for books by Dickens, and more books by Dickens, and Dickens was labouring night and day like a factory.

Nicholas Nickleby is perhaps the most typical of the tone of his earlier works. In form it is a very rambling, old-fashioned romance, the kind of romance in which the hero is only a convenience for the frustration of the villain. Nicholas is what is called in theatricals a stick. But any stick is good enough to beat a Squeers with. The wicked aristocrats, Sir Mulberry Hawk, Lord Verisopht and the rest are inadequate versions of the fashionable profligate. But this is not because Dickens in his vulgarity could not comprehend the refinement of patrician vice. There is no idea more vulgar or more ignorant than the notion that a gentleman is generally what is called refined. The error of the Hawk conception is that he is too refined. Real aristocratic blackguards do not swagger and rant so well. A real fast baronet would not have defied Nicholas in the tavern with so much oratorical dignity. A real fast baronet would probably have been choked with apoplectic embarrassment and said nothing at all. But Dickens read into this aristocracy a grandiloquence and a natural poetry which, like all melodrama, is really the precious jewel of the poor.

An exquisitely characteristic of Dickens is that the truly great achievement of the story is the person who delays the story. Mrs. Nickleby, with her beautiful mazes of memory, does her best to prevent the story of Nicholas Nickleby from being told. If Mrs. Nickleby is a fool, she is one of those fools who are wiser than the world. She stands for a great truth, the truth that experience is not in real life a saddening thing at all. The people who have had misfortunes are generally the people who love to talk about them. Experience is really one of the gaieties of old age, one of its dissipations. Mere memory becomes a kind of debauch. Experience may be disheartening to those who are foolish enough to try to co-ordinate it and to draw deductions from it. To happy souls like Mrs. Nickleby relevancy is nothing, and the whole of their past life is like an inexhaustible fairyland.

Dickens liked to have story within story. In this spirit he wished *Master Humphrey's Clock* to begin, and to be a big frame or bookcase for numberless novels. The clock started; but the clock stopped. *Master Humphrey's Clock* is now scarcely known except as the shell of one of the well-known novels. His *The Old Curiosity Shop* was published in accordance with the original *Clock* scheme. Perhaps the most typical thing about it is the title as to why the story should be called after the Old Curiosity Shop. Only two of the characters have anything to do with such a shop, and they leave it for ever in the first few pages. But we realize after a second thought that this title is something in the nature of a key to the whole Dickens romance. His tales always started from some splendid hint in the streets. And shops, perhaps the most poetical of all things, often set off his fancy galloping. Every shop, in fact, was to him the door of romance.

Around *Little Nell,* of course, a controversy raged and rages; some implored Dickens not to kill her at the end of the story. Some regret that he did not kill her at the beginning. The chief interest in this young person lies in the fact that she is an example, and the most celebrated example of what must have been a personal peculiarity, perhaps, a personal experience of Dickens.

In 1841 Dickens supplied *Barnaby Rudge*. It is an embodiment of the picturesque or even the pictorial element in Dickens. Barnaby Rudge, the idiot with his rags and his feathers and his raven, the bestial hangman, the blind mob—all make a picture, though they hardly make a novel. It is the next bubble in the pot, the next thing that burst out of that whirling, seething head. The tide of it rose and smoked and sang till it boiled over the Pot of Britain and poured over all America. In the January of 1842 he set out for the United States.

Dickens was a fierce democrat, but in his best vein he laughed at the cocksure Radical of common life, the red-faced man who said, "Prove it!" when anybody said anything. He fought for the right to elect: but he would not whitewash elections. He believed in Parliamentary government; but he did not pretend that Parliament is something much more heroic and imposing than it is. He fought for the rights of the grossly oppressed Nonconformists; but he spat out of his mouth the unction of that too easy seriousness with which they oiled everything, and held up to them like a horrible mirror the foul fat face of Chadband. He saw that Mr. Podsnap thought too little of places outside England. But he saw that Mrs. Jellaby thought too much of them. Dogmatic as he was, he never tied himself to any passing dogma. "He never admitted that economically, we must make hells of workhouses, any more than Rousseau would have admitted it. He never said the State had no right to teach children or save their bones, any more than Danton would have said it. He was a fierce Radical, but he was never a Manchester Radical. He used the test of Utility, but he was never a Utilitarian. While economists were writing soft words he wrote *Hard Times*, which Macaulay called "sullen socialism", because it was not complacent Whiggism. But Dickens was never a Socialist any more than he was an Individualist; and, whatever else he was, he certainly was not sullen. He was not even a politician of any kind. He was simply a man of very clear, airy judgment on things that did not inflame his private temper, and he perceived that any theory that tried to run the living State entirely on one force and motive was probably nonsense. Whenever the Liberal philosophy had embedded in it something hard and heavy and lifeless, by an instinct he dropped it out. He was too romantic, perhaps, but he would have to do only with real things. He may have cared too much about Liberty. But he cared nothing about "*Laissez-Faire*" (Chesterton 101-02).

With a more than American coolness, and a more than American impudence he sat down and wrote *Martin Chuzzlewit*. He wrote the notes of the American part of *Martin Chuzzlewit* while he was still in America; but it was a later decision presumably that such impressions should go into a book, and it was little better than an afterthought that they should go into *Martin Chuzzlewit.* In January, 1843, appeared the first number of the novel called *Martin Chuzzlewit.* In the July of 1844 Dickens went on an Italian tour, which he afterwards summarized in the book called *Pictures from Italy.* In the May of 1846 he ran over to Switzerland and tried to write *Dombey and Son* at Lausanne. He could not get on. He attributed this especially to his love of London and his loss of it, "the absence of streets and numbers of figures.... My figures seem disposed to stagnate without crowds about them." But he also attributed it more generally to the laxer and more wandering life he had led for the last two years, the American tour, the Italian tour, diversified only with slight literary productions. His ways were never punctual or healthy, but they were also never unconscientious as far as work was concerned. *Dombey and Son,* planned in all probability some time before, was destined to be the last of a quite definite series, the early novels of Dickens. *Dombey and Son* is the last novel in the first manner: *David Copperfield* is the first novel in the last. Yet even in *Dombey and Son* we can see the glimpse of a change, however faint, if we compare it with his first fantasies such as *Nicholas Nickleby* or *The Old Curiosity Shop*. The central story is still melodrama, but it is much more tactful and effective melodrama. Dickens gives us good ringing dialogue, very different from the mere rants in which Ralph Nickleby figures in the unimaginable character of a rhetorical moneylender. The book has not only a basic idea, but a good basic idea. There is a real artistic opportunity in the conception of a solemn and selfish man of affairs, feeling for his male heir, his first and last emotion, mingled of a thin flame of tenderness and a strong flame of pride. But with all these possibilities, the serious episode of the Dombeys serves ultimately only to show how fitted Dickens was for something opposite. *Dombey*, however, means first and foremost the finale of the early Dickens. This is the last farce; this is the last work in which a farcical license is tacitly claimed, a farcical note struck to start with. And in a sense his next novel may be called his first novel. But the growth of this great novel, *David Copperfield*, is a thing very interesting, but at the same time very dark, for it is a growth in the soul. "...Dickens's mind was in a stir of change; that he was dreaming of art, and even of realism. Hugely delighted as he invariably was with his own books, he was humble enough to be ambitious. He was even humble enough to be envious. In the matter of art, for instance, in the narrower sense, of arrangement and proportion in fictitious things, he began to be conscious of his deficiency, and even, in a stormy sort of way, ashamed of it; he tried to gain completeness even while raging at any one who called him incomplete. And in this matter of artistic construction, his ambition (and his success too) grew steadily up to the instant of his death. The end finds him attempting things that are at the opposite pole to the frank formlessness of "Pickwick". His last book, "The Mystery of Edwin Drood", depends entirely upon construction, even upon a centralized strategy. He staked everything upon a plot; he who had been the weakest of plotters, weaker than Sim Tappertit. He essayed a detective story, he who could never keep a secret; and he has kept it to this day. A new Dickens was really being born when Dickens died" (Chesterton 144-45).

Although there are many aspects of *David Copperfield*, the autobiographical aspect is the greatest. Unlike all the other books of Dickens, it is concerned with quite common actualities, but it is concerned with them warmly and with the war-like sympathies. It is not only both realistic and romantic; it is realistic because it is romantic. It is human nature described with the human exaggeration. All the characters seem a little larger than they really were, for David is looking up at them. And the early pages of the book are in particular astonishingly vivid. Dickens has excellently depicted the child enthroned in that humble circle which only in after years he perceives to have been humble. The early youth of David Copperfield is psychologically almost as good as his childhood. Dickens pierced the very core of the sensibility of boyhood. It was when he made David more afraid of a manservant than of anybody or anything else. The lowering Murdstone, the awful Mrs. Steerforth are not so alarming to him as Mr. Littimer, the unimpeachable gentleman's gentleman.

If *Dombey and Son* is the book before the transition and *David Copperfield* is typical of the transition itself, *Bleak House* is the book after the transition. *Bleak House* has every characteristic of his new realistic culture. The strong traces of an increase in social experience can be perceived in the book. Dickens began to understand something of what is strong and what is weak in the English upper class. Sir Leicester Dedlock is a far more effective condemnation of oligarchy than the ugly swagger of Sir Mulberry Hawk, because pride stands out more plainly in all its impotence and insolence as the one weakness of a good man, than as one of the million weaknesses of a bad one. Dickens, like all young Radicals, had imagined in his youth that aristocracy rested upon the hardness of somebody; he found that it rests upon the softness of everybody. It is very hard not to like Sir Leicester Dedlock, not to applaud his silly old speeches, so foolish, so manly, so genuinely English, so disastrous to England.

Dickens's next important book, after *Bleak House,* was *Hard Times* which strikes an almost unexpected note of severity. The characters are indeed exaggerated but they are bitterly and deliberately exaggerated; they are not exaggerated with the old unconscious high spirits of Nicholas Nickleby or Martin Chuzzlewit.

Dickens's *A Tale of Two Cities* (1859) was inspired by Carlyle's monumental account of French Revolution and planned with an intricate artifice suggestive of Wilkie Collins, the chief among the group of young authors enlisted by Dickens as contributors to *Household Words*. About it there is a grandiosity, as though Dickens had set himself to a task on lines to which his admirers were unaccustomed. There is too much of mystery and melodrama; but the opening scene in the stagecoach, the pictures of the bloodthirsty women of the Parisian proletariat, and the death of Sydney Carton have secured places in the memory of readers.

Great Expectations (1860-61) is told with a consistency and quietude of individuality which is rare in Dickens. But so far had he travelled along the road of a heavier reality, that he even intended to give the tale an unhappy ending, making Pip lose Estella for ever; and he was only dissuaded from it by the robust romanticism of Bulwer Lytton. But the best part of the tale—the account of the vacillations of the hero between the humble life to which he owes everything, and the gorgeous life from which he expects something, touches a very true and somewhat tragic part of morals; for the great paradox of morality is that the very vilest kind of fault is exactly the most easy kind (Chesterton 175).

In his *Our Mutual Friend* (1865) the plot is a tissue of crossed motives. The satire on snobbery and social ambitions is more heavy-handed than it had been in *Little Dorrit*. The powerful delineation of Headstone's tragic passion for Lizzie Hexam and the magnificent opening scene on the Thames demand special attention.

The Mystery of Edwin Drood (1870) was perhaps the most ambitious book that Dickens ever attempted. It is a detective story, and certainly a very successful one. *Edwin Drood* is not finished; for in the very middle of it Dickens died.

The key of the great characters of Dickens is that they are all great fools. There is the same difference between a great fool and a small fool as there is between a great poet and a small poet. The great fool is a being who is above wisdom rather than below it. A man can be entirely great while he is entirely foolish. We see this in the epic heroes, such as Achilles. We see this in all the great comic characters of all the great comic writers of whom Dickens was one. Almost all the characters of Dickens are colourful and alive—pompous hypocrites like Mr. Chadband in *Bleak House* and Mr. Pecksniff in *Martin Chuzzlewit*; snobs like Mrs. Merdle in *Little Dorrit* and the Veneerings in *Our Mutual Friend*; simple and likeable characters like Wemmick in *Great Expectations*; clever rogues like Sam Weller in *Pickwick* and Dick Swiveller in *The Old Curiosity Shop*; kindly and honest folk like Joe Gargery in *Great Expectations* and the Peggottys in *David Coperfield*; jolly old fellows like Captain Cuttle in *Dombey and Son* and the Cheeryble brothers in *Nicholas Nickleby*—all these mix with the normal characters whose adventures provide the plots of the novels, with grotesques like Mrs. Gummidge and Mr. Dick in *David Copperfield*, and with the giants of comedy like Mr. Micwaber and Mr. Pickwick himself.

Nobody in the world was ever less optimistic than Dickens in his treatment of evil or the evil man. Nobody ever made less attempt to whitewash evil than Dickens. Nobody black was ever less white than Dickens' black. If optimism means a general approval, the more a man becomes an optimist the more he becomes a melancholy man. Dickens knew very well the essential truth, that the true optimist can only continue an optimist so long as he is discontented. For the full value of this life can only be got by fighting; the violent take it by storm. Dickens was of all the Victorian novelists the man of the most comprehensive soul. He saw life, as no earlier novelist had seen it, from the point of view of the poor of a great city. His basic belief in the primary benevolent impulses of man—affection, charity, gaiety, fun, kindliness, spontaneity—brought within the compass of his sympathy any man or woman in whom he discerned the working of these impulses.

A SHORT OUTLINE OF DICKENS CHRONOLOGY

1812 (7 Feb.) Born at Landport, Hants, to John and Elizabeth Dickens.

1816-17 London.

1817-22 Chatham, Kent; early education.

1823 London.

1824 John Dickens in Marshalsea Debtors' Prison; Dickens employed in Warren's blacking warehouse.

1824-27 At Wellington House Academy.

1827-28 Employed as solicitors' clerk.

1829-31 A shorthand reporter, at Doctors' Commons; on *Mirror of Parliament;* on *True Sun.*

1833-34 First stories published in *Monthly Magazine.*

1834 (Aug.) – 1836 (Nov.) Reporter on *Morning Chronicle*; sketches published, collected as *Sketches by Boz*, two series, Feb. and Dec. 1836.

1836 (April) – 1837 (Nov.) *Pickwick Papers* (monthly).

(2 April) Marries Catherine Hogarth; lives at Furnival's Inn.

1837 (Jan.) – 1839 (Jan.) Edits *Bentley's Miscellany* (monthly, including *Oliver Twist*—published complete Nov. 1838).

(April) – 1839 (Dec.) At 48 Doughty Street.

(7 May) Mary Hogarth dies.

1838 (April) – 1839 (Oct.) *Nicholas Nickleby* (monthly).

1839 (Dec.) Moves to 1 Devonshire Terrace.

1840-41 *Master Humphrey's Clock* (weekly), including *The Old Curiosity Shop* and *Barnaby Rudge*; also monthly, April 1840-Nov. 1841.

1842 (Jan. – June) In North America. *American Notes* (Oct.).

1843 (Jan.) – 1844 (July) *Martin Chuzzlewit* (monthly).

(Dec.) *A Christmas Carol.*

1844 (July) – 1845 (June) Living in Italy.

(Dec.) *The Chimes.*

1845 (Sept.) First performance by the Amateurs; others in 1846-48, 1850-51.

(Oct.) – 1846 (March) Planning, editing and contributing to *Daily News.*

(Dec.) *The Cricket on the Hearth.*

1846 (May) *Pictures from Italy.*

(June – Nov.) Living in Switzerland.

(Oct.) – 1848 (April) *Dombey and Son* (monthly).

(Nov.) – 1847 (Feb.) Living in Paris.

(Dec.) *The Battle of Life.*

1847 (Nov.) Miss Coutts's 'Home for Homeless Women' opened.

1848 (Dec.) *The Haunted Man.*

1849 (May) – 1850 (Nov.) *David Copperfield* (monthly).

1850 (March) Starts *Household Words* (weekly), editing and contributing regularly.

1851 (Oct.) Moves to Tavistock House.

1852 (March) – 1853 (Sept.) *Bleak House* (monthly).

1854 (April – Aug.) *Hard Times* (weekly).

1855 (Dec.) – 1857 (June) *Little Dorrit* (monthly).

1856 (March) Buys Gad's Hill Place, Kent.

1858 (April) Begins public readings.

(May) Separates from Mrs. Dickens.

1859 (April – Nov.) *A Tale of Two Cities* (weekly and monthly).

(May) *All The Year Round* begins.

(June) *Household Words* ends.

1860 *The Uncommercial Traveller.*

(Oct.) Final removal to Gad's Hill Place.

1860 (Dec.) – 1861 (Aug.) *Great Expectations* (weekly).

1864 (May) – 1865 (Nov.) *Our Mutual Friend* (monthly).

1867 (Nov.) – 1868 (April) Public reading tour in USA.

1869 (April) Breakdown in provincial reading tour.

1870 (Jan. – March) Farewell season of public readings in London.

(April – Sept.) *The Mystery of Edwin Drood* (monthly; unfinished).

(9 June) Dies at Gad's Hill Place.

2

Hard Times: The Story Outline

The owner of an experimental private school in Coketown, Thomas Gradgrind, insists on teaching 'Facts' and 'Facts only'. Thomas Gradgrind, a 'man of realities,' is a man of 'facts and calculations.' He is a man always to proceed upon the principle that 'two and two are four, and nothing over.' With a rule and a pair of scales, and the multiplication table always in his pocket he is ready to weigh and measure 'any parcel of human nature.' Human nature is a mere question of figures, a case of simple arithmetic, to him. His keen feeling is that fancy and imagination have nothing to do with in a person's life and fact is everything. His own children are the models of his fact-oriented teaching. Even they are not allowed to learn nursery-rhymes and fairy-tales.

Mr. Bounderby is almost Mr. Gradgrind's bosom friend. Mr. Bounderby is a man perfectly devoid of sentiment. He believes that spiritual relationship towards another man is perfectly devoid of sentiment. He is a rich man: banker, merchant, manufacturer, and what not. He is a big, loud man with a stare, and a metallic laugh. He is a man made out of a coarse material, which seems to have been stretched to make so much of him. He is a man who could never sufficiently vaunt himself a self-made man. He is a man who is always proclaiming his old ignorance and his old poverty. He is a man who is the Bully of humility. A year or two younger than Mr. Gradgrind, Mr. Bounderby looks older.

To his utter surprise, one day while returning home from the school, Gradgrind sees his children, Louisa and Tom, trying to peep through the canvas-wall of a circus tent. He feels shocked to observe that his children are not sorry for going against the principles taught to them. After this surprising discovery, Gradgrind and his industrialized friend Mr. Josiah Bounderby start discussing as to the loophole which has caused such a disgrace. They concede that Louisa's schoolmate Sissy Jupe whose father is a stroller in the circus might have affected the children and induced them to enjoy circus. So, they decide to dismiss Sissy from the school to have precautionary measures against the possible influence on all the students of the school. Gradgrind and Bounderby set out to see Sissy's father. But reaching the place where Sissy's father stays they find him missing and come to learn that he has deserted his daughter and gone away. Gradgrind feels moved to see Sissy's plight and he decides to keep her under his tutelage and educate her in the condition that none from the circus party will seek to communicate with Sissy. Bounderby cannot agree with Gradgrind's decision as he thinks that Sissy would lay an obnoxous effect upon Gradgrind's children.

Mr. Bounderby is a bachelor. An elderly lady, Mrs. Sparsit, presides over his establishment, in consideration of a certain annual stipend. She is a prominent figure in attendance on Mr. Bounderby's car, as it rolls along in triumph with the 'Bully of humility', Mr. Bounderby, inside. Mrs. Sparsit is a highly connected lady. She has a great aunt living in those very times called Lady Scadgers. Mr. Sparsit, deceased, of whom she is the relict, has been by the mother's side what Mrs. Sparsit calls "a Powler". The late Mr. Sparsit, being by the mother's side a Powler, married the lady, being by the father's side a Scadgers. Lady Scadgers contrived the marriage. Mr. Sparsit inherits a fair fortune from his uncle, but owed it all before he came into it, and spent it twice over immediately afterwards. When he died, at twenty-four (the scene of his decease, Calais, and the cause, brandy), he did not leave his widow in affluent circumstances. And they had been separated soon after the honeymoon.

Sissy comes to stay at Gradgrind's house, Stone Lodge. There has been so little communication between Louisa and Sissy—both because life at Stone Lodge goes on monotonously round like a piece of machinery which discourages human interference, and because of the prohibition relative to Sissy's past career. They are almost strangers in the same house. Louisa wants to know how Sissy's father has left Sissy. Sissy, covering her eyes, and sobbing yet, reports the sad story: Sissy came home from the school in the afternoon, and found her father just come home too, from the booth. And he sat rocking himself over the fire, as if he was in pain. And Sissy asked him whether he had hurt himself, as he did sometimes, like they all did. He said, 'A little.' When she came to stoop down and look up at his face, she saw that he was crying. The more she spoke to him, the more he hid his face; and at first he shook all over, and said nothing but 'My darling!' and 'My love!' At last her father said that he had given no satisfaction again, and that he was a shame and disgrace, and she should have done better without him all along. She said all the affectionate things to him that came into her heart, and presently he was quiet and she sat down by him, and told him all about the school and everything that had been said and done there. When she had no more left to tell, he put his arms round her neck, and kissed her a great many times. Then he asked her to fetch some of the stuff he used, for the little hurt he had had, and to get it at the best place, which was at the other end of town from there. After kissing her again, he let her go. When Sissy wanted to take Merrylegs with her, her father shook his head and said, 'No, Sissy, no; take nothing that's known to be mine, my darling.' And she left him sitting by the fire. When she returned, he was gone.

Time passes on. Louisa and Tom grow young and Bounderby places his proposal to marry Louisa. Gradgrind blurts out that she is the subject of a proposal of marriage that has been made to him. He waits but Louisa utters not a word. This so far surprises him, as to induce him gently to repeat the words "a proposal of marriage..." to which she returns, without any visible emotion whatever, that she hears him and she is attending him surely. He comments that she looks even more dispassionate than he had expected. He informs her that Mr. Bounderby has made his proposal of marriage to him, and has entreated him to make it known to her, and to express his hope that she would take it into her favourable consideration. Louisa accepts the proposal, but betrays no love for Bounderby. Since Mr. Bounderby likes to take her thus, she tells her father that she feels satisfied to accept his proposal: 'Tell him, father, as soon as you please, that this was my answer. Repeat it, word for word, if you can, because I should wish him to know what I said.' She tells her father that his system of bringing up has suppressed any love and affection she might have had. Her father accepts her words as a complimentary testimonial to its efficacy. Mrs. Gradgrind feels pleased with the news, as far as she could be.

Louisa agrees to marry Bounderby mainly because of the fact that she does not like to disappoint his father who has every wish to see his daughter married to Bounderby, and her brother Tom expects it to happen anticipating that it would give him scope to have some advantages from Bounderby and enjoy his life. Louisa cannot ignore the interest of Tom also. Young Tom is ruined by his environment. He is presented as selfish, ill-natured, sensual, and completely mercenary. He is employed as a clerk in a bank owned by his sister's husband, Mr. Bounderby, and eventually steals money from the bank in order to cover his debts contracted in dissipation and idleness.

Mr. Bounderby is very happy with his marriage. He shifts his elderly housekeeper, Mrs. Sparsit, to the apartments of bank building. Mrs. Sparsit dislikes Louisa very much and always keeps an eye on her. While everything is going on peacefully at Gradgrind's and Bounderby's home, Gradgrind has been elected an M.P. from Coketown. With a letter of introduction by Gradgrind, Harthouse comes to meet Bounderby. Although Harthouse thinks Bounderby a fool, Louisa appears to him a remarkable lady. He thinks that Louisa is unhappy in her married life with Bounderby, and only Tom, Louisa's brother, is close to her and she enjoys his company. Coming to visit Bounderby's residence, Harthouse meets Tom there. Harthouse's flattery makes Tom feel himself important. Harthouse takes the advantage of Tom's love for drinking and extracts from him more information about Louisa's family life. Tom informs Harthouse about Louisa's family life. He tells Harthouse how Louisa married Bounderby, more or less to make his (Tom's) life easier and more pleasant. He imparts information to Harthouse about Louisa's education, which leads him to think that Louisa cannot be easily seduced. Harthouse tries to win her favour. On the other hand, Mrs. Sparsit starts secretly spying on Louisa and Harthouse. In their personal meeting, Harthouse tells Louisa that Tom is very ungrateful despite Louisa's great affection and favour for him. In his private conversation with Harthouse, Tom confesses his borrowing heavily from his sister, revealing extreme and callous inconsiderateness. When Harthouse offers to help him out of his economic problems, Tom says that money is no solution. Tom says that if he had got money at the time he needed it, he would not have been in his present plight. But Tom does not exactly define his plight. Harthouse urges Tom to show signs of gratitude to his sister. This delights Louisa enormously when Tom tells Louisa of his fondness for her. As it appears to Louisa that Tom's affectionate attitude towards her is linked with Harthouse's influence, her attitude towards Harthouse seems to soften.

Stephen Blackpool is a power-loom weaver. Stephen is tied to an impossible wife who has drunk herself into a state which defies marital happiness. Stephen loves another woman, Rachael and wants a divorce from his wife. Mr. Bounderby asks Stephen the purpose of his visit. Stephen is there to seek Bounderby's advice as to how he could be legally separated from his wife. Stephen informs him that they have been married nineteen years. Soon after their marriage she goes downhill, and returns at random intervals drunken and penniless. Bounderby, with Mrs. Sparsit in self-righteous support, informs him that only a thousand pounds or more could effect such a separation; otherwise nothing can be done. Stephen feels helpless, and wishes he were dead. Bounderby harangues him, telling him that he is turning or is being led into dangerous paths. Stephen descends the two white steps, shutting the black door with the brazen door-plate. He crosses the street with his eyes bent upon the ground, and thus is walking sorrowfully away, when he felt a touch upon his arm. It is an old woman, tall and shapely still, though withered by time, on whom his eyes falls when he stopped and turned. She is very cleanly and plainly dressed, has country mud upon her shoes, and is newly come from a journey. The old woman asks him whether he has seen the gentleman (Bounderby) in the house. The old woman appears to take it for granted that he leads a happy life indeed, and he has not the heart to disappoint her. He knows that there is trouble enough in the world. She enquires if Stephen's personal problems disrupt his work in the factory. Stephen says that they don't follow him there, and everything is accordant there. Stephen and the old woman are then in the black by-road near the place. The Hands are crowding in. The bell is ringing, and the serpent of smoke is a serpent of many coils. The strange old woman is delighted with the very bell. It is the beautifullest bell she has ever heard, as she says, and sounds grand. She says she must kiss the hand working in the factory for a dozen year. Stephen starts working. He has been at his loom full half an hour. He is thinking about that old woman. Having occasion to move round the loom for its adjustment, he glances through a window which is in his corner, and sees her still looking up at the pile of building, lost in admiration. He and Rachael live in a state of frustration.

Stephen refuses to join the union of working men, suffering ostracism because of this, but he insists on defending his fellow workers when Mr. Bounderby asks him about the union. He is accordingly black-listed. Bounderby sacks Stephen. Stephen pleads that this would mean his permanent unemployment in the industry; but Bounderby, knowing fully well the future reality of Stephen's life, remains unaffected.

One day while going back to his room, Harthouse sees Bounderby greatly troubled, and Bounderby informs him that his bank is robbed. Tom contrives a scheme to throw the blame on Stephen, a workman in Mr. Bounderby's factory.

Suspicion falls on Stephen Blackpool who has been seen outside the bank after his duty for two or three days and is reported to have disappeared on the night of robbery. Since it is Stephen who is used by Tom Gradgrind in his scheme to shift responsibility for the theft from the bank, Stephen is connected with the Gradgrind sequence. An old woman seen in Stephen's company is also suspected. The search for Stephen and the old lady, Mrs. Pegler, meets no success.

In the meantime, Louisa and Harthouse have developed an intimacy and they are often seen as talking in whisper on lonely places. Mrs. Sparsit makes a stay of some weeks in duration at Mr. Bounderby's retreat after the bank robbery. When ultimately she left the house, she is invited by Bounderby to visit the house every weekend. During the whole term of stay at Bounderby's house, Mrs. Sparsit is a pattern of consistency, continuing to take care and pity on Mr. Bounderby to his face; and to call his portrait, with the greatest acrimony and contempt, a 'Noodle', in private. Mrs. Sparsit is not a poetical woman. But she takes an idea in the nature of an allegorical fancy, into her head. Much watching of Louisa, and much consequent observation of her impenetrable demeanour, must have given her, as it were, a lift, in the way of inspiration. She erects in her mind a mighty staircase, with a dark pit of shame and ruin at the bottom; and down those stairs, from day to day and hour to hour, she sees Louisa descending. It becomes the task of Mrs. Sparsit's life, to look up at her staircase, and to watch Louisa coming down and down, but never turning back. But it is Louisa's conscience which abstains her from eloping with Harthouse and she comes to Gradgrind's house. She tells her father that his fact-oriented education has made her life chaotic. She opens her heart that it is because of the happiness of her father and brother that she married Bounderby to whom she has always felt contemptuous. She also makes him know of her proposed plan of elopement with Harthouse. After telling these things, Louisa faints. Meanwhile Mrs. Sparsit who overhears the secret conversation between Louisa and Harthouse about their plan for elopement and thinks that they will flee away imparts everything to Bounderby and the situation gets more complicated. Bounderby rushes to Gradgrind's house and insists that Louisa should return to his home. Gradgrind suggests that Bounderby should allow her to stay in Gradgrind's house until she recovers her nerves. But Bounderby leaves Gradgrind's house giving the ultimatum that Louisa should return before noon, on the following day. Disappointed Harthouse disappears after everything is made clear to him by Sissy.

In Louisa's absence, Mrs. Sparsit, in her effort to win favour of Bounderby, forcibly drags Mrs. Pegler to Bounderby in the suspicion that she has assisted Stephen in the bank robbery. But Mrs. Pegler turns out to be the mother of Bounderby. Bounderby bursts into fury because this proves his designed story about himself false that he was left by his mother in the hands of his drunken grandmother in his infancy.

Stephen leaves Coketown at the time when he is coincidentally suspected of the robbery in Bounderby's bank. Rachael writes a letter to Stephen to come back and clear himself from all charges which unduly falls upon him regarding the robbery. He tries to return to defend himself, but falls into an abandoned mineshaft on the way back. Louisa and Sissy discover Stephen into the pit. He was rescued and on the verge of dying Stephen tells Gradgrind that he is innocent about the robbery and that his son should be interrogated about it. But Tom is found to have disappeared from the place with the help of Sissy. Sissy, Louisa and Gradgrind meet Sleary under whose care Tom was staying. Gradgrind decides to shift Tom to some foreign place in order that he may be defended from any adverse consequences of law.

Before Tom could escape he is caught by Bitzer with all the evidences to present him as a culprit. Bitzer does not comply with Gradgrind's request to leave Tom so that he can escape from the country. He sticks to self-interest. He says that he was brought up in that catechism when he was very young. The model pupil of Gradgrind's school Bitzer believes in the fundamental principle of the Gradgrind philosophy that everything is to be paid for. Nobody is ever on any account to give anybody anything, or render anybody help without purchase. Gratitude is to be abolished, and the virtues springing from it are not to be indulged in. Every inch of the existence of mankind, from birth to death, is to be a bargain across a counter. But Sleary's presence of mind rescues Tom from the clutches of Bitzer. Bounderby dismisses Mrs. Sparsit because he is disgraced a lot by her act of carrying Mrs. Pegler in front of everybody. Bounderby dies after few years. Gradgrind gets wiser after realizing the loopholes of "Fact" education. Sissy gets married and lives happily with her children. To Louisa whose married life has proved a failure, Sissy remains the great source of comfort and delight.

3

Genesis, Vision, and Titling

If the first half of the 19th century considered itself the greatest of all the centuries, the second half of the 19th century discovered that it was the wickedest of all the centuries. The first half condemned and pitied the Middle Ages as barbarous, cruel, superstitious and ignorant; the second half saw no hope for mankind except in the recovery of the faith, the art, the humanity of the Middle Ages. In Macaulay's *History of England*, the world is so happy, so progressive, so firmly set in the right path, that the author cannot mention even the National Debt without proclaiming that the deeper the country goes into debt, the more it prospers. In Morris's *News from Nowhere* there is nothing left of all the institutions that Macaulay glorified except an old building, so ugly that it is used only as a manure market, that was once the British House of Parliament. Dickens's *Hard Times* was written in 1854, just at the turn of the half century; and in it Dickens writes with his eyes newly open and his conscience newly stricken by the discovery of the real state of England. In the book that went immediately before, *Bleak House*, he was still denouncing evils and ridiculing absurdities that were mere symptoms of the anarchy that followed the industrial revolution of the 18th and 19th centuries, and the conquest of political power by Commercialism in 1832. In *Bleak House* Dickens knows nothing of the industrial revolution: he imagines that what is wrong is that when a dispute arises over the division of the plunder of the nation, the Court of Chancery instead of settling the dispute cheaply and promptly, beggars the disputants and pockets both their shares. In *Hard Times* all is changed. The Chancery suitors who are driving themselves mad by hanging about the Courts in the hope of getting a judgment in their favour instead of trying to earn an honest living, are replaced by factory operatives in *Hard Times* who toil miserably and incessantly only to see the streams of gold they set flowing slip through their fingers into the pockets of men who revile and oppress them. Clearly this is not the Dickens who burlesqued the old song of the Fine Old English Gentleman, and saw in the evils he attacked only the sins and wickednesses and follies of a great civilization. This is Karl Marx, Carlyle, Ruskin, Morris, Carpenter, rising up against civilization itself as against a disease, and declaring that it is not our disorder but our order that is horrible; that it is not our criminals but our magnates that are robbing and murdering us: and that it is not merely Tom All Alone's that must be demolished and abolished, pulled down, rooted up, and made for ever impossible so that nothing shall remain of it but History's record of its infamy, but our entire social system. "For that was how men felt", as G.B. Shaw writes in his article "Hard Times" in *The Dickens Critics* (eds. G.H. Ford and L. Lane), "and how some of them spoke, in the early days of the Great Conversion which produced, first, such books as the *Latter Day Pamphlets* of Carlyle, Dickens's *Hard Times,* and the tracts and sociological novels of the Christian Socialists, and later on the Socialist movement which has now spread all over the world, and which has succeeded in convincing even those who most abhor the name of Socialism that the condition of the civilized world is deplorable, and that the remedy is far beyond the means of individual righteousness. In short, whereas formerly men said to the victim of society who ventured to complain, "Go and reform yourself before you pretend to reform Society", it now has to admit that until Society is reformed, no man can reform himself except in the most insignificantly small ways. He may cease picking your pocket of half crowns; but he cannot cease taking a quarter of a million a year from the community for nothing at one end of the scale, or living under conditions in which health, decency, and gentleness are impossible at the other, if he happens to be born to such a lot" (128). The occasional indignation in *Hard Times* has spread and deepened into a passionate revolt against the whole industrial order of the modern world. Here one may find no more villains and heroes, but only oppressors and victims, oppressing and suffering in spite of themselves, driven by a huge machinery which grinds to pieces the people it should nourish and ennoble, and having for its directors the basest and most foolish of us instead of the noblest and most farsighted.

John Holloway in the article "*Hard Times*: A History and a Criticism" in *Dickens and the Twentieth Century*, ed. by John Gross and Gabriel Pearson, writes: *Hard Times* "does not point to Utilitarianism as an ambitious philosophical theory of enlightened and emancipated thinking or of comprehensive social welfare and reform; nor to the genuine (if challengeable) idealism and dedicated high-mindedness of such an education as James Mill designed for his son (Greek at the age of three, and something that could at least pass as the full circle of human knowledge by adolescence). What Dickens seems to have had in mind was something much less far-reaching, and much more mundane and commonplace. The point comes out at once from Dickens's list of possible titles for the novel. This included: 'Two and Two are Four'; 'Simple Arithmetic'; 'A Mere Question of Figures'; and, the first of all, 'According to Cocker'. The last is William Cocker, the seventeenth century author whose *Arithmetic* was still in use as a school text. 'The celebrated Mr. Cocker', Dickens called him in a speech the year after *Hard Times* appeared" (159-60). But Harvey P. Sucksmith writes in *The Narrative Art of Charles Dickens*: "The autobiography of John Stuart Mill was published in 1874. Dickens can hardly have had direct knowledge about this, but it is possible that he could have learnt about it from Carlyle; part of his novel is a remarkable forecast of Mill's own story, an astonishingly accurate prediction of the psychological consequences of a given philosophical attitude rigorously carried through into an educational system. To any one ignorant of Mill's upbringing, Gradgrind's education of his children may appear a gross and incredible caricature; Mill's early chapters show that it is hardly an exaggeration at all.

What is more, Mill experienced a neurotic breakdown in his adolescence and was eventually compelled to acknowledge the claims of the emotions both in his own life and in his philosophical ideas. He gradually modified and softened the harsh and rigid utilitarianism of Bentham and his father" (170-71). *Hard Times* appeared the year before Spencer's *Principles of Psychology* and Bain's *The Senses and the Intellect* which mark the beginning of a biologically and physiologically oriented psychology that was to lead in turn to the new psychology of 19th century. The idea of repression is presented in its most complete and convincing form in *Hard Times*, which contains the fullest exposition of Dickens's general view of human psychology. He tries to show that the conflict between the reason, on the one hand, and the instincts, affections, and imagination, on the other, may be agonizingly real. Such a conflict may be resolved by the conscious acceptance of both 'head' and 'heart' or it may be driven underground through faulty education and result in the stunting of personality, mental breakdown, and even crime. The result of repressing affections, instincts, and imagination in favour of a one-sided rational development is the impoverishment of Bitzer's personality, the nervous collapse of Louisa with its sexual undertones, and the degeneration of Tom Gradgrind into selfishness and thieving.

The link between effect, structure, and vision can be seen in the genesis of the title of *Hard Times*. Dickens's list of alternative titles for this novel shows that Dickens is involved here in no less important a task than in clarifying the vision of his book.

Some evidence suggests that Dickens had decided on the theme of *Hard Times* before 20 January 1854, the date which heads the list of titles. On 23 January 1854, he reminded Miss Coutts: 'The main idea of it is one on which you and I and Miss Brown have often spoken.' Seven months earlier, he wrote to his sub-editor:

> I have thought of another article to be called "Frauds upon the Fairies", a *propos* of George Cruikshank's editing. Half playfully and half seriously, I mean to

> protest most strongly against alteration, for any purpose, of the beautiful little stories which are so tenderly and humanly useful to us in these times, when the world is too much with us early and late; and then to re-write "Cinderella" according to Total Abstinence, Peace Society, and Bloomer principles, and expressly for their propagation.

This article anticipates the ideas contained in 'Hard Heads and Soft Hearts' and 'Heads and Tales', two of the titles considered for *Hard Times*. Indeed, the idea behind 'Frauds upon the Fairies' goes back seven years to *Dombey and Son*:

> It being a part of Mrs. Pipchin's system not to encourage a child's mind to develop and expand itself like a young flower, but to open it by force like an oyster, the moral of these lessons was usually of a violent and stunning character: the hero—a naughty boy—seldom, in the mildest catastrophe, being finished off by anything less than a lion or a bear.

Hard Times takes the conflict between imagination and utility one stage further by eliminating fancy altogether from the process of education:

> Not that they knew, by name or nature, anything about an Ogre. Fact forbid!...
>
> No little Gradgrind had ever seen a face in the moon; it was up in the moon before it could speak distinctly. No little Gradgrind had ever learnt the silly jingle, Twinkle, twinkle, little star; how I wonder what you are! No little Gradgrind had ever known wonder on the subject, each little Gradgrind having at five years old dissected the Great Bear like a Professor Owen, and driven Charles's Wain like a locomotive engine-driver. No little Gradgrind had ever associated a cow in a field with that famous cow with crumpled horn who tossed the dog who worried the cat who killed the rat who ate the malt, or with that yet more famous cow who swallowed Tom Thumb: it had never heard of those celebrities, and had

> only been introduced to a cow as a graminivorous ruminating quadruped with several stomachs. (*HT*. I, III)

Moreover, the championing of fancy against fact of the utilitarian brand had been established as the policy of *Household Words* four years before *Hard Times*:

> No mere utilitarian spirit, no iron binding of the mind to grim realities, will give a harsh tone to our *Household Words*. In the bosoms of the young and old, of the well-to-do and of the poor, we would tenderly cherish that light of Fancy which is inherent in the human breast; which, according to its nurture, burns with an inspiring flame, or sinks into a sullen glare, but which (or woe betide that day!) can never be extinguished.... To show to all, that in all familiar things, even in those which are repellant on the surface, there is Romance enough, if we will find it out!

It seems that Dickens was formulating the theme of *Hard Times*, while he considered the alternative titles, but that he was working out this theme in terms of structure, effect, and vision.

Although neither Forster in his *Life* nor Butt and Tillotson in *Dickens at Work* supplied a full list of the titles in the manuscript or indicate their correct sequence, Dickens, in fact, drew up two lists of titles for this novel, one dated 20 January 1854, and the other in a letter of the same date which Forster quotes:

> 'I wish you would look' (20th of January 1854) 'at the enclosed titles for the *H.W.* story, between this and two o'clock or so, when I will call. It is my usual day, you observe, on which I have jotted them down—Friday! It seems to me that there are three very good ones among them. I should like to know whether you hit upon the same.' On the paper enclosed was written: 1. According to Cocker. 2. Prove It. 3. Stubborn Things. 4. Mr. Gradgrind's Facts. 5. The Grindstone. 6. Hard Times. 7. Two and Two are Four. 8. Something Tangible. 9. Our Hard-headed Friend. 10. Rust and Dust.

> 11. Simple Arithmetic. 12. A Matter of Calculation. 13. A Mere Question of Figures. 14. The Gradgrind Philosophy. The three selected by me were 2, 6, and 11; the three that were his own favourites were 6, 13 and 14; and as 6 had been chosen by both, that title was taken. (Quoted in Sucksmith 220)

Further, in a footnote to the passage, he adds what are in fact several titles from the manuscript:

> To show the pains he took in such matters I will give other titles also thought of for this tale. 1. Fact; 2. Hard-headed Gradgrind; 3. Hard Heads and Soft Hearts; 4. Heads and Tales; 5. Black and White.

Butt and Tillotson show considerable insight into what Dickens was about in the selection process and the final choice of *Hard Times*:

> These rejected titles and those in the manuscript... remain of interest, since they seem to indicate the limits within which the book would move. The irony implicit in *Something Tangible*, *A Matter of Calculation*, and *A Mere Question of Figures* suggests that the novel will open up areas of experience beyond the reach of Mr. Gradgrind's philosophy, and the importance of feelings, disregarded by the political economists, is represented in *Hard Heads and Soft Hearts*, while *Heads and Tales* seems to forecast the opposition of fact and fancy so prominent in the scenes at Sleary's Circus troupe.

The original list of titles in the manuscript is more than twice as long as the list in the letter; it is subdivided into two sections by a double line and, if we ignore the deletions, the second section very nearly corresponds to the list in the letter which reads almost like a fair copy. The only title which appears in the letter but not in the manuscript is "The Gradgrind Philosophy" which comes last and may have been added as an afterthought; this title is important in filling out the scheme Dickens had in mind. Harvey P. Sucksmith writes in *The Narrative Art of Charles Dickens*: "Proliferation there certainly is, one title suggesting another, and if, as Butt and Tillotson suggest, we do not see Dickens here in the initial stage of gestation yet it may still show another important stage in the creative process, that at which the original idea is clarified and crystallized in terms of vision, effect, and structure. Indeed, this attempt to be both comprehensive and precise accounts for the protean forms which his title takes on while these forms, in their turn, indicate the richness of the material he is handling. The process of clarification is not a mechanical association of ideas, not even a free association in the Freudian sense but something much nearer that controlled association which Jung describes as the genuine creative process" (221-22). There is a constant return to certain basic ideas which are amplified and enriched by the associations that have taken place. Consequently, Dickens's vision becomes but more complex as he strives to formulate a comprehensive view.

Dickens starts off from the idea of inflexibility as a feature of the Gradgrind system: 'Stubborn Things'. At intervals, he returns to this idea with the image of the grindstone which also adds the further ideas of harshness and abrasion: 'The Grindstone', 'Mr. Gradgrind's Grindstone'. The abrasive quality suggests the rough process of putting an edge on or sharpening to a fine point. Similarly, the idea of something mechanical, as the antithesis of the natural, is present in the image of the grindstone. As in every true symbol, both a positive and a negative potential are present, doubly important here, since catastrophe will develop organically from an over-positive assertion. Inflexibility and harshness are also combined in 'Hard Times'. The very name 'Gradgrind' suggests all three ideas of inflexibility, harshness, and abrasion.

The inflexibility in his first title, 'Stubborn Things', immediately suggests Dickens's second title, 'Fact', a further key idea in his concept of the Gradgrind system. In Book II, Chapter II of *Hard Times*, Dickens refers to the utilitarian political economists as 'The hard Fact fellows'. In a letter, he explains the satire of *Hard Times*:

> My satire is against those who see figures and averages, and nothing else—the representatives of the wickedest

> and most enormous vice of this time—the men who, through long years to come, will do more to damage the real truths of political economy than I could do (if I tried) in my whole life.
>
> (To Mr. Charles Knight. 30 Jan. 1854. *HD*, 329)

That Dickens is attacking the utilitarian political economy in the figure of Gradgrind can be seen in the title, 'Mr. Gradgrind's Philosophy'. The obsession with an inflexible system of facts is stressed in the author's notes for *Hard Times*: 'Mr. Gradgrind. Facts and Figures. "Teach these children nothing but facts. Nothing but facts. Nothing but facts."' Dickens identifies facts with the image of the grindstone, that is, with the ideas of inflexibility, harshness, and abrasion: 'Mr. Gradgrind's (grindstone) Facts.' Inflexibility and harshness then combine with the kind of intellect dealing in facts and figures, 'Hard-headed Gradgrind', an idea returned to in 'Our Hard-headed Friend'. Sucksmith writes in *The Narrative Art of Charles Dickens*: "With the theme beginning to embody itself in character, the harsh inflexible intellect suggests its antitheses, in feeling, 'Hard Heads and Soft Hearts', and in imagination, 'Heads and Tales'. As a result, the basic dramatic conflict of the novel appears and perhaps the character of Sissy and the tragedy of Louisa Gradgrind are born. All this in its turn suggests further structure. The basic dramatic conflict of the novel, 'Black and White', is to be resolved..." (223-24).

A series of titles which follows shows Dickens trying to realize the theme in terms of structure and effect. One of these titles, also cancelled, suggests something may have been overlooked by the Gradgrind system and expresses what is lacking, ironically enough, in mathematical terms: 'Unknown Quantities'. The other titles, two of which have also been cancelled, all ironically state the extreme Gradgrind position: 'Two and Two are Four', 'Prove It', 'According to Cocker', 'Prove it!', 'Something Tangible', 'Simple Arithmetic', 'A (mere) Matter of Calculation', 'A Mere Question of Figures'. Sucksmith comments: "Obviously, these titles hint at *hubris* and peripety, possibly at discovery also, worked into a pattern of structural irony and poetic justice" (224).

Another sequence of associations, which leads to the final selection of a title and adds an important dimension to the vision of the novel, begins with the grindstone image. The title, 'The Grindstone', suggests 'The Time Grinder' which is stressed by underscoring. 'The Grindstone' has grown out of 'Hard-headed Gradgrind' and after the antithesis, 'Hard Heads and Soft Hearts', which follows immediately, 'The Time Grinder' suggests itself. Through this final image, as Sucksmith writes, "time enters into Dickens's vision as an inflexible and relentless agency of fate which will wear away the cocksure hardness of the Gradgrind system. This idea is returned to in the curious title, 'Rust and Dust'" (224).

Dickens consciously elaborates the idea of time as the machine of an ironic fate. Time will really decide the development of character and the final destiny of the Gradgrind children. This cosmic view is ironically contrasted with Gradgrind's puny sense of time when he deceives himself into thinking that he is settling his daughter's future on the opportune occasion of Bounderby's proposal: 'Children grow up. Time, a manufacturer. Passes them through his mill. Time for Mr. Gradgrind "to talk to" Louisa—Tom' (Working Notes for *HT*. I, XIV). That Dickens saw time as the agency of an ironic and punitive fate in *Hard Times* is confirmed in the concluding paragraph of Chapter XIV by a classical reference which was deleted in proof:

> She tried to discover what kind of woof Old Time, that greatest and longest-established Spinner of all,—one of the few I have heard of who is not at once a Croesus and a Victim—would weave from the threads he had already spun into a woman. But, his factory is a secret place, his work is noiseless, and his Hands are mutes. (I, XIV)

'Hard Times' first appears almost immediately after 'The Times' and while Dickens is alternating between 'Mr. Gradgrind's Grindstone' and 'The (universal) General Grindstone', between the Gradgrind and the cosmic views of the system. The title, *Hard Times*, thus compresses the ideas of inflexibility, harshness, and abrasion together with the concepts of time as industrial setting, as historical period, and as the medium of fate.

Hard Times is a special novel in the canon, this is partly, at last, because it is also the angriest. Like *Gulliver* before or *1984* after, it is conceived and sustained in anger. This is no doubt why it exudes energy and even exaltation, despite the muffling of Dickens's normal poetic effects. Its energy is specifically satiric, with anger unleashed and driven to extremes. Coketown is the whole place; and its rich manufacturers are proud of its dirt, and declare that they like to see the sun blacked out with smoke, because it means that the furnaces are busy and money is being made; whilst its poor factory hands have never known any other sort of town, and are content with it as a rat is with a hole. Mr. Bounderby is the self-made humbug. England is full of Bounderbys and Gradgrinds; and people are all to a quite appalling extent in their power. Bounderby is an extreme example of a self-made man in the tradition soon to receive a powerful further impetus from Samuel Smiles (*Self-Help*, 1859)—witness the mutated 'Ecce Homo' in 'behold your Bounderby', a blasphemy which nothing but savage seriousness could sustain. Gradgrind is an extreme instance of a kindly man, intending as a father nothing but good, but wholly perverted by his deadly ideas. Blackpool is an extreme example of a worker, honourable and even noble in nature, pursued by relentless impersonal forces to his downfall and death. Behind these three instances is a sick society, where Gradgrind's children merely enact, in terrifyingly human terms, the extreme logic prescribed by their world.

If *The Old Curiosity Shop* was written to amuse and entertain the readers, *Hard Times* was written to make them uncomfortable; and it will make them uncomfortable though it will perhaps interest them more, and certainly leave a deeper scar on them. As G.B. Shaw said in his article "Hard Times" in *The Dickens Critics* (eds. G.H. Ford and L. Lane): "...you need not fear to find Dickens losing his good humor and sense of fun and becoming serious in Mr. Gradgrind's way. On the contrary, Dickens in this book casts off, and casts off for ever, all restraint on his wild sense of humor" (130). He had always been inclined to break loose. But in *Hard Times* he begins at last to exercise quite recklessly his power of presenting a character in the most fantastic and outrageous terms, putting into its mouth from one end of the book to the other hardly one word which could conceivably be uttered by any sane human being, and yet presenting with an unmistakable and exactly truthful portrait of a character that one recognizes at once as not only real but typical.

Because Dickens presents his truth with some colour of caricature the essential value and truth of Dickens's writings have been unwisely lost sight of by many thoughtful persons. The things he presents are always true. Ruskin says that he wishes that Dickens could think it right to limit his brilliant exaggeration to works written only for public amusement; and when he takes up a subject of high national importance, such as that which he handled in *Hard Times*, that he would use severer and more accurate analysis. Ruskin writes in his "A Note on *Hard Times*" in *The Dickens Critics*: "The usefulness of that work [*Hard Times*]...is with many persons seriously diminished because Mr. Bounderby is a dramatic monster, instead of a characteristic example of a worldly master; and Stephen Blackpool a dramatic perfection, instead of a characteristic example of an honest workman. But let us not lose the use of Dickens's wit and insight, because he chooses to speak in a circle of stage fire. He is entirely right in his main drift and purpose in every book he has written; and all of them, but especially *Hard Times*, should be studied with close and earnest care by persons interested in social questions. They will find much that is partial, and because partial, apparently unjust; but if they examine all the evidence on the other side, which Dickens seems to overlook, it will appear, after all their trouble, that his view was the finally right one, grossly and sharply told" (47-48).

4

A Chapter-wise Critical Summary

BOOK I. SOWING

CHAPTER I: ONE THING NEEDFUL

In a school room, in addition to a class of boys and girls, there are three grown up and mature persons present. A hard and dry looking man is emphasizing to the children the prime need of teaching and learning nothing but facts, 'the one thing needful'. The man is none but Mr. Thomas Gradgrind.

The chapter communicates both a description and a judgment of a concept of education. This concept is defined in a speech and then evaluated in terms of the speaker's appearance and the setting. Because of the brevity of this chapter, we are all the more susceptible to the effect of its highly rhetorical patterning, particularly the manipulation of certain repeated words, notably *fact, square,* and *emphasis*. In Gradgrind's speeches the word "Facts" is capitalized, to signify his almost religious devotion to "Facts". The economy of *Hard Times* is a special and brilliant effect in the Dickens theatre, and it is offered as loudly and distinctly, and as proudly, as any of Dickens's other effects. Who could fail to hear this in the very first chapter:

> 'Now, what I want is, Facts. Teach these boys and girls nothing but Facts. Facts alone are wanted in life. Plant nothing else, and root out everything else. You can only form the minds of reasoning animals upon Facts: nothing else will ever be of any service to them. This is

the principle on which I bring up these children. Stick to Facts, Sir!'

The skeletal qualities establish themselves in the first chapter which prepares its reader with facts. Like other opening chapters in Dickens's novels it broods over the action which follows it, yet not in his accustomed way. The opening, 'Facts, facts, facts...' is very different from the fog in Dickens's *Bleak House*, the prison in *Little Dorrit*, the marshes in *Great Expectations*, the London river in *Our Mutual Friend*. The first chapter of *Hard Times* differs chiefly from these others by being abstract, since abstraction is here the quintessence of the book. 'Facts, facts, facts....' Mr. Gradgrind fires at the souls of his victims and we encounter the children, Louisa, Tom, Bitzer, as the living dead. Bitzer indeed is almost a zombie, while Louisa drifts, a shade less palely, through her lonely despair.

CHAPTER II: MURDERING THE INNOCENTS

Thomas Gradgrind is a 'man of realities'. Thomas Gradgrind is a man of 'facts and calculations'. He is a man always to proceed upon the principle that 'two and two are four, and nothing over'. With a rule and a pair of scales, and the multiplication table always in his pocket he is ready to weigh and measure 'any parcel of human nature'. Human nature is a mere question of figures, a case of simple arithmetic, to him. He has no nonsensical belief in him.

Thomas Gradgrind presents himself before 'the little pitchers', the boys and girls of his model school, who are to be filled so full of facts. He seems a kind of "cannon loaded to the muzzle with facts, and prepared to blow them clean out of their regions of childhood at one discharge". He seems a galvanizing apparatus, too, charged with a grim mechanical substitute for the tender young imaginations that are to be stormed away.

A horse figures prominently in the classroom scene when the tyranny of fact is being demonstrated. Mr. Gradgrind asks who is 'girl number twenty'. "Sissy jupe, Sir" explains number twenty, blushing, standing up, and curtseying. Mr. Gradgrind objects against the name, "Sissy", and asks her to call herself

Cecilia. Mr. Gradgrind enquires what Sissy's father is. Sissy or Cecilia says that she belongs to the horse-riding, the circus troupe. Mr. Gradgrind frowns and waves off the objectionable calling with his hand. He orders that she mustn't say anything about the horse-riding in the school. Then she is asked to give her definition of a horse. Sissy is thrown into the greatest alarm by this demand. She cannot define a horse though she belongs to Sleary's horse-riders.

Mr. Gradgrind tells the pupils, 'the little pitchers', that as Sissy is unable to define a horse she possesses of no facts, in reference to one of the commonest of animals. The square finger of Mr. Gradgrind, moving here and there, lights suddenly on Bitzer, perhaps because he chances to sit in the same ray of sunlight which irradiates Sissy. The boys and girls sit on the face of the inclined plane in two compact bodies, divided up the centre by a narrow interval. Sissy, being at the corner of a row on the sunny side, comes in for the beginning of a sunbeam, of which Bitzer who is at the corner of a row on the other side, a few rows in advance, catches the end. But Sissy is so dark-eyed and dark-haired, that she seems to receive a deeper and more lustrous colour from the sun, when it shines upon her. Bitzer is so light-eyed and light-haired that the self-same rays appear to draw out of him what little colour he ever possesses. His "cold eyes would hardly have been eyes, but for the short ends of lashes which, by bringing them into immediate contrast with something paler than themselves, expressed their form". His short-cropped hair may have been a mere continuation of the sandy freckles on his forehead and face. His skin is so unwholesomely deficient in the natural tinge that he looks as though if he were cut he would bleed white.

The moral and spiritual differences are rendered here in terms of sensation, and the symbolic intention emerges out of metaphor and the vivid evocation of the concrete. What may, perhaps, be emphasized is that Sissy stands for vitality as well as goodness—they are seen, in fact, as one; she is generous, impulsive life, finding self-fulfilment in self-forgetfulness—all that is the antithesis of calculating self-interest. There is an essentially Laurentian suggestion about the way in which 'the dark-eyed and dark-haired' girl, contrasting with Bitzer, seems to receive a 'deeper and more lustrous colour from the sun', so opposing the life that is lived freely and richly from the deep instinctive and emotional springs to the thin-blooded, quasi-mechanical product of Gradgrindery. Though Bitzer is 'colourless' or 'light' at every reappearance, this suggestion is rarely brought to imaginative life after the beginning; but the more important point is that Sissy is never again vividly seen in these or indeed in any 'vivid terms of sensation'. Mr. Gradgrind has a 'square forefinger', a 'square wall of a forehead', a 'square coat', and all these indicate Gradgrind's rigid, inflexible nature.

As Thomas Gradgrind asks Bitzer to give the definition of a horse, Bitzer defines it: "Quadruped. Graminivorous. Forty teeth, namely twenty-four grinders, four eye-teeth, and twelve incisive. Sheds coat in the spring; in marshy countries, sheds hoofs, too. Hoofs hard, but requiring to be shod with iron. Age known by marks in mouth."

The schoolroom contrast of Sissy Jupe and Bitzer is a contrast between the education, practical but often inarticulate which is gained by living and doing, and the education, highly articulated, which is gained by systemization and abstraction. The instinctive, un-intellectual, unorganized life is the ground of genuine feeling and of all good relationships.

The Third Gentleman steps forth. He is a government officer, and in his own way, 'a professed pugilist'. The 'government officer' is intended by Dickens as a representative of the newly formed Department of Practical Art, and he is presented as a monster of pedantry. To the gentleman, "Taste" is only another name for "Fact". The gentleman declares that it is a new principle, a discovery, a great discovery. When the gentleman asks the pupils whether they would use a carpet having a representation of flowers upon it, only a few feeble stragglers say 'Yes' and among them is Sissy Jupe. To meet up the questions, Sissy says that she is very fond of flowers and she should like to carpet her room with representations of flowers and it wouldn't hurt them if tables and chairs are put upon them: "They would be the pictures of what was very pretty and pleasant, and I would fancy—." A vigorous objection rises up against Sissy's 'I would fancy.' "Ay, ay, ay! but you mustn't fancy", cries the gentleman, "You are not, Cecilia Jupe," Thomas Gradgrind solemnly repeats, "to do anything of that kind". "Fact, fact, fact!" says the gentleman. And "Fact, fact, fact!" repeats Thomas Gradgrind. The gentleman advises Cecilia *alias* Sissy to be in all things regulated and governed by fact, and she must discard the word "Fancy" altogether as she has nothing to do with it: "This is the new discovery. This is fact. This is taste." Sissy curtseys, and sits down.

Mr. M'Choakumchild then begins in his best manner to give his first lesson. Dickens' satirical description is very amusing: "He had been put through an immense variety of paces and had answered volumes of head-breaking questions. Orthography, etymology, syntax, and prosody, biography, astronomy, geography, and general cosmography, the sciences of compound proportion, algebra, land-surveying and levelling, vocal music, and drawing from models, were all at the ends of his ten chilled fingers.... If he had only learnt a little less, how infinitely better he might have taught much more!" Mr. M'Choakumchild starts the preparatory lesson, looking into all the vessels (the pupils) ranged before him, one after another, to see what they contain. The satiric tone of the novelist and the fundamental tenor of the novel are insinuated in the following words: "Say good M'Choakumchild. When from thy boiling store, thou shalt fill each jar brim full by-and-by, dost thou think that thou wilt always kill outright the robber Fancy lurking within—or sometimes only maim him and distort him!"

CHAPTER III: A LOOPHOLE

Mr. Gradgrind starts walking homeward from the school with considerable satisfaction. It is his school, and he intends it to be a model. He intends every child in it to be a model—just as the young Gradgrinds are all models. There are five young Gradgrinds and all they are models. They have been lectured at, from their tenderest years. Almost as soon as they could run alone, they had been made to run to the lecture room. The first object with which they had an association, or of which they have a remembrance, is a large black board with a dry Ogre chalking ghastly white figures on it. No little Gradgrind has ever seen a face in the moon; it was up in the moon before it could speak distinctly. No little Gradgrind has ever learnt the silly jingle, 'Twinkle, twinkle, little star; how I wonder what you are!' No little Gradgrind has ever known wonder on the subject. Mr. Gradgrind directs his steps towards his matter-of-fact home, Stone Lodge. He has virtually retired from the wholesale hardware trade before he builds Stone Lodge, and is now looking about for a suitable opportunity of making an arithmetical figure in parliament. Stone Lodge is situated on a moor within a mile or two of a great town called Coketown.

Stone Lodge is a very regular feature on the face of the country. It is a calculated, cast up, balanced and proved house. A lawn and garden and infant avenue, all ruled straight like a botanical account-book. "Iron clamps and girders, fireproof from top to bottom; mechanical lifts for the housemaids, with all their brushes and brooms; everything that heart could desire." The little Gradgrinds have cabinets in various departments of science too. They have a little conchological cabinet, and a little metallurgical cabinet, and a little mineralogical cabinet; and the specimens are all arranged and labeled. Mr. Gradgrind walks on in a hopeful and satisfied frame of mind. He is an affectionate father, after his manner; but he would probably have described himself as "an eminently practical" father. He has a particular pride in the phrase "eminently practical" which is considered to have a special application to him. He has reached the neutral ground upon the outskirts of the town, which is neither town nor country and yet is either spoiled, when he hears the sound of music. A flag, floating from the summit of the temple, proclaims to mankind that it is "Sleary's Horse-riding" which claims their suffrages. Thomas Gradgrind takes no heed of these trivialities. He passes on as a practical man ought to pass on. But, the turning of the road takes him by the back of the booth where a number of children have been congregated in stealthy attitudes, striving to peep into the circus show. This brings him to a stop. He is irritated that the circus-vagabonds might be attracting the young rabble from his model school.

A space of stunted grass and dry rubbish being between him and the young rabble, he takes his eyeglass out of his waistcoat to look for any child he knows by name, and may order off. Phenomenon is almost incredible though distinctly seen. He then beholds none but his own metallurgical Louisa, peeping with all her might through a hole in a deal board, and his own mathematical Thomas abasing himself on the ground to catch but 'a hoof of the graceful equestrian Tyrolean flower-act'. He feels dumb with amazement. He crosses to the spot and lays his hand upon them, and says "Louisa!! Thomas!!" Both rise, red and disconcerted. But, Louisa looks at her father with more boldness than Thomas does. Indeed, Thomas does not look at him, but gives himself up to be taken home like a machine. Mr. Gradgrind asks, leading each away by a hand, what they were doing there, in the name of wonder, idleness, and folly. Louisa replies shorty that they wanted to see what it was like. In her reply to Gradgrind's questions, Louisa is rather bold. She is a child of fifteen or sixteen. She is pretty. When Gradgrind rebukes Tom taking it for granted that he brought his sister to a scene like this, Louisa quickly says that she brought him there. Mr. Gradgrind cannot accept it that Tom and Louisa, who should be replete with facts and who have been trained to mathematical exactness may be seen in that degraded position.

Louisa and Tom feel stifled with Gradgrind's fact-oriented Benthamite utilitarianism and emptiness is embodied in Louisa's speeches:

> "I was tired, father. I have been tired a long time", said Louisa.
> "Tired? Of what?" asked the astonished father.
> "I don't know of what—of everything, I think."
> "Say not another word", returned Mr. Gradgrind.
> "You are childish. I will hear no more."

He has been reflecting all the while on what Mr. Bounderby would say about this delinquency. At the mention of the name of Mr. Bounderby, Louisa steals an intense and searching look at her father. He sees nothing of it, for before he looked at her, she had again cast down her eyes.

The ground for the little catastrophe is carefully prepared by Gradgrind's arrogant dismissal of the circus. His rejection of the imaginative and affective side of human nature sets in motion against him the machinery of the natural law. The ensuing catastrophe is the kind that Aristotle recommends. It contains both a discovery and a peripety and possesses the proper qualities of surprise and probability. Surprise is not only registered through 'phenomenon almost incredible' but the specific reference to 'his own metallurgical Louisa' and 'his own mathematical Thomas'. It brings out all the irony in the neat reversal of Gradgrind's expectations as father and educationist. The spiritual myopia of Gradgrind is suggested by the business of the eyeglass which he needs to make out what his children are up to under his very nose. Thus the physical action expresses and underlines the wider spiritual message. Moreover the incident is related organically to the rest of the novel both in form and in content. It foreshadows the major double catastrophe in which daughter and son show so alarmingly the unexpected yet quite inevitable effects of the Gradgrind system of education on their adult lives.

CHAPTER IV: MR. BOUNDERBY

Mr. Bounderby is almost Mr. Gradgrind's bosom friend. Mr. Bounderby is a man perfectly devoid of sentiment. He believes that spiritual relationship towards another man is perfectly devoid of sentiment. He is a rich man: banker, merchant, manufacturer, and what not. He is a big, loud man with a stare, and a metallic laugh. He is a man made out of a coarse material, which seems to have been stretched to make so much of him. He is a man who could never sufficiently vaunt himself a self-made man. He is a man who is always proclaiming his old ignorance and his old poverty. He is a man who is the Bully of humility. A year or two younger than Mr. Gradgrind, Mr. Bounderby looks older.

We will later know that Bounderby is an arch-hypocrite. Although he wishes it to be believed that he fought his way up from the gutter, he had his perfectly secure childhood.

In the formal drawing-room of Stone Lodge, Mr. Bounderby delivers some observations to Mrs. Gradgrind on the circumstance of its being his birthday. Mrs. Gradgrind is a colourless ineffective woman. She is feeble, mentally and bodily. She is always taking physic without any effect. Mr. Bounderby stands before the fire, "partly because it was a cool spring afternoon though the sun shone; partly because the shade of Stone Lodge was always haunted by the ghost of damp mortar; partly because he thus took up a commanding position, from which to subdue Mrs. Gradgrind." Mr. Bounderby says that he hadn't a shoe to his foot. As to a stocking, he didn't know such a thing by name. He passed the day in ditch, and the night in a pigsty. That's the way he spent his tenth birthday. He proclaims that he was born in a ditch. He fought through his poverty. He says that he has been a determined character and he is a self-made person. He says that his mother left him to his grandmother and his grandmother was the wickedest and the worst old woman that ever lived. She had even taken his shoes off and sold them for drink. The grandmother kept a chandler's shop and kept him in an egg box, 'the cot of infancy'. He ran away; then he became a young vagabond and, in that stage of life, everybody of all ages knocked him about and starved him. He was to pull through it though nobody threw him out a rope. Eventually he rose to his present position after having worked as an errand-boy, vagabond, labourer, porter, clerk, chief manager, small partner, and now he is Josiah Bounderby of Coketown. Being heated when he arrives at this climax, Josiah Bounderby of Coketown stops. He stops just as his eminently practical friend, still accompanied by the two young culprits, Louisa and Tom, enters the room. On seeing him, Mr. Gradgrind stops also, and gives Louisa a reproachful look that plainly says, "Behold your Bounderby." As Mr. Bounderby wants to know the matter, Louisa mutters, haughtily, without lifting up her eyes, that they were peeping at the circus and father caught them.

Mrs. Gradgrind is not a scientific character. She usually dismisses her children to their studies with the general injunction to go and be 'somethingological'. Mrs. Gradgrind's stock of facts in general is woefully defective, but "Mr. Gradgrind in raising her to her high matrimonial position had been influenced by two reasons. Firstly, she was most satisfactory as a question of figures; and secondly, she had 'no nonsense' about her. By nonsense he meant fancy; and truly it is probable she was as free from any alloy of that nature, as any human being not arrived at the perfection of an absolute idiot, ever was."

Mr. Gradgrind resumes that he is very much vexed by this discovery. He has systematically devoted himself to the education of the reason. The reason is the only faculty to which education should be addressed. And yet, it would appear from this unexpected circumstance as if something has crept into Thomas's and Louisa's minds which has never been intended to be developed, and in which their reason has no part.

Bounderby says that the curiosity has its rise in idle imagination which is a very bad thing for anybody, but a cursed bad thing for a girl like Louisa. Bounderby suddenly locates that one of those strollers' children, Sissy, in the school is the cause behind such type of curiosity. Both agree that the disobedience must have been caused by the influence of Cecilia Jupe, whom they decide to dismiss from the school. Mr. Gradgrind goes upstairs for the address of Sissy's father. Mr. Bounderby opens the door of the children's study and looks into that serene floor-clothed apartment. Louisa languidly leans upon the window looking out, without looking at anything. Louisa is physically aware of Bounderby, and the awareness revolts her. Young Thomas stands sniffing revengefully at the fire. Adam Smith and Malthus, two younger Gradgrinds, are out at lecture in custody. Little Jane, after manufacturing a good deal of moist pipeclay on her face with slate-pencil and tears, has fallen asleep over vulgar fractions.

'"It's all right now, Louisa: it's all right, young Thomas", said Mr. Bounderby; "you won't do so any more. I'll answer for its being all over with father. Well, Louisa, that's worth a kiss, isn't it?" Louisa, slowly walked across the room, and ungraciously raised her cheek towards him, with her face turned away.' Bounderby went his way. But she stands on the same spot, rubbing the cheek he had kissed, with her handkerchief, until it is burning red. She is still doing that, five minutes afterwards. Tom sulkily remonstrates that she would rub a hole in her face. Louisa feels so contaminated that she says that he may cut the piece out with his penknife and she wouldn't cry.

The chapter throws light on Bounderby's forged story about his past life and on his character. We do not miss Dickens' satirical mode of narration here. Louisa's reaction after Bounderby's kiss bears more implication than what is apparent.

CHAPTER V: THE KEYNOTE

The keynote is fact, and fact-immersed Coketown. Coketown, to which Bounderby and Gradgrind are walking, is a triumph of fact. It has no greater taint of fancy in it than Mrs. Gradgrind herself. Coketown is a town of red brick, or brick that would have been red if the smoke and ashes had allowed it. It is a town of unnatural red and black. It is a town of machinery and tall chimneys, out of which interminable serpents of smoke trail themselves for ever and ever. It has a black canal in it, and a river—that runs purple with ill-smelling dye. It is a town of vast piles of building full of windows rattling and trembling all day. It is a town where the piston of the steam engine work monotonously up and down in a state of melancholy madness. It contains several large streets very like one another, and many small streets still more like one another, inhabited by people equally like one another to whom everyday is the same as yesterday and tomorrow, and every year the counterpart of the last and the next.

Coketown is a town severely workful. The solitary exception is the New Church, a stuccoed edifice with a square steeple over the door, terminating in four short pinnacles like florid wooden legs. All the public inscriptions in the town are painted alike, in severe characters of black and white. The jail might have been the infirmary, the infirmary might have been the jail. Everywhere in the material aspect and in the immaterial of the town is fact, fact, and fact. The M'Choakumchild school is all fact, and the school of design is all fact, and the relations between master and man are all fact.

Mr. Gradgrind and Mr. Bounderby are walking through Coketown for Pod's End where Sissy's father lives. As they stop for a moment, looking around to enquire about the location, Cecilia Jupe reaches there running round the corner of the street at a quick pace and with a frightened look. Gradgrind stops her and she reports that she was run after and she wanted to get away. Bitzer comes round the corner with blind speed. When Sissy complains that Bitzer frightened her with his cruel faces, Bitzer says that he asked her if she would know how to define a horse and offered to tell her again, and she ran away, and he ran after her that she might know how to answer when she would be asked. He then turns about and retreats, as ordered by Gradgrind. Mr. Gradgrind asks Sissy to take them to her father as they are going there. Sissy is carrying a bottle of the nine oils to rub her father with. She says that the circus people always use the nine oils when they get any hurts in the ring. They reach Pod's End and they stop, at twilight, at the door of a mean little public house, with dim red lights in it. It is the house where Sissy and her father reside, and where other members of the circus troupe are also living.

Mr. Gradgrind, though hard enough, is by no means so rough a man as Mr. Bounderby. His character is not unkind all things considered. Coketown is an image of a kind of death in life. Dickens presents the keynote in effective economy with theatricality:

> Fact, fact, fact, everywhere in the material aspect of the town; fact, fact, fact, everywhere in the immaterial. The M'Choakumchild school was all fact, and the school of design was all fact, and everything was fact between the lying-in hospital and the cemetery, and what you

couldn't state in figures, or show to be purchasable in the cheapest market and saleable in the dearest, was not, and never should be, world without end, Amen.

CHAPTER VI: SLEARY'S HORSEMANSHIP

The name of the public-house is the Pegasus's Arms. Underneath the winged horse upon the sign-board, 'The Pegasus's Arms' is inscribed in Roman letters. Beneath that inscription again, in a flowing scroll, the painter has touched off the lines: Good malt makes good beer,/ Walk in, and they draw it here;/ Good wine makes good brandy,/ Give us a call, and you'll find it handy.

As it has grown too dusky outside, to see the sign, and as it has not grown light enough within to see the picture, Mr. Gradgrind and Mr. Bounderby receive no offence from these idealities. They follow Cecilia up some steep corner-stairs without meeting any one, and stop in the dark while she goes on for a candle. The highly trained performing dog, Merrylegs, has not barked yet. Sissy says, with a face of great surprise, that her father is not in their room, and if they wouldn't mind walking in, she would find him directly. They walk in; and Sissy, having set two chairs for them, speed away with a quick light step. It is a mean, shabbily-furnished room, with a bed in it. They hear the doors of rooms above, opening and shutting as Sissy enters from one to another in quest of her father. She comes again in the room in a great hurry, opens a battered and mangy old hair trunk and finds it empty. She looks round with her hands clasped and her face full of terror. She says that her father must have gone to the Booth, and she would like to go there to fetch him.

A young man, Mr. E.W.B. Childers appears at the door. Mr. Gradgrind tells him that Sissy has gone to fetch her father, but he can no longer wait and so he would leave a message for her father with Childers. Mr. Bounderby puts in that they are the kind of people who know the value of time and the circus people are the kind of people who do not know the value of time. But Childers informs them that Mr. Jupe had missed his tip in the ring very often, lately. Although Mr. Gradgrind and

Mr. Bounderby cannot form any idea about missing a tip, Childers further informs them that the previous night, he missed his tip at the banners, too, and was loose in his ponging. Childers pursues that Mr. Jupe sent his daughter out on an errand about an hour before, and then was seen to slip out himself with his hat over his eyes and a bundle tied up in a handkerchief under his arm. Sissy would never believe it of him, but he has cut away and left her. Sissy would not believe it because they were never asunder and he seemed to dote upon her. Childers resumes that Mr. Jupe always had it in his head that Sissy should be taught proper education, and the idea never got out of his head. Even he had been picking up a bit of reading, writing and ciphering for her for last seven years. Mr. Gradgrind says that, on the contrary, he is there to tell Sissy's father that her connexions make her not an object for the school, and that she must not attend any more. While Mr. Gradgrind is talking to Mr. Bounderby as to what to decide about Sissy if her father has really left her, the various members of Sleary's company gather together from the upper regions. Last of all Mr. Sleary appears. Mr. Gradgrind tells Sleary that he would have something to propose to Sissy.

Sissy comes running into the room as she had run out of it. And when she sees them all assembled, and sees their looks, and cannot see her father, she breaks into a most deplorable cry, and takes refuge on the bosom of the most accomplished tight-rope lady. Mr. Gradgrind announces that although he is there to inform her father that she cannot be received at the school any more, in consequence of some practical objections, he is willing to take charge of the girl and to educate her, and provide for her, on the condition that she must terminate her relationship with the circus people. Mr. Gradgrind then tells Sissy that the only observation he would make to her is that it is highly desirable to have a sound practical education, and that even her father himself appears, on her behalf, to have known and felt that much. The words have a visible effect upon her. She stops in her wild crying. The whole company perceives the force of the change in Sissy. Sissy asks how her father would find her then. Mr. Gradgrind works it out that

Mr. Sleary would then let him know where she has gone and he should have no power of keeping her against her father's wishes and he would have no difficulty in finding him (Gradgrind) as he is well-known. Gradgrind's proposal is accepted by Sissy and the entire circus troupe. But Bounderby opposes Gradgrind's proposal and suggests to think over the proposal before putting it into effect; and meantime, Sissy would stay with him at his house.

Sissy takes her farewell of the whole company. Everybody blesses her in a variety of voices from all the room. But the riding-master's eye has observed the bottle of the nine oils in her bosom, and he interposes to leave the bottle to him.

She bursts into tears and requests to let her keep it for her father till he comes back: "He will want it when he comes back. He had never thought of going away, when he sent me for it. I must keep it for him, if you please!"

The world of the circus party is marked by fellow-feeling and there is an untiring readiness to help and pity one another. Mr. Sleary really feels a paternal interest in Sissy and this attitude is to be contrasted with Bounderby's contemptuous attitude. There is a remarkable gentleness and childishness about these people, a special inaptitude for any kind of sharp practice, deserving often of as much respect, and always of as much generous construction, as the everyday virtues of any class of people in the world.

The dignity and wit and finesse with which the sexual freedom of the circus women is described in the chapter needs no exegesis—we are reminded that the limited Dickens was also the rebellious Dickens. Dickens embodies the kind of gratuitous kindness which derives from spontaneous fellow-feeling and cannot be accounted for by the Utilitarian calculus. This kind of spontaneity is by no means unrelated to the brilliant circus tricks of the performers. The kindness of the horse riding is embodied chiefly in the figure of Sleary, and we are accordingly conscious mostly of the meanings enforced by this character. Their skills have no value for the Utilitarian calculus, but they express vital human impulse, and they minister to vital human needs.

CHAPTER VII: MRS. SPARSIT

Sissy is staying at Bounderby's house. Mr. Bounderby is a bachelor. An elderly lady, Mrs. Sparsit, presides over his establishment, in consideration of a certain annual stipend. She is a prominent figure in attendance on Mr. Bounderby's car, as it rolls along in triumph with the 'Bully of humility', Mr. Bounderby, inside. Mrs. Sparsit is a highly connected lady. She has a great aunt, living in those very times, called Lady Scadgers. Mr. Sparsit, deceased, of whom she is the relict, has been by the mother's side what Mrs. Sparsit calls "a Powler". The late Mr. Sparsit, being by the mother's side a Powler, married the lady, being by the father's side a scadgers. Lady Scadgers contrived the marriage. Mr. Sparsit inherited a fair fortune from his uncle, but owed it all before he came into it, and spent it twice over immediately afterwards. When he died, at twenty-four (the scene of his decease, Calais, and the cause, brandy), he did not leave his widow in affluent circumstances. And they had been separated soon after the honeymoon. "That bereaved lady, fifteen years older than he, fell presently at deadly feud with her only relative, Lady Scadgers; and, partly to spite her ladyship, and partly to maintain herself, went out at a salary. And here she was now, in her elderly days, with the Coriolanian style of nose and dense black eyebrows which had captivated Sparsit, making Mr. Bounderby's tea as he took his breakfast."

Mrs. Sparsit's "sir", in addressing Mr. Bounderby, is a word of ceremony, rather exacting consideration for herself in the use, than honouring him. Mr. Bounderby informs Mrs. Sparsit about Mr. Gradgrind's whim of bringing up the 'tumbling-girl', Cecilia Jupe. He says that it is clear to him that the 'little puss', Louisa, would get small good out of such companionship. He further informs her in course of their conversation that he is going to take Tom into his office to have him under him after Tom has finished his educational cramming. Mr. and Miss Gradgrind being then announced, he receives Mr. Gradgrind with a shake of the hand, and Miss

Gradgrind with a kiss. On coming in the room, Sissy curtseys to Mr. Bounderby, Mr. Gradgrind, and also to Louisa. But in her confusion she omits Mrs. Sparsit. Observing this, the blustrous Bounderby rebukes her sternly. Bounderby gives the introduction of Mrs. Sparsit: that she acts as the mistress of his house, and that she is a highly connected lady. He warns Sissy that if ever she did not behave towards that lady in her most respectful manner, he would give her a bit punishment. Mr. Gradgrind tells him, in a conciliatory voice, that he hopes that that was merely an oversight. Bounderby accepts Mr. Gradgrind's suggestion, but tells Mrs. Sparsit that he would not allow even oversights towards her.

Mr. Gradgrind informs Sissy that he has made up his mind to take her into his house to employ her about Mrs. Gradgrind, while not in attendance at the school. Mr. Gradgrind says that he should have the satisfaction of causing her to be strictly educated; and she would be a living proof of the advantages of his education. He would like to reclaim and form her anew. When Sissy says that she used to read to her father about the Fairies, the Dwarf, and the Hunch-back, and Genies, Mr. Gradgrind silences her and asks her never to breathe a word of 'such destructive nonsense' any more. He tells Bounderby that she would require rigid training, and he would observe it with interest. So, Mr. Gradgrind and Louisa take Cecilia Jupe off with them to Stone Lodge.

Bounderby invents elaborate degradations for his own early years, and compares these with the imagined glories of the Sparsit past. In this way both the hypocrites, Bounderby and Mrs. Sparsit, can draw satisfaction from completely fictitious accounts of themselves. Mrs. Sparsit thus embraces the grandeur and rejects the implication of relative seniority. A.E. Dyson says in *The Inimitable Dickens: Hard Times* "is a skeletal novel; ...The very humour is skull-like. What could be funnier than the pairing of Bounderby and Mrs. Sparsit, two humbugs perfectly calculated to serve each other right?" (186).

CHAPTER VIII: NEVER WONDER

Louisa has been overheard to begin a conversation with her brother, by saying "Tom, I wonder"—upon which Mr. Gradgrind, who is the person overhearing, says, "Louisa, never wonder!" "Herein lay the spring of the mechanical art and mystery of educating the reason without stooping to the cultivation of the sentiments and affections. Never wonder. By means of addition, subtraction, multiplication, and division, settle everything somehow, and never wonder."

There is a library in Coketown, to which general access is easy. Mr. Gradgrind greatly torments his mind about what the people read in that library. It would be a disheartening circumstance and a melancholy fact to him to think that even the readers there persist in wondering: They wonder about human nature, human passions, human hopes and fears, the struggles, triumphs and defeats, the cares and joys and sorrows, the lives and deaths of common men and women. They sometimes sit down to read mere fables about men and women.

Young Thomas Gradgrind is in the hair-cutting chamber at twilight. Young Thomas is sitting astride of a chair before the fire, with his arms on the back, and his sulky face on his arms. Louisa sits in the darker corner by the fireside, looking at him and often looking at the bright sparks as they drop upon the hearth. Tom expresses his hatred against his life at Stone Lodge:

> "I am sick of my life, Loo. I hate it altogether, and I hate everybody except you,"
>
> "As to me," said Tom, "I am a Donkey, that's what I am. I am as obstinate as one, I am more stupid than one, I get as much pleasure as one, and I should like to kick like one."

Tom has paused to find a sufficiently complimentary and expressive name for the parental roof, and seems to relieve his mind for a moment by the strong alliteration: 'jolly old-Jaundiced Jail'. He says that he cannot think how he would live in the house without Louisa. Louisa says, after silently watching the sparks awhile, that as she is getting older, and nearer growing up, she "often sits wondering before the fire, and thinks how unfortunate it is for her that she can't reconcile him to home better than she is able to do". Tom says that she is the only pleasure he has. Tom's disgust against Fact and Figures is evident as he says, "I wish I could collect all the Facts we hear so much about...and all the Figures, and all the people who found them out: and I wish I could put a thousand barrels of gunpowder under them, and blow them all up together!" He expresses his hope that when he would go to live with Bounderby, he would have his revenge. He would enjoy a little, and go about and see something, and hear something. Louisa says that Mr. Bounderby thinks the way their father thought, and is a great deal rougher, and not half so kind. Tom says that he knows very well how to manage and smooth Bounderby. Louisa is his tram-card: "It's you. You are his little pet, you are his favourite; he'll do anything for you. When he says to me what I don't like, I shall say to him, 'My sister Loo will be hurt and disappointed, Mr. Bounderby.'" Louisa was looking at the fire. Tom says that it would be getting away from home. Tom says that he would be very unwilling, both to leave her, and to leave her in Stone Lodge. But he must go whether he likes it or not; and he should better go where he could take some advantage of her influence, than where he should lose it altogether. To a question by Tom, Louisa says that she does not see anything in the fire, particularly, but since she has been looking at it, she has been wondering about him and herself, grown up. '"Wondering again!" said Tom. "I have such unmanageable thoughts", returned his sister, "that they will wonder".' Mrs. Gradgrind who has opened the door without being heard happens to overhear Louisa's words and scolds her in no uncertain terms for wondering when she has expressly been warned by her father never to wonder. She rebukes Tom that it is really shameful that a boy brought up as he has been should be found encouraging his sister to wonder. When Louisa denies Tom's participation in the offence their mother says that unless she has been encouraged, it is morally and physically impossible that she could have done it. "I was encouraged by nothing, mother, but by looking at the red sparks dropping out of the fire, and whitening and dying. It made me think, after all, how short my life would be, and how little I could hope to do in it." "Nonsense!" says Mrs. Gradgrind, rendered almost energetic. She says that if such stuff is to reach their father's ears she would not hear the last of it. It is poor Mrs. Gradgrind's perpetual fear of fancy as a dreaded intruder. Whenever and however it manifests itself, she fears she will never hear the last.

The fire gazing scene in the chapter when Louisa and Tom are at their father's hearth, a place where the 'fanciful imagination' is a 'treason', is very significant. Louisa seems transfixed by the flames, and she speaks slowly, and in a curious tone, as if she were reading what she asked in the fire, and it were not quite plainly written there. When Tom looks into the fire to see what engrosses his sister, he finds nothing; to him it looks "as stupid and blank as everything else looks". Their exchange of words shows that the fire brings on wonder. Tom is looking for some substantial relief from the mulish drudgery of his life. But as Louisa's response shows, the fire-gazing reaches deeper into the psychic life, inducing the very wonder upon which circus-going and all imaginative enterprise are founded.

CHAPTER IX: SISSY'S PROGRESS

Sissy Jupe has not an easy time of it, between Mr. M'Choakumchild and Mrs. Gradgrind, and is not without strong impulses, in the first months of her probation, to run away. Life in general is opened to her as such a closely ruled ciphering-book, that assuredly she would have run away, but for only one restraint. But this restraint is the result of no arithmetical process. It is self-imposed in defiance of all calculation. The girl believes that her father has not deserted her; she lives in the hope that he would come back, and in the faith that he would be made the happier by her remaining where she is. Being reported by M'Choakumchild, Mr. Gradgrind observes that the case of Sissy shows the necessity of infinite grinding at the mill of knowledge; and that Jupe "must be kept to it". So Jupe is kept to it, and becomes low-spirited, but no wiser.

There has been so little communication between Louisa and Sissy—both because life at Stone Lodge goes on monotonously round like a piece of machinery which discourages human interference, and because of the prohibition relative to Sissy's past career. They are almost strangers in the same house. Louisa says, "You are more useful to my mother, and more pleasant with her than I can ever be", "You are pleasanter to yourself, than I am to *myself*." Sissy pleads, "I am—O so stupid!" Louisa tells her she would be wiser by-and-by. Sissy says that all through school hours she makes mistakes. Louisa asks, "Mr. and Mrs. M'Choakumchild never make any mistakes themselves, I suppose, Sissy?" "O no!" she eagerly and innocently replies. "They know everything."

Mr. M'Choakumchild knows a little about everything, but has never learned how to communicate anything but knowledge for its own sake. Sissy reports to Louisa her difficulties in understanding him.

Louisa wants to know how Sissy's father has left Sissy. Sissy, covering her eyes, and sobbing yet, reports the sad story: Sissy came home from the school in the afternoon, and found her father just come home too, from the booth. And he sat rocking himself over the fire, as if he was in pain. And Sissy asked him whether he had hurt himself, as he did sometimes, like they all did. He said, 'A little.' When she came to stoop down and look up at his face, she saw that he was crying. The more she spoke to him, the more he hid his face; and at first he shook all over, and said nothing but 'My darling!' and 'My love!'

Now Tom comes lounging in, and stares at the two with a coolness not particularly savouring of interest in anything but himself. Tom informs Louisa that their father has brought Bounderby home. Tom wants her to go into the drawing-room because it may open a good chance of old Bounderby's asking him to dinner.

Then Sissy resumes in a lower voice: At last her father said that he had given no satisfaction again, and that he was a shame and disgrace, and she should have done better without him all along. She said all the affectionate things to him that came into her heart, and presently he was quiet and she sat down by him, and told him all about the school and everything that had been said and done there. When she had no more left to tell, he put his arms round her neck, and kissed her a great many times. Then he asked her to fetch some of the stuff he used, for the little hurt he had had, and to get it at the best place, which was at the other end of town from there. After kissing her again, he let her go. When Sissy wanted to take Merrylegs with her, her father shook his head and said, 'No, Sissy, no; take nothing that's known to be mine, my darling.' And she left him sitting by the fire. When she returned, he was gone.

The episode in which Sissy Jupe tells Louisa the story of her father's one outburst of anger has a crucial function in the novel. The 'Sympathetic induction of emotion' is the basis of all other forms of sympathy which Dickens uses. He was well aware of the form when he comments, on 'the child's unconscious sympathy with youth' and an 'old man's enthusiasm...felt in with the only creature to whom he was linked by ties of long association'. This form is described by McDougall as follows: Active sympathy...is of prime importance for the development of the sentiment of affection between equals.... It involves a reciprocal relation between at least two persons; either party to the relation not only is apt to experience the emotions displayed by the other, but he desires also that the other shall share his own emotions; he actively seeks the sympathy of the other, and, when he has communicated his emotion to the other, he attains a peculiar satisfaction which greatly enhances his pleasure and his joy...the sharing of our emotion by another intensifies our own emotion by way of the fundamental reaction of primitive sympathy. Louisa is sharing Sissy's distress about her father, the reciprocal principle which McDougall stresses. We see 'the sympathetic induction of emotion' at work in 'the trembling of Sissy's lip repeated in Louisa's face'.

CHAPTER X: STEPHEN BLACKPOOL

In the hardest working part of Coketown, in the innermost fortifications of that ugly citadel, among the multitude of

Coketown, generically called the "Hands", lives Stephen Blackpool, forty years of age. Stephen looks older, but he has had a hard life. He has known a peck of troubles in his life. He is usually called Old Stephen, in a kind of rough homage to the fact. He is a rather stooping man, with a knitted brow, a pondering expression of face. He has a hard-looking head sufficiently capacious, on which his iron-grey hair lay long and thin. He holds no station among the Hands who can make speeches and carry on debates. He is a good power-loom weaver, and a man of perfect integrity.

The lights in the great factories, which look, when they are illuminated, like Fairy palaces, are all extinguished. The bells have rung for knocking off for the night, and has ceased again. The Hands, men and women, boy and girl, are clattering home. Old Stephen is standing in the street, with the old sensation upon him which the stoppage of the machinery always produces—the sensation of its having worked and stopped in his own head. He is waiting to see Rachael. It is a wet night, and many groups of young women pass him, with their shawls drawn over their bareheads and held close under their chins to keep the rain out. He knows Rachael well, for a glance at any one of these groups is sufficient to show him that she is not there. At last, there are no more to come; and then he turns away in disappointment, thinking that he has missed her. But, he has not gone the length of three streets, when he sees another of the shawled figures in advance of him. Making his pace at once much quicker and much softer, he darts on until he is very near this figure, and then calls "Rachael!" Rachael turns, being then in the brightness of a lamp; and raising her hood a little, shows a quiet oval face, dark and rather delicate, irradiated by a pair of very gentle eyes, and further set off by the perfect order of her shining black hair. Her face is not a face in its first bloom of youth. She is a woman of thirty-five years of age. He looks at her with some disappointment in his face, but with a respectful and patient conviction that must be right in whatever she does. Stephen praises her beauty that she looks as young as ever she has been.

Stephen laments that his life is a muddle, always a muddle and he can never get beyond it. They have walked some distance, and are near their own homes. The woman's is the first reached. She goes, with her neat figure and her sober womanly step, down the dark street, and he stands looking after her until she turns into one of the small houses. When she is lost to his view, he pursues his homeward way, glancing up sometimes at the sky, where the clouds are sailing. He takes the end of the candle from a shelf, lights it at another end of candle on the counter, without disturbing the mistress of the shop who is asleep in her little room, and then he goes upstairs into his lodging. Going to the hearth to set the candle down upon a round three-legged table there, he stumbles against something. As he recoils, looking down at it, it raises itself up into the form of a woman in a sitting attitude. She is his wife. His disabled, drunken wife is barely able to preserve her sitting posture by steadying herself with one begrimed hand on the floor, while the other is so purposeless in trying to push away her tangled hair from her face. She is a creature so foul to look at, but so much fouler than that in her moral infamy, that it is a shameful thing even to see her. After an impatient oath or two, and some stupid clawing of herself with the hand for support, she gets her hair away from her eyes sufficiently to obtain a sight of him. Then she sits swaying her body to and fro, and making gestures with her unnerved arm. Her face is stolid and drowsy. She cries, "I'll sell thee off again, and I'll sell thee off again, and I'll sell thee off a score of times!" He is sitting on the side of the bed, with his face hidden in his hands. As she staggers to it, he avoids her with a shudder, and passes to the opposite end of the room. She throws herself upon the bed heavily, and soon starts snoring hard. He sinks into a chair, and moves but once all that night. It is to throw a covering over her; as if his hands are not enough to hide her, even in the darkness.

Three new characters have been introduced in this chapter and we come to know of Stephen's domestic plight. The reference to "Fairy palaces" is in some sense ironic, that these factories are merely temples to fact which denies the existence both of fairies and of their architecture as absurd castles in the air. It is a trenchant parody of the whole romantic sensibility as it becomes an aestheticizing indifference to human pain.

CHAPTER XI: NO WAY OUT

The Fairy palaces burst into illumination, before pale morning showed the monstrous serpents of smoke trailing themselves over Coketown. Stephen bends over his loom, quiet, watchful, and steady. So many hundred Hands are working in this Mill. The day grows strong, and shows itself outside, even against the flaming lights within. The work goes on until the noon-bell rings. More clattering upon the pavements rises up. The looms, and wheels, and Hands all are out of gear for an hour. Stephen comes out of the hot mill into the damp wind and cold wet streets. He is feeling haggard and worn.

Stephen turns from his own class and his own quarter, taking nothing but a little bread as he walks along, towards the hill on which his principal employer, Mr. Bounderby, lives. Bounderby lives in a red house with black outside shutters, green inside blinds, a black street door, up two white steps, BOUNDERBY (in letters very like himself) upon a brazen plate, and a round brazen door-handle underneath it, like a brazen full-stop. Mr. Bounderby is at his lunch. So Stephen had expected. Bounderby is given the message. There was nothing troublesome against Stephen Blackpool, and so he is allowed.

Mr. Bounderby asks Stephen the purpose of his visit. Stephen is there to seek Bounderby's advice as to how he could be legally separated from his wife. Stephen informs him that they have been married nineteen years. Soon after their marriage she goes downhill, and returns at random intervals drunken and penniless. Bounderby, with Mrs. Sparsit in self-righteous support, informs him that only a thousand pounds or more could effect such a separation; otherwise nothing can be done. Stephen feels helpless, and wishes he were dead. Bounderby harangues him, telling him that he is turning or is being led into dangerous paths.

Dickens voices his indignation at the costliness of divorce, which remains a privilege of the rich. He might have been thinking already, in 1854, of the possible collapse of his own home life, and he may have wished publicly to assert his position in favour of the easier dissolution of all unhappy marriages. Yet the case of Blackpool and his wife is so different from that of Charles and Catherine Dickens that the link is by no means certain.

Dickens's sentences are assiduously paced and the antithetical structure is automatic and tenacious. One can quote the following lines: "Stephen bent over his loom, quiet, watchful, and steady. A special contrast...to the crashing, smashing, tearing piece of mechanism at which he laboured." The contrast of opposed syntactic triads, the quiet and steady adjectives against the grating kinetic participles, has a tightness unfamiliar in Dickens's usual prose. There are ironies in the passage, for that "special contrast" asserted between hero and machine is partly subverted by the similar three pronged grammar of their balanced descriptions, and is in fact contradicted by that extra-syntactic parallel throughout the novel which insists that men in the society are slowly being turned into machines.

CHAPTER XII: THE OLD WOMAN

Stephen descends the two white steps, shutting the black door with the brazen door-plate. He crosses the street with his eyes bent upon the ground, and thus is walking sorrowfully away, when he felt a touch upon his arm. It is an old woman, tall and shapely still, though withered by time, on whom his eyes fall when he stopped and turned. She is very cleanly and plainly dressed, has country mud upon her shoes, and is newly come from a journey. The old woman asks him whether he has seen the gentleman (Bounderby) in the house. The old woman appears to take it for granted that he leads a happy life indeed, and he has not the heart to disappoint her. He knows that there is trouble enough in the world. She enquires if Stephen's personal problems disrupt his work in the factory. Stephen says that they don't follow him there, and everything is accordant there. Stephen and the old woman are then in the black by-road near the place. The Hands are crowding in. The bell is ringing, and the serpent of smoke is a serpent of many coils. The strange old woman is delighted with the very bell. It is the beautifullest bell she has ever heard, as she says, and sounds grand. She says she must kiss the hand working in the factory for a dozen year.

Stephen starts working. He has been at his loom full half an hour. He is thinking about that old woman. Having occasion to move round the loom for its adjustment, he glances through a window which is in his corner, and sees her still looking up at the pile of building, lost in admiration. Heedless of the smoke and mud and wet, she is gazing at it. The old woman who will later prove to be Bounderby's mother contributes to the fairy world of the novel.

Stephen comes out of the factory. He feels it is better to have no home in which to lay his head, than to have a home and dread to go to it. He eats and drinks, for he is exhausted—but he little knows or cares what. He wanders about in the chill rain, thinking and thinking, and brooding and brooding. He thinks of the waste of the best part of his life, of the change it makes in his character for the worse every day, tormented by a demonic wife. He thinks of Rachael. He thinks of how she has contentedly pursued her own lone quiet path—for him—and how he has sometimes seen a shade of melancholy on her blessed face that smites him with remorse and despair. Filled with such thoughts he has an unwholesome sense of growing larger, of being placed in some new and diseased relation towards the objects among which he passes, of seeing the iris round every misty light turn red—he goes home for shelter.

CHAPTER XIII: RACHAEL

A candle is faintly burning in the window of Stephen's lodging. From the outside of his home Stephen gloomily passes to the inside, with suspended breath and with a slow footstep. He goes up to his door, opens it, and enters the room. Quiet and peace are there; Rachael is there, sitting by the bed. She turns her head. Her face lightens Stephen's mind. She sits by the bed, watching and tending his wife. Everything is in its place and order as he has always kept it. The little fire is newly trimmed. The hearth is freshly swept. It appears to him that he sees all this in Rachael's face, and looks at nothing besides. While looking at her face, it is shut out from his view by the softened tears that filled his eyes. He has seen how earnestly she looks at him, and how her own eyes are filled too, with tears. Rachael turns towards the bed. There are wounds about the neck of the 'self-made outcast', Stephen's wife. Rachael is dressing them. She steeps a piece of linen in a basin, into which she pours some liquid from a bottle, and lays it with a gentle hand upon the sore. The three-legged table has been drawn close to the bedside, and on it there are two bottles. This is one.

Stephen feels a violent fit of trembling, and then sinks into his chair. After a time he controls himself, and is fixedly looking towards Rachael. His eyes are moistened, and she seems to him as if she has a glory shining round her head. Rachael says she has the hope that when his wife would get better she would leave him to himself again, and do him no more hurt. Then Rachael keeps silence, for she wants Stephen to sleep. He closes his eyes, more to please her than to rest his weary head. His imperfect consciousness fades away at last, and he dreams a long, troubled dream. Rachael also falls asleep in the chair to the bed. He wakes only to see his wife, craving for drink, taking up the bottle of poison with which Rachael had been dressing her wounds. He sits spell-bound, making no move to stop her. However, at that critical moment, Rachael starts up and averts the danger. As it is early morning now, she has to leave. Stephen hopes that one day, even in death perhaps, he and Rachael might be together.

Stephen's subconscious thoughts are revealed here in Freudian terms. Rachael is a character too white to be real. This is a gripping chapter in respect of the plot structure of the novel.

CHAPTER XIV: THE GREAT MANUFACTURER

Time is the great manufacturer which 'lays his icy hands' on everything and everyone. Time goes on in Coketown like its own machinery. Mr. Gradgrind is conscious that Louisa is becoming almost a young woman and Thomas almost a young man. Time passes Tom into Bounderby's bank and makes him an inmate of Bounderby's house. Time, the same great manufacturer, always with an immense variety of work on hand, in every stage of development, passes Sissy onward in his mill, and works her up into 'a very pretty article'. Time makes Mr. Gradgrind Member of Parliament from Coketown.

Mr. Gradgrind expresses his hopeless opinion to Sissy that her continuance at the school any longer would be useless. The result of her probation there has greatly disappointed him. She could not acquire, under Mr. and Mrs. M'Choakumchild, anything like that amount of exact knowledge which Gradgrind looked for. In Mr. Gradgrind's opinion, she is extremely deficient in her facts. Her acquaintance with figures is very limited. She is altogether backward, and below the mark. Sissy agrees to the opinion and timidly says that she has tried hard, but could not learn. Mr. Gradgrind thinks that the circumstances of her early life are too unfavourable to the development of her reasoning powers. Sissy could not check her tears. Mr. Gradgrind affectionately says that he does not complain of her and that she is an affectionate, earnest, good young woman. He also says that she is useful to Mrs. Gradgrind, and she is serviceable in his family also. He therefore hopes that Sissy could make herself happy in those relations. He says that he has heard from Louisa that Sissy has still preserved the bottle of nine oils for her father, and that proves Sissy's lack of success in the training of the science of arriving at exact results. He really likes Sissy too well to have a contempt for her.

Gradgrind tells Louisa that he has to talk to her about something very important and that he would like to do so after breakfast the next day. Mr. Gradgrind kisses Louisa and goes away; and Louisa returns to the serene apartment of the hair-cutting character. Leaning her elbow on her hand, she looks at the short-lived sparks that so soon subsided into ashes. Tom looks in at the door. He is looking like a young gentleman of pleasure, and not quite a prepossessing one. He asks Louisa whether their father has said anything particular to her very recently. Tom informs her that their father is with Bounderby that night and they are having a regular confab together up not in the house but at the Bank, probably to keep Mrs. Sparsit's ears as far off as possible. He expresses his joy that what would happen would be a splendid thing for him and it would be 'uncommonly jolly'. He presses her in his arm, and kisses her cheek. She returns the kiss, but is still looking at the fire.

Louisa gives Tom an affectionate good-night, and goes out with him to the door, whence the fires of Coketown could be seen, making the distance lurid. She stands there, looking steadfastly towards them, and listening to his departing steps. It seems as if, first in the fire within the house, and then in the fiery haze without, she tries to "discover what kind of woof Old Time, that greatest and longest-established Spinner of all, would weave from the threads he had already spun into a woman". But Time's factory is a secret place, his work is noiseless, and his Hands are mutes. Dickens turns poetic in his description of the 'Great Manufacturer' in rhetorical language.

CHAPTER XV: FATHER AND DAUGHTER

Mr. Gradgrind's room is quite a blue chamber in its abundance of blue books. His observatory is a stern room, with a deadly statistical clock in it. Louisa repairs on the appointed morning. When she sits down near her father's table, she sees through a window the high chimneys and the long tracts of smoke looming in the heavy distance gloomily. Mr. Gradgrind tells his daughter that she has been so well trained that he is happy to say that he has perfect confidence in her good sense. He expresses his belief that she is not impulsive, she is not romantic and she is accustomed to view everything from the strong dispassionate ground of reason and calculation. And he expresses his hope that she would view and consider only from that ground what he is going to communicate. He blurts out that she is the subject of a proposal of marriage that has been made to him. He waits but Louisa utters not a word. This so far surprises him, as to induce him gently to repeat the words "a proposal of marriage..." to which she returns, without any visible emotion whatever, that she hears him and she is attending him surely. He comments that she looks even more dispassionate than he had expected. He informs her that Mr. Bounderby has made his proposal of marriage to him, and has entreated him to make it known to her, and to express his hope that she would take it into her favourable consideration.

The scene is characteristically rich in invention: Dickens amplifies his single point with a fine variety of devices. When Gradgrind is momentarily nonplussed by Louisa's rational calmness, the readers feel that he is surprised because he really does have good instincts; he knows there is something wrong with this marriage, that Louisa ought to have to be persuaded by rational arguments, just as he has had to persuade himself by rational arguments. But he can't face this fact yet.

There is silence between them, father and daughter. The deadly statistical clock sounds very hollow. The distant smoke looks very black and heavy. "Father", asks Louisa, "do you think I love Mr. Bounderby?" Mr. Gradgrind feels extremely discomfited by her unexpected questions like whether he thinks Louisa love Mr. Bounderby or whether he asks her to love Bounderby or Bounderby asks her to love him. Gradgrind advises her to consider the question as she has been accustomed to consider every other question, simply as one of tangible Fact. Louisa is, in round numbers, twenty years of age and Mr. Bounderby is, in round numbers, fifty. There is some disparity in their age, but, he thinks that in their means and positions there is none; on the contrary, he says that he finds that there is a great suitability in the marriage. He further counteracts the disparity of their ages with copious and universal statistics. To Louisa's question, "Shall I marry him?" Gradgrind answers that precisely she should. He adds that it is satisfactory to him, as her father to know that she does not come to the consideration of that question with the previous habits of mind, and habits of life, that belong to many young women. Louisa accepts the proposal, but betrays no love for Bounderby. Since Mr. Bounderby likes to take her thus, she tells her father that she feels satisfied to accept his proposal:

'Tell him, father, as soon as you please, that this was my answer. Repeat it, word for word, if you can, because I should wish him to know what I said.' She tells her father that his system of bringing up has suppressed any love and affection she might have had. Her father accepts her words as a complimentary testimonial to its efficacy. Mrs. Gradgrind feels pleased with the news, as far as she could be.

The phrasing of Louisa is veiled enough for the modest reader to miss the point if he wishes. Louisa, having failed repeatedly to get her father to acknowledge the need for love in marriage, stares out of the window at the factory chimneys of Coketown so fixedly that he asks her why she's looking at them. Gradgrind asks if she is "consulting with the chimneys of the Coketown works".

> 'There seems to be nothing there but languid and monotonous smoke. Yet when the night comes, Fire bursts out, father!' she answered, turning quickly.
>
> 'Of course I know that, Louisa. I do not see the application of the remark.'

This is a new kind of frankness, even if it escapes Mr. Gradgrind, and a new kind of woman. Louisa's hours of fire-gazing drew her to a sense of wonder and provided Dickens with an icon for her constrained but vital energies. But these energies have stagnated, and she can now find symbolic expression for them only in the smouldering, incendiary nature of the Coketown furnaces waiting for their violent discharge. Louisa's world is very much like Paul's constrained world in *Dombey and Son.*

Sissy feels emotionally affected by Louisa's passive acceptance of the proposal. When Mr. Gradgrind has presented Louisa before Sissy, Sissy has suddenly turned her head, and looks, in wonder, in pity, in sorrow, in doubt, in a multitude of emotions, towards Louisa. Louisa has known it, and seen it, without looking at her. From that moment she is impassive, proud and cold—held Sissy at a distance—changed to her altogether. Sissy's tenderness is repulsed because of a moment's pity and amazement, which Louisa, understandably, cannot accept. We saw that Louisa and Sissy developed a sympathetic bond between each other. The rejection of this sympathetic bond with Sissy on the part of Louisa marks a special crisis of the book and leads to Louisa's catastrophe. The resumption of the sympathetic relationship with Sissy marks a further crisis and results in the denouement. Without a full appreciation of the sympathetic link between Sissy and Louisa we cannot grasp either Louisa's character or the function of Sissy in the novel.

CHAPTER XVI: HUSBAND AND WIFE

Mr. Bounderby feels disquietude on hearing Louisa's acceptance. It is occasioned by the necessity of imparting the happy news to Mrs. Sparsit. He could not make up his mind how to present the news to her or what the consequences of the step might be. However, he has no choice but to do it; so, after attempting several letters, and failing in them all, he resolves to do it by word of mouth. He enters his own house with anything but a courageous air.

Mr. Bounderby sits looking at Mrs. Sparsit, as she picks out holes for some inscrutable ornamental purpose, in a piece of cambric. Mr. Bounderby says that he is going to astonish her with the news that he is going to marry 'Tom Gradgrind's daughter'. Mrs. Sparsit returns that she hopes he should be happy. Bounderby resumes that under the circumstances, he thinks it would not be agreeable to a character like hers to remain in his house, but better to go to his Bank where there are apartments, where 'a born-and-bred lady' would be rather a catch than otherwise if the same annual compliment would be acceptable there. Mrs. Sparsit says that if the position she would assume at the Bank is one that she could occupy without descending lower in the social scale, she has nothing to object to it. Bounderby says that she would have her private apartments, coals and candles, and all the rest of it; and she would have her maid to attend upon her, and her light porter to protect her, and she would be able to have her liberty more. Mrs. Sparsit accepts his offer gratefully with many acknowledgments for past favours.

The marriage was appointed to be solemnized in eight weeks' time. Mr. Bounderby starts visiting Stone Lodge every evening, as an accepted wooer. Love is made in the form of bracelets; and, on all occasions it takes a manufacturing aspect. Settlements are made. An extensive assortment of Facts appropriates honour to the contract. The marriage is all Fact, from first to last. The deadly statistical clock in the Gradgrind observatory knocks every second with *his accustomed regularity* (emphasis added). So the day of marriage came, as all other days come to people sticking to reason only; and when it came, they were married in the church. Being united in holy matrimony, they go home to breakfast at Stone Lodge. There is an improving party assembled on the auspicious occasion. Bounderby makes a pompous and egotistical speech, and the pair leaves for Lyons for their honeymoon. Tom alone is elated at the turn of events.

In this chapter the plot development gets a new thrust and the character of Louisa takes a peculiar twist. Dickens's pungent satire is revealed in the words about the marriage: "The business was all fact, from first to last." To the interest seeking Tom it is something "uncommonly jolly".

BOOK II. REAPING

CHAPTER I: EFFECTS IN THE BANK

It is a sunny midsummer day in Coketown. Seen from a distance in such weather, Coketown looks shrouded in a haze of its own, which appears impervious to the sun's rays. Mrs. Sparsit is in her afternoon apartment at the Bank. Office-hours are over. Mr. Bounderby has been married a year. And Mrs. Sparsit has never released him from her determined pity a moment.

The Bank offers no violence to the wholesome monotony of the town. Mrs. Sparsit is conscious that by coming in the evening among the desks and writing implements, she sheds a feminine as well as aristocratic grace upon the office. Seated, with her needlework or netting apparatus, at the window, she has a self-laudatory sense of correcting, by her ladylike deportment, the rude business aspect of the place. With that impression of herself, Mrs. Sparsit considers herself, in some sort, the Bank Fairy. A deaf serving-woman and the light porter Bitzer attend Mrs. Sparsit.

Mrs. Sparsit's tea is set for her on a little table. The light porter places the tea-tray on it, knuckling his forehead as a form of homage. "He was a very light porter indeed; as light as in the days when he blinkingly defined a horse, for girl number twenty." This is his usual hour for having a confidential chat with Mrs. Sparsit. Mrs. Sparsit enquires about the news of the day. Bitzer guesses that she is going to ask him something particular. He makes a pretence of arranging the rulers, inkstands, and so forth, while that lady is having her tea, glancing through the open window, down into the street. Mrs. Sparsit asks him whether the clerks are trustworthy, punctual and industrious. Bitzer answers in the affirmative, adding the words, "the usual exception". Bitzer holds the respectable office of general spy and informer in the establishment, for which volunteer service he receives a present at Christmas, over and above his weekly wage. He has grown into an extremely clear-headed, cautious, prudent young man, who is safer to rise in the world. His mind is exactly regulated. He has no affections or passions. All his proceedings are the result of the nicest and coldest calculation.

Bitzer tells Mrs. Sparsit that he doubts Tom very much and he does not like his ways at all. He opines that Tom is a dissipated, extravagant idler. Bitzer needs no recreations in life and to him it is stuff and nonsense to want recreations. He says that he does not want recreations, he never did, and he never would. As to people's combining together, by watching and informing upon one another, he says that one could earn a trifle now and then, whether in money or goodwill, and improve their livelihood. To improve the livelihood would be the first consideration of a rational creature. It would become quite nauseous, concerning their wives and families. Bitzer says, "I don't want a wife and family."

A stranger knocks, and repeats his knock so loudly that the light porter hastens down to open the door. The visitor strolls to the window. He is as unmoved by his entry as man could possibly be. He stands whistling to himself with all imaginable coolness, with his hat still on, and a certain air of exhaustion upon him, in part from excessive gentility. Mrs. Sparsit observes in her womanly way that he would be thirty-five, and thinks the attributes for him: "good-looking, good figure, good health, good teeth, good voice, good breeding, well-dressed, dark hair, bold eyes". Mrs. Sparsit does not forget to inform him that her husband was a Powler, and that she had long adapted herself to the governing power of her life. The stranger says that he is the bearer of a letter of introduction to Mr. Bounderby the banker. He asks a fellow and he directs him to the Bank. He says that his letter is from Mr. Gradgrind whom he has had the pleasure of knowing in London. Mrs. Sparsit recognizes the hand, and gives Mr. Bounderby's address, with all needful clues and directions in aid. In course of the conversation between Mrs. Sparsit and the stranger, the latter comes to know that Mr. Bounderby's wife is too young, around twenty years of age. After the visitor's departure, Mrs. Sparsit wants to know Bitzer's opinion about him. Bitzer says that he seems to spend much money on clothes and Mrs. Sparsit agrees to him. When Bitzer says that the visitor might be given to gambling, Mrs. Sparsit says that gambling is not good and it is immoral. Without a candle in the room, Mrs. Sparsit sits at the window, not until the light porter announced that her nocturnal sweetbread is ready. The stranger is Mr. James Harthouse. The chapter is a satire on Bitzer, Mrs. Sparsit, and Coketown and its people, to some extent.

CHAPTER II: MR. JAMES HARTHOUSE

After a few dashes in the public meeting way, Mr. Gradgrind and a council of political sages approves of Jem, James Harthouse. It is resolved to send him down to Coketown, to become known there and in the neighbourhood. Hence the letter Jem had last night shown to Mrs. Sparsit. Mr. Bounderby sees the letter, superscribed, "Josiah Bounderby, Esquire, Banker, Coketown. Specially to introduce James Harthouse, Esquire. Thomas Gradgrind."

Within an hour of the receipt of this dispatch and Mr. James Harthouse's card, Mr. Bounderby puts on his hat and goes down to the Hotel. There he meets Harthouse. Bounderby tells Harthouse that Coketown is not the kind of place he has been accustomed to, and therefore he would like to tell him something about Coketown. Bounderby says that the smoke in Coketown is 'meat and drink' to the people, being the healthiest thing in all respects, and particularly for the lungs. Bounderby says that the work in the mills in Coketown is the pleasantest work, the lightest work and the best-paid work. As to the Hands, there is not a Hand in this town, man, woman, or child, who does not have one ultimate object in life and the object is to be fed on turtle soup and venison with a gold spoon, though the object could never to be fulfilled. Bounderby does not forget to inform him about his humble origin that he is a bit of dirty riff-raff, and a genuine scrap of tag, rag and bobtail.

Bounderby invites James to his house to introduce him to his wife, Mr. Gradgrind's daughter. They go out without further discourse. Mr. Bounderby fetches the new acquaintance to his private red brick dwelling. In the drawing-room there presently enters Louisa, the most remarkable girl Mr. James Harthouse has ever seen. She is so constrained, and yet so careless. She is so reserved, and yet so watchful. She is so cold and proud, and yet so sensitively ashamed of her husband's braggart humility. In face she is as remarkable as in manner. Her features are handsome. But their natural play is so locked up, that it seems impossible to guess at their genuine expression.

From the mistress of the house, James glances to the house itself. There is no mute sign of the hand of a woman in the room. No graceful little adornment, no fanciful little device anywhere expresses her influence. Bounderby is obviously proud of his marriage with her. He says that his wife is his junior, and further adds that he does not know what she has seen in him to marry him, but she saw something in him or she wouldn't have married him. Harthouse enters into a friendly sort of conversation with Louisa. In course of his conversation with her, he says he has gone through several types of boredom in his life and that he has come to the conclusion that there is no point in acquiring any particular opinions and convictions. He tells Louisa that his motto in life is: "What will be, will be."

Harthouse observes that throughout the conversation Louisa remains absolutely impassive. At no stage the features of her face relaxes. He wonders whether there is anything at all that could move her face. Just then Louisa's brother appears on the scene. On seeing him, Louisa smiles joyfully, and Harthouse comes to the conclusion that her brother is the only creature she cares for. After that Harthouse begins to show a good deal of interest in Tom, and Tom feels much flattered by the attentions of him.

CHAPTER III: THE WHELP

Although Tom has been brought up under one continuous system of unnatural restraint, he could not but become a hypocrite. Although he has never been brought up always under guidance, he is incapable at last of governing himself. Although his imagination has been strangled in his cradle, still he has grown up without discipline. When Harthouse goes back to hotel from Bounderby's house, he takes Tom with him. Tom feels quite elated in Harthouse's company who offers him his hospitality with excellent tobacco and liquor. Under the influence of wine and tobacco to which he is unused, yet assuming a man-of-the-world air, Tom proves himself to be an over-talkative, gullible hypocrite. He tells Harthouse how Louisa married Bounderby, more or less to make his (Tom's) life easier and more pleasant. He tells Harthouse too of Louisa's introspection, and of "the system", and of Mrs. Sparsit's long-standing, but unrequited devotion to Mr. Bounderby.

"Whelp" is a cliché, and the word was first used by Harthouse, and then adopted by the novelist in his authorial capacity. The word is used with ironical intent, suggesting some inadequacy in the speaker's habits of thought. Dickens plays on Gradgrind's "facts" to this effect. But in the case of

Harthouse's "whelp" he has taken a moral cliché from Tom who is morally unreliable, and invested it with his own authority as narrator. This gives away the fact that Tom is being forced into a new role.

CHAPTER IV: MEN AND BROTHERS

Stephen Blackpool the good workman and Slackbridge the Union agitator form a separate story line which has been generally condemned as fairly thin and crude and not very well adjusted to the central fable. The sincerity of Dickens' social feeling is not to be called in doubt. Few men have been so vividly struck as he was by the sufferings of the poor, by the unfairness of fate, and by the frequent cruelty of privileged people.

At a union meeting, Slackbridge, a violent agitator, is addressing a large number of Hands. He urges the workers that they must rally round one another as one united power, and crumble into dust the oppressors that too long has battened and exploited them. In many great respects Slackbridge is essentially below the fellow workers. He is not so honest, he is not so manly, he is not so good humoured like them. And he substitutes cunning for their simplicity, and passion for their safe solid sense. He is an ill-made, high-shouldered man.

Slackbridge is speaking over a particular worker, Stephen Blackpool, who denies to join the workers' union, Union Aggregate Tribunal. The cunning leader calls the union to expel Stephen and to treat him as an outcast. Few members suggest that Stephen should be given a chance to explain himself. A plain speaking man, Stephen says that he does not see what good would emerge out of the union activities. He says that, considering his troubled and miserable life that he has been leading for many years, he feels no interest to join the union. Slackbridge dubs Stephen a traitor and he forces Stephen to be sent to Coventry by his workmates. Thus Stephen Blackpool easily falls into the loneliest of lives, the life of solitude among a familiar crowd. He becomes a stranger at his work, on his way to it and from it. By general consent, they even avoid that side of the street on which he habitually walk; and leave it, of all the working men, to him only.

Stephen has been a quiet silent man for many years. He associated but little with other men. It is even harder than he could have believed possible. He is separated in his own conscience by all his fellows from a baseless sense of shame and disgrace. The first four days of his endurance are days so long and heavy. Not only does he see no Rachael all the time, but he avoids every chance of seeing her. He knows that if Rachael is seen in his company, the union would take her to task also. He has been quite alone during the four days, and has spoken to no one. But some day while he is leaving his work at night, a young man of a very light complexion, Bitzer, accosts him in the street. After enquiring his name and his present predicament, Bitzer informs Stephen that Mr. Bounderby wants to speak to him and he is sent to fetch him. Stephen turns about to the red brick castle of his master, Mr. Bounderby.

CHAPTER V: MEN AND MASTERS

Stephen is bidden into the drawing-room of Mr. Bounderby's house. A tea-table is set. Other than Mr. Bounderby, Louisa, her brother, and Harthouse are present in the room. Stephen makes his obeisance to them, closing the door and standing near it, with his hat in his hand. Bounderby thinks that he would be able to emanate from Stephen some inside information about the union and its leaders. But Stephen refuses to act as an informer. Bounderby thinks that Stephen is afraid to do it. Bounderby tells Harthouse that he had warned Stephen against the mischievous strangers who are always about, and he tells Stephen that he is going in the wrong direction. He also says that he is still a slave to the union leaders, and that he is afraid to open his lips about them. Stephen protests that he is not afraid of the union leaders. Stephen refuses to say anything about Slackbridge and the union combination, or about his own refusal to join it. About his own decision what he says is that it is a promise to someone not to associate himself in the union.

Bounderby blusters that he can have half a dozen leaders like Slackbridge put on trial and get them transportation for life. Stephen replies that the "muddle" would remain a muddle even if a hundred Slackbridges were to be transported in the deepest ocean. He tells Bounderby of the general confusion, monotony and lack of proper direction of the workers' energies, and of their not sharing in the apparent prosperity of Coketown. Stephen says that the masters should see the workers not as machines, but as human beings with feelings, sentiments and souls. In fact, in his own quiet way, Stephen condemns the whole fabric of *laissez faire*. It should be observed also that the Lancashire dialect used by Stephen has a twofold effect. In the author's view, it stresses the speaker's simplicity and, as an indirect implication, his sincerity and virtuousness, and thus makes his words more genuine and weighty. But in fact, it also creates a certain distance between the man who is speaking and the author, who does not assume the whole responsibility for his protest. Bounderby sacks Stephen. Stephen pleads that this would mean his permanent unemployment in the industry; but Bounderby, knowing fully well the future reality of Stephen's life, remains unaffected. Stephen leaves him, saying: "Heaven help us all in this world."

Dickens thought that there should be the right to strike, but almost always wrong to use it. He dislikes the extremists on both sides. He hates employers like Bounderby, and he distrusts trade union organizers such as Slackbridge. He is in favour of all attempts to encourage better industrial relations and for conciliation on both sides. Stephen's words to Bounderby supporting the workers is an attack upon the *laissez faire* system of letting business do what it pleases. But Dickens says that neither side can be always and forever right without reference to the other side. He is arguing for what he conceives to be justice to both capital and labour; he is arguing for co-operation; he is saying that Victorian society does not award justice to labour; he is saying that something drastic needs to be done, or revolution will erupt and ruin all.

CHAPTER VI: FADING AWAY

It is falling dark when Stephen comes out of Bounderby's house. No sooner had the thought occurred to him that he had encountered a curious old woman on his previous visit to Bounderby's house than he heard a step behind him and turning saw her in Rachael's company. The old woman says that she met Rachael by chance when she was standing outside Bounderby's house. Stephen has to conquer an instinctive propensity to dislike the old woman. Her manner is as honest and simple as a manner possibly could be. He pursues the subject that interests her in her old age. The lady wants to know about Bounderby's wife. Stephen says that he has seen the lady, young and handsome, with fine dark thinking eyes and a still way of appearance. Stephen informs Rachael that Bounderby's work and he are parted, that he has lost his job. All three are walking. The old woman is so decent and contented that they both feel an interest in her. She is too sprightly to allow of their walking at a slow pace on her account. Stephen invites the other two to his house and to have a cup of tea. They comply with his request, and the three move on to the house where he lodges.

Stephen lights a candle, sets his little tea-board, gets hot water from below, and brings in small portions of tea and sugar, a loaf, and some butter from the nearest shop. The bread is new and crusty, the butter fresh, and the sugar lump, of course—in fulfillment of the standard testimony of the Coketown magnates. Rachael makes the tea and the visitor enjoys it mightily. When Stephen wants to know the old lady's name, she announces herself as "Mrs. Pegler". Mrs. Pegler's husband was already dead, by Mrs. Pegler's calculation, when Stephen was born. When asked about her children, the old lady says that she had a son who did well, wonderfully well, but somehow she has "lost" him. The landlady comes stumbling up the narrow stairs, and calling Stephen to the door, whispers in his ear. Mrs. Pegler catches a word (Bounderby) as it was muttered. She cries in a suppressed voice to hide her and not to let her be seen and not to let Mr. Bounderby come up till she has got away. Stephen assures her that it is Mrs. Bounderby and not the gentleman. Stephen takes the candle, goes downstairs, and in a few moments returns, lighting Louisa into the room. She is followed by the whelp, Tom. For the first time in her life Louisa has come into one of the dwellings of the Coketown Hands. For the first time in her life she is face to face with anything like individuality in connexion with them. She stands for some moments looking round the room. From the few chairs, the few books, the common prints, and the bed she glances to the two women, and to Stephen. Louisa says that she is there to talk to Stephen in consequence of his losing the job of Mr. Bounderby. Louisa says that Stephen has fallen into suspicion with his fellow-weavers because he has made a promise to someone as to not to be one of them and that she is sure that it must have been to Rachael that he has made that promise. Rachael bursts into tears. Rachael says that she prayed him to avoid trouble for his own good, but that has caused a broil. Stephen is determined to keep his promise to Rachael as she is, in his own words, the 'Angel' of his life. Louisa turns her head to him, and bends it with a deference that is new in her. She looks from him to Rachael, and her features soften. Stephen says that he must quit the place and try to find a job somewhere else.

A purse appears in Louisa's hand. The rustling of a bank-note is audible, as she unfolds one and keeps it on the table. She offers it as a kind of help to Stephen for being unemployed. Stephen says that to show that he is not a man without reason and gratitude, he would take only two pound under the self-imposed condition to pay it back. Seeing his sister ready to depart, Tom gets up, rather hurriedly, and tells his sister that he should like to talk to Stephen a moment. He asks Stephen to step out on the stairs. Tom instructs Stephen to wait for him near Bounderby's bank in the evening after finishing his duty in the factory. Stephen has still to work in the factory for two or three days to complete the weaving already assigned. Stephen promises to wait as per Tom's instructions for the few days. Tom says that he would hear something to his own advantage, and that Bitzer would be the messenger to carry his message.

Mrs. Pegler remains in her corner until Mrs. Bounderby and Tom are gone and Stephen comes back with the candle in his hand. She is in a state of inexpressible admiration of Mrs. Bounderby. Stephen and Rachael escort Mrs. Pegler to the door of the Travellers' Coffee House, where they part from her. They walk back together to the corner of the street where Rachael lives.

Stephen works in the mill the next day, and the next, uncheered by a word from any one there. At the end of the third day, his loom stands empty. He has overstayed his hour in the street outside the Bank, on each of the two first evenings. But nothing has happened there, good or bad. He resolves to wait full two hours, on the third and last night. Stephen observes Mrs. Sparsit sitting at the first floor window as he had seen her before, and that the light porter Bitzer is there. When Bitzer first comes out, Stephen thinks he might be looking for him. But the light porter only casts his eyes upon him slightly and says nothing. We see that the honest and upright Stephen is made a victim by the union leader and he is further going to be a victim of Tom's evil design.

CHAPTER VII: GUNPOWDER

In his desultory fashion Harthouse makes headway among the "Hard Facts" fraternity. He is getting increasingly interested in the hidden and pent-up emotions of Louisa who is living then at her husband's newly acquired property in the countryside outside Coketown. He has succeeded in convincing Louisa that his attitude to life, the attitude of 'honesty in dishonesty', is the most practical one. His philosophy seems to have relieved Louisa who has all her life been suppressed and inhibited. One day Harthouse asks for Louisa's permission to speak to her about something personal. He points out that she has done many favours to Tom because of her affection for him. Louisa admits his brother's increasing addiction to gambling, and her obvious help with his debts. In his private conversation with Harthouse, Tom also confesses his borrowing heavily from his sister, revealing extreme and callous inconsiderateness. When Harthouse offers to help him out of his economic problems, Tom says that money is no solution. Tom says that if he had got money at the time he needed it, he would not have been in his present plight. But Tom does not exactly define his plight. Harthouse urges Tom to show signs of gratitude to his sister. This delights Louisa enormously when Tom expresses his fondness for her. As it appears to Louisa that Tom's affectionate attitude towards her is linked with Harthouse's influence, her attitude towards Harthouse seems to soften.

In the scene Tom is seen sitting on the terrace with Harthouse, picking roses and tearing them to pieces with his teeth. The sorry state of Tom's soul is implied by such behaviour, and it is fully explained in the later interview between Louisa Gradgrind and her father, when she strikes herself on the bosom and asks 'what have you done, O father, what have you done, with the garden that should have bloomed once, in this great wilderness here?'

CHAPTER VIII: EXPLOSION

James Harthouse sits in the pleasant bay window of his dressing room. He has established a confidence with Mrs. Bounderby from which her husband was excluded. Yet he has not any earnest wickedness of purpose in him for the time being. His motto is: "What will be, will be." The next day, Harthouse gets through the day to his own satisfaction, as is to be expected under the fatiguing circumstances; and comes riding back at six o'clock. While returning on horseback from a public engagement, he suddenly encounters Mr. Bounderby who informs him that his Bank was robbed the previous night and it was robbed in an extraordinary manner, with a false key. Harthouse asks the amount. Mr. Bounderby, in his desire to make the most of it, really seems mortified by being obliged to reply that it is not much, not more than a hundred and fifty pounds. Bounderby says that it is not the sum but the fact, the fact of the Bank being robbed, and that is the important circumstance. Bounderby reports that Tom locked in his safe a hundred and fifty odd pound, and some time in the night, some fellows, somehow, got to Tom's safe, forced it, and abstracted the contents. Being then disturbed, they made off; letting themselves out at the main door, and double locking it again with a false key, which they leave in the street near the Bank. He violently explodes that a Hand is suspected to be involved in it, and the suspect is none but Stephen Blackpool. Bounderby says that Stephen had been seen loitering near the bank for two or three days in the evenings before his departure from Coketown. An old woman who seems to have been coming into Coketown and watched the Bank a whole day might be Stephen's accomplice. Louisa who is also present in the scene inwardly remembers that on the occasion of her visit to Stephen, there was an old woman in his room that night and she had shrunk from observation. Bounderby then tells Louisa that Mrs. Sparsit's nerves have been acted upon by the Bank robbery, and she would stay in his residence a day or two.

Mrs. Sparsit's greatest point, first and last, is her determination to pity Mr. Bounderby. And she has a curious propensity to call Mrs. Bounderby "Miss Gradgrind". Her repetition of this mistake covers her with modest confusion, but indeed, as she says, it seems so natural to say Miss Gradgrind. In the drawing-room after dinner, Mr. Bounderby tries the case of the robbery, examines the witnesses, makes notes of the evidence, finds the suspected persons guilty, and sentences them to the extreme punishment of the law. When that is done, Bitzer is sent to town with instructions to ask Tom to come home.

Long after Louisa had lain down, she watches and waits for her brother's coming home. That night Louisa is not feeling comfortable as the suspicion that the robbery might have been committed by her brother has crossed her mind on account of Tom's gambling habits. It is past midnight when she heard the bell at the gate. She feels as though she would have been glad that it rings on until daylight. All is silent again. She waits about some quarter of an hour. Then she arises, puts on a loose robe, and goes out of her room in the dark, and up the staircase to her brother's room. His door is shut. She softly opens it and approaches his bed with noiseless steps. She knows that he only feigns to be asleep, but she says nothing to him. Tom starts by-and-by as if he were just then awakened. Louisa asks Tom if he has anything to tell her. She appeals to him that if ever he loved her, he should tell her if he has anything concealed. She asks Tom to tell her the truth, and promises not to reproach him; instead, she would remain compassionate and faithful to him and try to save him at any cost. She turns her ear to his lips, but he remains doggedly silent. Louisa stands for some time at the bedside before she slowly moves away. She softly closes the door and returns to her room. Then Tom looks cautiously up and finds her gone. He creeps out of bed, fastens his door, and throws himself upon his pillow again. He is tearing his hair, morosely crying, hatefully but impenitently spurning himself. The chapter expresses Louisa's excellent opinion about Stephen and that her grave suspicion regarding the bank robbery falls on Tom. With her pretension and hypocrisy, Mrs. Sparsit is a comic character.

CHAPTER IX: HEARING THE LAST OF IT

Mrs. Sparsit is prowling about Bounderby's house where she is staying. How she gets from story to story is a mystery beyond solution. A subtle hint of Mrs. Sparsit's cat-like nature is found in the following words: "A lady so decorous in herself, and so highly connected, was not to be suspected of dropping over the banisters or sliding down them, yet her extraordinary facility of locomotion suggested the wild idea. Another noticeable circumstance in Mrs. Sparsit was, that she was never hurried. She would shoot with consummate velocity from the roof to the hall, yet would be in full possession of her breath and dignity on the moment of her arrival there. Neither was she ever seen by human vision to go at a great pace."

Mrs. Sparsit takes very kindly to Mr. Harthouse, and has some pleasant conversation with him soon after her arrival. Mrs. Sparsit tells him that although it used to be considered that Miss Gradgrind was wanting in animation, she is admitting that Miss Gradgrind appears considerably and strikingly improved in that respect. Mrs. Sparsit's demeanour towards Mr. Bounderby is so modest and humble that it makes Bounderby swell with a sense of importance and exaltation, and he starts harbouring irritation towards Louisa who, as he thinks, is always indifferent to his needs and moods. Mrs. Sparsit is provoking friction between the uncouth Bounderby and his quiet passive wife, thus throwing Louisa and Harthouse more on each other's company.

Bitzer brings a note to say that Mrs. Gradgrind is very ill at Stone Lodge. Louisa returns hastily to her old home. Sissy is tending her mother. When Louisa wants to hear of her mother, she says that it is something new when somebody wants to hear of her. Mrs. Gradgrind is incoherent in her talk. When Louisa asks her whether she is feeling pain, she says that there is a pain somewhere in the room, but she cannot positively say that she has got it. When Sissy brings Louisa's sister in the room, Louisa observes the intimacy between Sissy and her sister. Her mother wants to talk to Louisa alone. Left alone with her mother, Louisa sees her lying with an awful lull upon her face, "like one who was floating away upon some great water, all resistance over, content to be carried down the stream." Louisa puts the shadow of a hand to her lips again, and recalls her.

Mrs. Gradgrind says that whenever she says anything on any subject, she has never heard the last of it: and consequently, that she has long left off saying anything. She says that Louisa and her brother have learnt 'Ologies' a great deal, of all kinds from morning to night and if there is any 'Ology' left, of any description, she would not be able to hear its name. She resumes that there is something, not an 'Ology' at all, that their father has missed, or forgotten: "I don't know what it is. I have often sat with Sissy near me, and thought about it. I shall never get its name now. But your father may. It makes me restless. I want to write to him, to find out for God's sake, what it is. Give me a pen, give me a pen." The power of restlessness is gone. She fancies, however, that her request has been complied with. The pen she could not have held is in her hand. It matters little what figures of wonderful no-meaning she begins to trace upon her wrappers. The hand soon stops in the midst of them. Mrs. Gradgrind dies.

The chapter marks a crucial development of the plot in the novel. Mrs. Sparsit is still a source of comedy. Mrs. Gradgrind's "somethingological" concern or obsession with

"Ology" hints at Dickens's fundamental satirical intent on utilitarian statistics; and it is pathetic also. Something different from fact "Ology" had crept in her mind because of Sissy's constant company, but all is in vain.

CHAPTER X: MRS. SPARSIT'S STAIRCASE

Mrs. Sparsit makes a stay of some weeks in duration at Mr. Bounderby's retreat. When ultimately she left the house, she is invited by Bounderby to visit the house every weekend. During the whole term of stay at Bounderby's house, Mrs. Sparsit is a pattern of consistency, continuing to take care and pity on Mr. Bounderby to his face; and to call his portrait, with the greatest acrimony and contempt, a 'Noodle', in private.

Mrs. Sparsit is not a poetical woman. But she takes an idea in the nature of an allegorical fancy, into her head. Much watching of Louisa, and much consequent observation of her impenetrable demeanour, must have given her, as it were, a lift, in the way of inspiration. She erects in her mind a mighty staircase, with a dark pit of shame and ruin at the bottom; and down those stairs, from day to day and hour to hour, she sees Louisa descending. It becomes the task of Mrs. Sparsit's life, to look up at her staircase, and to watch Louisa coming down and down, but never turning back. If Louisa had once turned back, it might have been the death of Mrs. Sparsit in spleen and grief. She sees that Louisa has been descending steadily the staircase.

Louisa sits by Mr. Harthouse, in an alcove in the garden. Louisa is talking very low. Harthouse stands leaning over her, as they whisper together, and his face almost touches her hair. Mrs. Sparsit is straining her hawk's eyes to the utmost from her chamber window. Mrs. Sparsit is too distant to hear a word of their discourse. Louisa and Harthouse are talking about the robbery. Louisa cannot believe that Stephen has committed the robbery and she seeks Harthouse's opinion about it. Harthouse says that all the evidence points to Stephen. Then Louisa and Harthouse stroll away among the lanes in the twilight; Louisa is leaning on his arm, and "she little thought how she was going down, down, down, Mrs. Sparsit's staircase".

CHAPTER XI: LOWER AND LOWER

Mr. Gradgrind, apprised of his wife's death, comes back from London, and buries her in a business-like manner. He then returns with promptitude and resumes his parliamentary duties.

In Mrs. Sparsit's eyes, the figure (Louisa) descends the great stairs, steadily, steadily; always verging, like a weight in deep water, to the black gulf at the bottom.

Mrs. Sparsit keeps unwinking watch on Louisa. Although Mrs. Sparsit visits Bounderby's house only weekend, all the week she maintains her cat-like observation of Louisa, through her husband, through her brother, through James Harthouse, through the outsides of letters and packets, through everything animate and inanimate that at any time went near the stairs. Mrs. Sparsit gets baffled by the reserve of Louisa's nature. Sometimes it seems to her that Louisa is about to rest her foot on the last step of the staircase and fall into the pit. But there are times when Mr. James Harthouse is not sure of winning Louisa. There are times when he cannot read the face he has studied so long.

Days wear away. Mr. Bounderby is to be called away from home by business for three or four days. On a Friday Bounderby informs that to Mrs. Sparsit at the Bank. Bounderby tells her that she should visit his house as usual and his absence would not make any difference to her visit. Mrs. Sparsit says that she would go in that his will is a law to her; otherwise, she is not feeling sure that it would be quite so agreeable to Miss Gradgrind to receive her. Before going to Bounderby's house that weekend, Mrs. Sparsit invites Tom at the bank to have some food and drink in her company with a view to eliciting information about Harthouse and Louisa. Tom has long been a down-looking young fellow, but this characteristic had so increased recently, that he never raises his eyes to any face for three seconds together. Mrs. Sparsit consequently has her ample means of watching his looks. From

Tom, Mrs. Sparsit comes to know that Harthouse is out for Yorkshire, on a shooting expedition, and that he would return on the following day and Tom would receive him in the evening at the railway station.

On Saturday, Mrs. Sparsit sits at her window all day long looking outside. But, above all, her attention is on her staircase. As the evening comes, she puts on her bonnet and shawl, and goes quietly out for the railway station. She stands at a point where she might remain unnoticed. Tom is in attendance, and is loitering about until the expected train comes in. But Mr. Harthouse is seen nowhere. Tom waits until the crowd has dispersed, and the bustle is over. Then he takes counsel with porters. He decides to wait until the next train should come in, after an hour and forty minutes. The thought occurs to Mrs. Sparsit that it is a device on the part of Mr. Harthouse to keep Tom out of the way and she comes to the conclusion that Harthouse is with Louisa in Bounderby's residence at that moment. The station for the country house is at the opposite end of the town. The road is not easy. But Mrs. Sparsit is very quick to reach Bounderby's house. She glides out of her carriage. She goes up to the house, keeping within the shrubbery, and goes round it, peeping between the leaves at the lower windows. There are no lights yet, and all is silent. She tries the garden with no better effect. She thinks of the wood, and moves towards it stealthily. She softly crushes her way through the thick undergrowth. She hears low voices close at hand, his voice and hers. She becomes sure that they are Louisa and Harthouse; and the appointment at the station was a device to keep Tom away. Louisa and Harthouse are yonder, by the felled tree. Bending low among the dewy grass, she advances closer to them. She draws herself up, and stands behind a tree. She notices that Harthouse has reached there on horse back, and must have passed through the neighbouring fields for his horse is tied to the meadow side of the fence. Mrs. Sparsit overhears Harthouse speaking to Louisa in amorous tones. Calling her "My dearest love", Harthouse says that he could not stay away knowing she is alone in the house. Louisa urges him to go away. She commands Harthouse to go away. But she sits still and even her manner of speaking is not hurried. Mrs. Sparsit sees with delight that Harthouse's arm embraces her. A little later, both Louisa and Harthouse start. It was rain, beginning to fall fast, in heavy drops. Mrs. Sparsit sees him detain Louisa with his encircling arm, and hears him tell her how he loves her, and how she is the stake for which he ardently desires to play away all that he has in life. Mrs. Sparsit watches Louisa coming out of the wood, and sees her enter the house. Mrs. Sparsit stands hidden in the density of the shrubbery. Louisa, cloaked and muffled, comes out of the house. Mrs. Sparsit feels sure that Louisa eloped. She is sure that Louisa fell from the lowermost stair, and was swallowed up in the gulf.

Indifferent to the rain, and moving with a quick determined step, Louisa struck into a side-path parallel with the ride. Mrs. Sparsit follows in the shadow of the trees, at but a short distance. When Louisa stops to close the side-gate without noise, Mrs. Sparsit stops. When she goes on, Mrs. Sparsit goes on. Mrs. Sparsit knows that a train for Coketown would come through presently. Tumbling her shawl into a new shape and putting it on over her bonnet, Mrs. Sparsit changes her usual appearance. So disguised, she has no fear of being recognized when she follows up the railroad steps. Louisa sits waiting in a corner. Mrs. Sparsit sits waiting in another corner. The seizure of the station announces the train. Louisa puts into one carriage, Mrs. Sparsit puts into another. The tremendous rain occasioned infinite confusion when the train stopped at its destination. Gutters and pipes has burst. Drains have over-flowed, and streets are underwater. When the train arrived at Coketown, Mrs. Sparsit thinks that Louisa would get into a coach. She decides that she must see the coach number, and hear the order given to the coachmen. But, Mrs. Sparsit is wrong in her calculation. Louisa gets into no coach, and is already gone. Mrs. Sparsit has no resource but to burst into tears of bitterness and say, "I have lost her!"

Perhaps the most vividly memorable part of the whole novel is that of Mrs. Sparsit spying on Louisa and Harthouse, and following the fleeing Louisa, through the thunderstorm, to the railway station and to Coketown. It is the culmination of one of the great imaginative strokes of the book, Dickens's likening of her temptation to the descent of a great staircase, into chaos at its foot. He extracts the image, with great skill and economy, from Louisa's own 'what does it matter?' and then imposes it on Mrs. Sparsit, and modulates it, with a truly poetic movement, into the 'deep water' and universal deluge of the railway scene. The whole scene of the flight, in its fluent modulation of imagery and its melodrama charged with human weight, is Dickens at his most characteristic and his best.

CHAPTER XII: DOWN

Mr. Gradgrind is at home for the vacation in Parliament has started. He sits writing in the room with the deadly statistical clock. The noise of the rain cannot disturb him much. When it thundered very loudly, he glances towards Coketown, having it in his mind that some of the tall chimneys might be struck by lightning. But he feels utterly amazed to see Louisa who enters the room and without any preliminaries, says that she wishes to speak to him. Louisa looks so colourless, so disheveled, so defiant and despairing, that he is afraid of her. She drops into a chair before him, and puts her cold hand on his arm.

Louisa curses the hour in which she was born. She says that her father's education through which she had been brought up has taken away the graces of her soul, the sentiments of her heart and the bliss of life: "What have you done, O father, what have you done, with the garden that should have bloomed once, in this great wilderness here?" She says that she does not mean to reproach him. She says that what he had never nurtured in her has never nurtured in himself. If he had only neglected her, she would have been a much better and much happier creature. On hearing this, after all his care, Mr. Gradgrind bows his head upon his hand and groans aloud. Louisa says that had she been allowed to exercise fancy of the heart, she should have been "a million times wiser, happier, more loving, more contented, more innocent and human in all good respects" than her present state of being. She has almost repulsed and crushed her better angel into a demon. “What I have learned has left me doubting, misbelieving, despising, regretting, what I have not learned; and my dismal resource has been to think that life would soon go by, and that nothing in it could be worth the pain and trouble of a contest.”

Louisa says that her father proposed her husband to her, and she married him. She never made a pretence to Bounderby or her father that she loved him. She was not wholly indifferent, for she had a hope of being pleasant and useful to Tom. Tom had been the subject of all the little tenderness of her life; perhaps he became so because she knew so well how to pity him. Louisa resumes that when she was irrevocably married, there rose up into rebellion against the tie, the old strife, made fiercer by all those causes of disparity which arose out of the two individual natures, and which no general laws would ever rule or state for her.

Louisa says that what she said is not to reproach him or complain against him. There is something else which she wants to inform him. She has had a new acquaintance with a man, light, polished and easy. The man understands her, and can read her thoughts. There seems to be a near affinity between them. The man gains her confidence. Her father’s face is ashy white, and he holds her in both his arms. Louisa says that she has done no worse and she has not disgraced her father. She says plainly that she may be in love with the man. That very night, her husband being away, he has been with her, declaring himself her lover. Louisa says, “I do not know that I am sorry, I do not know that I am ashamed, I do not know that I am degraded in my own esteem. All that I know is, your philosophy and your teaching will not save me.... Save me by some other means!” He tightens his hold in time to prevent her sinking on the floor, but she cries out in a terrible voice, “I shall die if you hold me! Let me fall upon the ground!” Louisa collapses and sinks to the floor. Mr. Gradgrind sees the pride of his heart and the triumph of his system, lying an insensible heap, at his feet.

Louisa’s feeling of frustration is fraught with some tragic potentiality. Lousia pours forth her accusations from the pressure of self-realization, from a sense of wasted life. If in the beginning Mr. Gradgrind asserted the efficacy of education based on facts, the same teaching has boomeranged upon himself in the end when he realizes that the summation of his facts is going to crush his own daughter. The scene may be called the most moving one in the novel.

BOOK III. GARNERING

CHAPTER I: ANOTHER THING NEEDFUL

Louisa awakes from a torpor. Her eyes languidly opens on her old bed at home, and her old room. She could scarcely move her head for pain and heaviness. Her eyes are strained and sore, and she is very weak. A curious passive inattention has taken possession of her. The presence of her little sister who is attending upon her cannot attract her notice for some time. Even when their eyes meet, and her sister approaches the bed, Louisa lies for minutes looking at her in silence. Her sister has withdrawn. She lies with her face towards the door. It opens and her father enters. He has a jaded anxious look upon him. He sits down at the side of the bed, tenderly asking how she is, and dwelling on the necessity of her keeping very quiet after her agitation and exposure to the weather last night. He speaks in a subdued and troubled voice, very different from his usual dictatorial manner; and is often at a loss for words. Gradgrind tells her that he is feeling much grieved by her revelations and that he holds himself fully responsible for the circumstances. He says that the ground on which he stood had ceased to be solid under his feet. The only support on which he leaned had given way in an instant, and he is stunned by the discoveries. He says that he had proved his system to himself, and he had rigidly administered it; and therefore he must bear the responsibility of its failures. He entreats Louisa to believe that he had meant to do right.

Louisa says that she knows that he had intended to make her happy and that she had never blamed him, and she never should. Gradgrind says that some person holds that there is a wisdom of the Head, and that there is a wisdom of the Heart, but he had not supposed so; he had supposed the head to be all-sufficient, but it might not be all-sufficient. He says, in a forlorn manner, that he is an unhappy man to see her plight. He holds that he has a misgiving that some change might have been slowly working about him in his house, by mere love and gratitude: that what the Head had left undone and could not do, "the Heart may have been doing silently". He looks upon her once more, and goes out of the room.

Louisa hears a light tread near the door, and it is Sissy who is standing beside her. Sissy's tenderness and affection for Louisa has overcome Louisa's resistance to her, and Louisa softens. Louisa then expresses her regret to Sissy that she had been so proud and so hardened, so confused and troubled, so resentful and unjust to every one and to herself, that everything was stormy, dark, and wicked to her. Louisa then appeals to Sissy: "Forgive me, pity me, help me! Have compassion on my great need and let me lay this head of mine upon a loving heart!" Sissy feels greatly touched by Louisa's words, and they develop a new relationship with each other.

We saw that Louisa and Sissy developed a sympathetic bond between each other. In the chapter "FATHER AND DAUGHTER" we felt the rejection of the sympathetic bond with Sissy on the part of Louisa and it marked a special crisis of the book and led to Louisa's catastrophe. The resumption of the sympathetic relationship with Sissy in this chapter marks a further crisis and results in the denouement. Without a full appreciation of the sympathetic link between Sissy and Louisa we cannot grasp either Louisa's character or the function of Sissy in the novel.

CHAPTER II: VERY RIDICULOUS

Harthouse is positively agitated. He is horribly bored by existing circumstances. After putting his horse at Coketown through the storm, he waited up all night. The dawn came, the morning came, and the day came, and neither message nor letter came. He went down to the country house. There he got the report that Mr. Bounderby was away, Mrs. Bounderby was in town, and she left for town suddenly the previous evening. In these circumstances he decides to follow Mrs. Bounderby to town. But the thought never occurs to him that Louisa would go to her father's house, Stone Lodge.

Back at the hotel, when he has been trying to read a newspaper in vain, for half an hour, the waiter informs him that a young lady wishes to see him. Harthouse hurries into the gallery. He sees an unknown young woman, plainly dressed, very quiet and very pretty. He conducts her into the room. Her face is innocent and youthful and pleasant. She seems to have her mind entirely preoccupied with the occasion of her visit. The lady concerned is Sissy. Sissy asks Harthouse to keep her visit secret, and to keep secret what she is going to say. Sissy reports that Louisa arrived at her father's house the previous night, in great agitation, and was insensible all through the night. Sissy hopes that she might be sure that he would not see Louisa again. Sissy says that the first object of her meeting him is to assure him that he must believe that there is no hope of his ever speaking with Louisa again. Harthouse looks at Sissy with an incredulous smile upon his lips. But her mind looks over and beyond him, and the smile is quite thrown away. He takes a little time for consideration. Very clearly but emphatically Sissy says that she has no commission from Louisa other than the commission of her love for Louisa, and Louisa's love for her. She adds that she has no other trust than that she has been with Louisa since her coming home, and that Louisa has given her (Sissy) confidence. She further adds that she has no further trust, than that she knows something of Louisa's character and her marriage with Bounderby. Harthouse says that he cannot give up the expectation of seeing Louisa further. Sissy appeals to Harthouse to depart from Coketown that very night and never to return to it. Although Harthouse states the fact that he has been in Coketown on 'a public kind of business' and it would make him so ridiculous to back out suddenly in an incomprehensible way, Sissy says that he should comply with the request to make amends to Louisa for the wrong and the harm that he has done to her. Harthouse says that no man ever was placed in a more ridiculous position than he is, by Sissy. He says that although he is not a moral sort of fellow, he had no particular evil intention towards Louisa, and that, whatever had happened, was the result of the growing intimacy between them. He complies with the request to leave Coketown for good.

Sissy rises to depart. Harthouse wants to know her name and whether she is related to the Gradgrind family. Sissy introduces herself as "Sissy Jupe" and says that she is only a forlorn girl separated from her father who had been a stroller, and taken pity on by Mr. Gradgrind, and she has been living in Mr. Gradgrind's house ever since. Sissy is gone. In the very circumstances of life, Harthouse considers himself nothing but 'a Great Pyramid of failure'. He picks up a pen and writes three notes, one to his brother, another to Bounderby, and the third to Mr. Gradgrind, informing them that he is leaving Coketown for good. A secret sense of having failed and been ridiculous oppresses him so much.

Harthouse comes into the novel to tempt Louisa, and it is enough that the temptation should be plausible and strong. Dickens has merely to remove him from Coketown, and this again is easy; it is enough to allow the minimal good in his nature—helped along by the stirring of humour, and the natural desire to be well rid of complications—to respond to Sissy's appeal.

CHAPTER III: VERY DECIDED

Regarded as a classical ruin, Mrs. Sparsit is an interesting spectacle on her arrival at her journey's end. Mrs. Sparsit reaches London where Bounderby happened to be at that time, and tells him that his wife has eloped with Harthouse. Utterly heedless of the wear and tear of her clothes and constitution, and adamant to her pathetic sneezes, Mr. Bounderby immediately crams her into a coach, and bears her off to Stone Lodge.

Mr. Bounderby tells Mr. Gradgrind that Mrs. Sparsit has something to say to him and that would strike him dumb. Mr. Gradgrind speaks of a very special letter he had written to Mr. Bounderby, in reference to Louisa. Mr. Bounderby informs Mr. Gradgrind that Mrs. Sparsit, by accident, in a situation overheard a conversation out of doors between her daughter and his precious gentleman-friend, Mr. James Harthouse. Gradgrind tells Bounderby that he has known what has passed in the conversation, and he informs that the moment Louisa could detach herself from that interview, she hurries by the train to town and runs from town to his house through a raging storm, and presents herself before him in a state of distraction; and from then, Louisa is in his house. Mr. Bounderby silently gazes about him for some moments, in every direction except Mrs. Sparsit's direction. Bounderby demands apology from Mrs. Sparsit who takes refuge in tears, seeing no way to defend herself. Bounderby orders Mrs. Sparsit to go to her apartment at the bank without delay. Bounderby extends his right hand to the weeping lady, and escorts her to the conveyance.

Bounderby complains that he is not at any time as dutifully and duly treated by Louisa, as Josiah Bounderby of Coketown ought to be treated by his wife. Mr. Bounderby takes particular pains to harden himself at all points. It is his amiable nature. Mr. Gradgrind says that he has his doubts whether he (Gradgrind) had understood Louisa and whether he had been quite right in the manner of her education. Then Bounderby gives his definition of Education: "Education! I'll tell you what education is—To be tumbled out of doors, neck and crop and put upon the shortest allowance of everything except blows. That's what I call education." Mr. Gradgrind assures him that he has no desire to be controversial. What Gradgrind says is that he sought to repair what was amiss, if he possibly can; and he hopes that Bounderby would assist him in a good spirit, for he has been very much distressed.

Gradgrind says that he has intended to recommend that Bounderby should allow Louisa to remain at Stone Lodge on a visit, and be attended by Sissy who understands her, and on whom Louisa has her trusts. Bounderby says that he is given to understand by Gradgrind that his daughter does not properly know her husband's merits, and is not impressed with such a sense as would become her. Gradgrind urges him that his impression is unreasonable. Gradgrind asks him to allow Louisa a period of repose and reflection at Stone Lodge, which may tend to a gradual alteration for the better in many respects. Bounderby takes the suggestion as an insult to him. He blusters that if Louisa would not return to his house by twelve o'clock at noon the next day, he would send her clothes and so forth over at Stone Lodge and Gradgrind would have to take charge of her permanently for the future. Gradgrind urges him to reconsider his decision before committing himself to it. Before leaving Gradgrind's house, Bounderby says that he has given him his decision, and he has got no more to say. At five minutes past twelve o'clock next day, he directs Mrs. Bounderby's property to be carefully packed up and sent to Stone Lodge. He advertises his country house for sale by private contract. He then resumes, what may be called, a bachelor life.

Mrs. Sparsit's hope to see Louisa at the bottom of the pit, down her staircase, fails dishearteningly. Mr. Gradgrind adds a little grace to himself and he rises a little in reader's estimation. Bounderby's blustering manner makes him more ridiculous.

CHAPTER IV: LOST

Stephen Blackpool is suspected of complicity in the robbery at Bounderby's Bank. Bounderby offers Twenty Pounds reward for the apprehension of Stephen Blackpool. Stephen is described by dress, complexion, estimated height, and manner, as minutely as he could be. It is described how Stephen had left Coketown, and in what direction he had been last seen going. The whole matter is printed in great black letter on a staring broadsheet; Bounderby causes the walls to be posted with a number of placards in the dead of night, so that it should strike upon the sight of the whole population at one blow. The factory-bells need to ring their loudest that morning to disperse the workers who stand in the tardy daybreak, collected round the placards, devouring them with eager eyes.

Slackbridge, the delegate, gets an opportunity to address the workers too that night, concerning Stephen. He congratulates the workers on their previous decision, which had been taken at Slackbridge's suggestion, to cast Stephen out for ever. He describes Stephen as a thief, a plunderer, a proscribed fugitive, a fester and a wound upon the noble character of the Coketown operative. He proposes to the workers on the part of the union to get it resolved in that meeting that "Stephen Blackpool, weaver, referred to in this placard, having been already solemnly disowned by the community of Coketown hands, the same are free from the shame of his misdeeds, and cannot as a class be reproached with his dishonest actions!" The general assemblage subscribes to 'the gospel' according to Slackbridge, and gives three cheers for him.

Rachael, hurt by the kind of public humiliation of Stephen, goes to see Bounderby and claims that Stephen is innocent and reports him about the visit of Tom and Louisa to Stephen's lodging two or three days before Stephen's departure from Coketown. Bounderby cannot believe it and he takes Rachael to Stone Lodge. Louisa confirms Rachael's words, that she and Tom had visited Stephen and she offered financial help to him. Louisa, assisted by Sissy, tries her best to eradicate Rachael's suspicion about Louisa's intention behind calling upon Stephen and offering him financial help. Rachael tells Bounderby that she knows where Stephen is at present, and that she has written a letter to him to come and clear himself of the charges made against him. She says that Stephen would be back within two days.

But Stephen does not return. On the fourth day Rachael meets Bounderby with a letter written by Stephen. The letter contains Stephen's address, and it is known from the letter that Stephen had secured a job at a working colony about sixty miles away from Coketown. Bounderby sends messengers to that place to fetch Stephen, but the messengers come back with the information that after receiving Rachael's letter Stephen had immediately left the place and nobody knows where he is. Even after six or seven days, there is no sign of Stephen.

CHAPTER V: FOUND

Every night, Sissy goes to Rachael's lodging. Sissy sits with her in her small neat room. All day Rachael toils, whatever her anxieties. The monotony is unbroken. Even Stephen Blackpool's disappearance is becoming as monotonous a wonder as any piece of machinery in Coketown. Rachael tells Sissy that she holds a firm confidence in Stephen, a man so faithful to everything honest and good, that even if he was never to be heard of any more, and she was to live to be a hundred years old, she would never once leave trusting Stephen. She says that she has had the mistrust that some one has put Stephen out of way, as by his coming back of his own accord, and showing himself innocent before them all, someone would be confounded. That is why he might be stopped, and it would not be unlikely to think that he might be murdered. Sissy suggests that if no news reaches the next day, i.e. Saturday, on Sunday morning they should walk in the country.

Sissy and Rachael are drawn together like twin souls, and sit in semi-darkness waiting; it is a symbolic role for virtue to play. They sustain each other, using their strong inner convictions against circumstances. Rachael says that without Sissy's companionship and faith in Stephen she might even have gone mad. But why does Sissy believe in Stephen? Not because she knows Stephen but because she knows Rachael, and has formed an absolute trust in Stephen through her faith in Rachael's judgment. This in turn prompts Rachael's solemn reassertion of faith in Stephen; she does know him, and has never for one moment doubted his truth. It is tempting to see the passage as sentimental, or even conventional, but this would surely be a mistake. Sissy is not just propping up a sister-woman relationship with easy reassurances; her profession of belief in Rachael is as serious and considered as Rachael's reply. The confidence Rachael holds in her heart against all discouragement is not likely to be wrong. Rachael caps this careful phrasing with a claim still more positive: 'God knows my heart, I have never once left trusting Stephen Blackpool!'

As Sissy and Rachael are passing Mr. Bounderby's house on foot, and somehow they look round involuntarily, the bright gaslight over Mr. Bounderby's steps shows them Mrs. Sparsit in a coach, in an ecstasy of excitement, struggling to open the door. Mrs. Sparsit seeing them at the same moment calls to them to stop. They see Mrs. Pegler coming out of the coach.

Mr. Bounderby appears, accompanied by Mr. Gradgrind and Tom, with whom he had been holding conference upstairs. Mr. Bounderby looks more astonished than hospitable, at sight of the uninvited party of some twenty-five neighbours in his dining-room. Mr. Bounderby's visage exhibits an extraordinary combination of all possible colours and expressions of discomfiture as old Mrs. Pegler is disclosed to his view.

Mr. Bounderby roars against Mrs. Sparsit, asking explanation as to why she has interferred into his family affairs. Mrs. Pegler asks not to blame her (Mrs. Pegler) as it was not her fault. She tells her darling son, Josiah, that she suggested Mrs. Sparsit over and over again that what she was doing would not be agreeable to him. But she threatened her that if she (Mrs. Pegler) resisted her, she should be brought by constables. Mrs. Pegler reminds him that she has never broken the condition laid down: that she has never said that she is his mother, and that she has always admired him at a distance. Even when she has visited the town sometimes to take 'a proud peep' at him, she has done it unbeknown, and gone away. Mr. Gradgrind observes with severity that he is surprised to see that in her old age she is not ashamed to claim Mr. Bounderby for her son, after her unnatural and inhuman treatment of him. She says that she herself has brought up Josiah (Bounderby) as best as she could, handicapped as she was by her stark poverty. And it comes to light that Bounderby's grandmother had died before he was born. It is disclosed from the words of Mrs. Pegler that Bounderby had pensioned his mother off on thirty pounds a year, and he laid the condition that she was to remain in the countryside and never introduce herself for his mother. The spectators greedily take in every syllable of Mrs. Pegler's appeal, and at each succeeding syllable become more and more astonished. It is plain to all present there that Bounderby's story about his mother and grandmother is a pack of damned lies. Although Bounderby could not deny the account given by Mrs. Pegler, he says that he is not bound to explain his family affairs to anyone. Thus he dismisses the crowd from his house. However, Mrs. Pegler was offered a bed at her son's (Bounderby's) house.

All is revealed. The Bully of humility is proved to be a simple liar. Dickens's methods here are the traditional ones which we are familiar with from, for instance, Fielding's account of the overthrow of Thwackum and Square in *Tom Jones*. But it took no miracle of flexibility on Dickens's part to 'reconcile' this kind of characterization with central fable of his novel, for the completely successful rendering of Gradgrind's self-discovery is not notably more complex and more inward than the rendering of Bounderby.

CHAPTER VI: THE STARLIGHT

Louisa and Sissy have got the apprehension which they have not spoken to each other that Tom might be the actual culprit in the Bank robbery and he might have manipulated things as to cause Stephen's death.

The Sunday was a bright Sunday in autumn, clear and cool, when early in the morning Sissy and Rachael met, to walk in the country. Sissy and Rachael are put down at a station about midway between the town and Mr. Bounderby's retreat. Under their feet, the grass is fresh; beautiful shadows of branches flicker upon it, and speckle it. Hedgerows are luxuriant; everything is at peace. Engines at pits' mouths, and lean old horses that had worn the circle of their daily labour into the ground, are alike quiet. Sissy and Rachael are walking on across the fields and down the shady lanes. They follow paths and tracks, however slight. "It is so still here, Rachael, and the way is so untrodden, that I think we must be the first who have been here all the summer." As Sissy says it, her eyes are attracted by another of those rotten fragments of fence upon the ground. She gets up to look at it, and she notices footsteps. She runs back, and catches Rachael round the neck. Rachael has already started up. There is a hat lying in the grass. They go forward together. Rachael takes it up, shaking from head to foot. She breaks into a passion of tears and lamentations: Stephen Blackpool is written in his own hand on the inside. They are afraid to look, but they examine it, and find no mark of violence, inside or out the hat. It has been lying there some days, for rain and dew had stained it, and the mark of its shape is on the grass where it had fallen. They look fearfully about them, without moving, but could see nothing more. Sissy has unclasped her hand, and is in the act of stepping forward when Rachael caught her in both arms with a scream that resounded over the wide landscape. Before them, at their very feet, is the brink of a black ragged chasm hidden by the thick grass. They spring back, and fall upon their knees, each hiding her face upon the other's neck. They feel that he is down there. Rachael is making her terrific screaming. It is impossible to hush her; and it is deadly necessary to hold her, or she would fling herself down the shaft. Sissy at last brings her to be silent, and to look at her with a tearless face of stone. Sissy creeps towards it on her hands and knees, and calls to him as loud as she could call. She listens, but no sound replies. She calls again. Still there is no answering sound. She does this, twenty, thirty times. She takes a little clod of earth from the broken ground and throws it in. She could not hear it fall.

Sissy runs from field to field, and lane to lane, and place to place, as she has never run before. She comes to a shed by an engine-house where two men were lying in the shade, asleep on straw. One of the men is in a drunken slumber, but on his comrade's shouting to him that a man has fallen down the Old Hell Shaft, he starts out to a pool of dirty water, puts his head in it and comes back sober. A whole village is up. Windlasses, ropes, poles, candles, lanterns, all things necessary, are being brought into one place, to be carried to the Old Hell Shaft. It seems then hours and hours since she has left the lost man lying in the grave where he has been buried alive. She cannot bear to remain away from it any longer—it is like deserting him—and she hurries swiftly back, accompanied by half-a-dozen labourers, including the drunken man whom the news has sobered, and who is the best man of all. When they come to the Old Hell Shaft, they find it as lonely as she had left it. The men called and listened as she had done, and examined the edge of the chasm, and settled how it had happened, and then sat down to wait until the implements they want should come up. After they have waited some time, straggling people who have heard of the accident begin to come up. Then the real help of implements begin to arrive. In the midst of that,

Rachael returned; and with her party there is a surgeon, who has brought some wine and medicines. But, the expectation among the people that Stephen would be found alive is very slight. A large ring is made round the Old Hell Shaft, and appointed men to keep it. Besides volunteers, only Sissy and Rachael are at first permitted within this ring. Later in the day, when the message brings an express from Coketown, Mr. Gradgrind and Louisa, and Mr. Bounderby, and Tom, are also there.

The sun is four hours lower than when Sissy and Rachael had first sat down upon the grass, before a means of enabling two men to descend securely was rigged with poles and ropes. Difficulties arise in the construction of that machine, simple as it was. Requisites have been found wanting. It is five o'clock in the afternoon of the bright autumnal Sunday, before a candle was sent down to try the air, while three or four rough faces stand crowded close together, attentively watching it. The candle is brought up again, feebly burning, and then some water was cast in. Then the bucket was hooked on and it was lowered away. As the rope goes out, tight and strained, and the windlass creaks, there is not a breath among the one or two hundred men and women looking on. The signal is given and the windlass stops, with abundant rope to spare. Apparently so long an interval ensues with the men at the windlass standing idle, that some woman shrieked that another accident had happened. But the surgeon who held the watch sternly admonishes them to keep silence. He has not well done speaking, when the windlass is reversed and works again. Practised eyes know that it did not go as heavily as it would if both workmen had been coming up, and that only one was returning. The rope came in tight and strained. Ring after ring is coiled upon the barrel of the windlass. All eyes are fastened on the pit. The sobered man is brought up and he leaps out briskly on the grass. He reports that Stephen is hurt so very bad that they did not know how to get him up. Under the surgeon's directions, some men bring a hurdle, on which others make a thick bed of spare clothes covered with loose straw, while he himself contrives some bandages and slings from shawls and handkerchiefs.

Ring after ring is coiled upon the barrel of the windlass safely, and the connecting chains appear, and finally the bucket with the two men holding on at the sides and tenderly supporting between them the figure of a poor, crushed, human creature. At first, none but the surgeon went close to it. He did what he could in its adjustment on the couch. But the best that he could do was to cover it. That gently done, he calls to him Rachael and Sissy. And at that time the pale, worn, patient face is seen looking up at the sky, with the broken right hand lying bare on the outside of the covering garments, as if waiting to be taken by another hand. He had fallen into the pit while coming to Coketown in response to Rachael's letter to clear himself of the charges related to the bank robbery. They give him drink, moisten his face with water, and administer some drops of cordial and wine. Though he lies quite motionless looking up at the sky, he smiles, seeing Rachael: "Ah Rachael it is all a muddle. From first to last, a muddle." She stoops down on the grass at his side, and bends over him until her eyes are between his and the sky, for he could not so much as turn them to look at her. Stephen says that he would like to talk to Gradgrind who is then brought to his side. Stephen appeals, "Sir, yo will clear me an' mak my name good wi' aw men. This I leave to yo." Gradgrind is troubled and asks how. Stephen tells him to ask his son: "I leave none ahint me: not a single word. I ha seen an' spok'n wi' yor son, one night. I ask no more 'o yo than that yo clear me-an' I trust to yo to do't."

They carry him very gently along the fields, and down the lanes, and over the wide landscape. Rachael is always holding the hand in hers. Very few whispers break the mournful silence. It is soon a funeral procession. The star has shown him where to find the God of the poor. Stephen dies. The story is to be read as a parable, or a tract for the times. If it is not read thus, Stephen's fall down Old Hell Shaft and the star he thought he could see as he lay there dying, is as trite and tasteless a piece of false piety as an author has ever committed: "The star had shown him where to find the God of the poor;

and through humility, and sorrow, and forgiveness, he had gone to his Redeemer's rest."

CHAPTER VII: WHELP-HUNTING

Before the ring formed round the Old Hell Shaft is broken, one figure had disappeared from within. When Mr. Gradgrind is summoned to the couch, Sissy, attentive to all that happened, slips behind 'that wicked shadow', Tom, and whispers in his ear something. Without turning his head, Tom confers with her a few moments, and vanishes. Thus Tom has gone out of the circle before the people move. When the father reaches home, he sends a message to Mr. Bounderby desiring his son to come to him directly. The reply is that Mr. Bounderby, having missed him in the crowd, and seeing nothing of him since, had supposed him to be at Stone Lodge. In the morning, Gradgrind goes down to the Bank himself as soon as it is opened, and seeing his son's place empty goes back along the street to meet Mr. Bounderby on his way there. To Bounderby he says that for reasons he has found it necessary to employ his son at a distance for a little while. He also says that he is charged with the duty of vindicating Stephen Blackpool's memory, and declaring the thief. Mr. Bounderby, quite confounded, stands stock-still in the street after his father-in-law has left him. Mr. Gradgrind returns home, locks himself in his room, and keeps it all that day. When Sissy and Louisa tap at his door, he does not open it. He eats nothing all day, and has no candle after dark. They hear him walking to and fro late at night. But, in the morning he appears at breakfast at the usual hour, and takes his usual place at the table. Aged and bent he looks, and quite bowed down; and yet he looks a wiser man and a better man, than in the days when he wanted nothing but Facts.

The thought is unbearable to him that the bank robbery committed by his son has made another man a victim of it. At the same time his anxiety is that Tom should somehow be saved from the legal consequences of the crime. Before he leaves the room, he appoints a time for Sissy and Louisa to go to him; and so, with his grey head drooping, goes away. Louisa says that Tom must have made some representation to Stephen Blackpool which induces him to do in good faith and honesty, what he had never done before, and to wait about the Bank those two or three nights before he left the town. Sissy informs Mr. Gradgrind that, having heard Stephen's last words to him, she goes to Tom when no one sees, and asks him to escape at once. Tom was in a tremble before she whispered to him, and he started and trembled more then, and said, 'Where can I go? I have very little money, and I don't know who will hide me!' Sissy thought of her father's old circus and knew where Mr. Sleary had gone at that time of year and she read of him in a paper only the other day. Then Sissy asks him to hurry there, and tell his name, and ask Mr. Sleary to hide him. And Sissy sees him shrink away among the people. It is the more hopeful as the town to which Sissy has directed him is within three hours' journey of Liverpool, whence he can be swiftly dispatched to any part of the world. It is consented that Sissy and Louisa should repair to the place in question by a circuitous course, alone; and that the unhappy father, setting forth in an opposite direction, should get round to the same bourne by another and wider route. It is further agreed that he should not present himself to Mr. Sleary, lest his intentions should be mistrusted, or the intelligence of his arrival should cause his son to take flight anew.

Sissy and Louisa travelled all night. The first thing they see on entering the town is the skeleton of Sleary's circus. The company had departed for another town more than twenty miles off, and had opened there the previous night. Ultimately it is one o'clock when they reach there. They go, with fluttering hearts, to the well-remembered booth. The flag with the inscription SLEARY'S HORSE-RIDING is there; and the Gothic niche is there; but Mr. Sleary is not there. Mr. Gradgrind arrives within an hour afterwards. As anticipated by Sissy, Mr. Sleary is taking care of Tom's safety in every possible way. He has been disguised as a member of the circus troupe and he is playing the role of a black-servant in one of the circus-acts. Mr. Gradgrind feels terribly depressed to see Tom, one of his model children, cutting a mocking figure in a circus. He questions Tom as to the how and why of the bank robbery. Tom replies that a certain number of people holding positions of trust are bound to prove dishonest and that he is one of them. Tom says that he forced the safe himself over night, and shut it ajar before he went away. He had had the key that was found, made long before. He dropped the key that morning, so that it might be supposed to have been used. In fact, he did not take the money all at once and he had been stealing money in small sums from time to time. Tom has been treated as a cipher all along, and now the statistical "reality" has taken its own whelpish turn. This revenging attitude in the case of Tom Gradgrind is even prepared for earlier in the novel, when Tom explains that he has been treated for so long as a mule or donkey that "I should like to kick like one" (I, VIII).

Tom is feeling happy that he would be sent abroad because he is feeling miserable in the circus. Louisa is crying to him that she has forgiven him, and she loves him still, and that he would one day be sorry to have left her so, and glad to think of her words while far away. Suddenly they see someone ran against them. Mr. Gradgrind and Sissy, who are both before Tom while his sister yet clinging to his shoulder, stop and recoil. There is Bitzer, out of breath. His thin lips part. His thin nostrils distend. His white eyelashes are quivering. His colourless face looks more colourless than ever as if he ran himself into a white heat. There he stands, panting and heaving, as if he has never stopped since the night. "I'm sorry to interfere with your plans", says Bitzer, shaking his head. He must have young Tom and he mustn't be got away by horse-riders. Bitzer says that he has recognized Tom who is in a smock frock, and he must have him. Then he takes possession of Tom.

CHAPTER VIII: PHILOSOPHICAL

Bitzer holds 'the paralyzed culprit', Tom, by the collar, and stands in the Ring, blinking at his old patron, Mr. Gradgrind, through the darkness of the twilight. Interrupting Mr. Gradgrind's words about Bitzer's self-interest, Bitzer retorts that he is sure that Mr. Gradgrind knows that "the whole social system is a question of self-interest". He says that he was brought up in that catechism when he was very young. It is a fundamental principle of the Gradgrind philosophy that everything is to be paid for. Nobody is ever on any account to give anybody anything, or render anybody help without purchase. Gratitude is to be abolished, and the virtues springing from it are not to be indulged in. Every inch of the existence of mankind, from birth to death, is to be a bargain across a counter. "And if we didn't get to Heaven that way, it was not a politico-economical place, and we had no business there." Bitzer's bloodless arguments menace the broken Gradgrind.

Sleary forges a stratagem, involving an intelligent dog. He pretends to be on Bitzer's side and says that he would have Tom and Bitzer conveyed to the railway station. While they are in Sleary's carriage, the trained horse starts dancing at a signal from the carriage-driver, without moving an inch further, and it obliges Bitzer to get down. One of the trained circus-dogs then takes charge of Bitzer and would not let him move a step in any direction. Thus Sleary succeeds in getting Tom off to Liverpool. Sleary tells Gradgrind the story of how Tom has escaped, and the overwhelmed Gradgrind offers any amount of money as a reward to Mr. Sleary. But Sleary accepts nothing but a five-pound note for the carriage-driver, a collar for the dog, a set of bells for the horse, brandy and water for himself, and a little refreshment for the whole circus-troupe.

Later he tells Gradgrind that Sissy's father must be dead, as the dog Merrylegs returned to the circus to die. Sleary then expounds his philosophy of life to the humiliated Gradgrind.

The kindness of the horse riding is embodied chiefly in the figure of Sleary, and we are accordingly conscious mostly of the meanings enforced by this character. The scenes in which Sleary helps Gradgrind get Tom out of the country derive their meaning from the eminently theatrical contrast between practical hard-headed Gradgrind, now menaced by his prize pupil Bitzer and sloppy, lisping Sleary. That is, the main accent is on brandy and water; positively 'triumphant activity' comes only in the miniature comic form of the polka-dancing horse. Dickens's point is the surprising *practicality* of the incompetent-seeming Sleary, and the surprising *usefulness* of the horse that can dance the polka. This does not in any important way *feel* inconsistent with Dickens's earlier view of the Horse-riding which emphasizes, as Dr. Leavis points out, the fact that the skills of the Horse-riding contain their end within themselves and are therefore 'wasteful' in terms of Gradgrind's algebra.

CHAPTER IX: FINAL

Mr. Bounderby feels that Mrs. Sparsit had audaciously anticipated him and presumed to be wiser than he. He feels inappeasably indignant with her for her triumphant discovery of Mrs. Pegler. At last he makes the discovery as to how to discharge Mrs. Sparsit. He decides to punish Mrs. Sparsit according to her deserts. Since the Pegler affair, Mrs. Sparsit has covered her pity for Mr. Bounderby with a veil of quiet melancholy and contrition. It has become her habit to assume a woeful look. Mr. Bounderby rebukes Mrs. Sparsit that she may be highly connected, but she cannot be permitted to bother and badger a man in his position, and he is not going to put up with it. He says that a different sort of establishment altogether would bring out a lady of her powers. In unambiguous terms Mrs. Sparsit expresses her contempt against him and even mentions that she has often stood before his portrait and calls him a 'noodle'.

We are given a glimpse of the future: Bounderby dies in a fit in the Coketown street. The white-haired decrepit Gradgrind bends his inflexible theories to appointed circumstances, making his facts and figures subservient to Faith, Hope, and Charity. He exonerates Stephen's name from the charge of bank-robbery and publishes the guilt of his son, although with extenuation. With the pangs of remorse, Tom dies premature out of a fever, with the name of Louisa on his lips.

Rachael, after a long illness once again joins the Coketown Hands at the factory. She looks a woman of pensive beauty, always dressed in black, but sweet-tempered and serene, and even cheerful. She still remains compassionate on Stephen's degraded drunken wife who is sometimes seen in the town secretly begging of her, and crying to her. Sissy has become a wife, a mother lovingly watchful of her children, ever careful that they should have a childhood of the mind no less than a childhood of the body. Louisa, herself alone, is to feel happy in the love and friendship of Sissy and her children, helping a little to bring happiness and kindness into the world around her.

Sissy, like a character in a morality play, illustrates all the ideas opposite from the utilitarian philosophy and she is the character—along with the circus people, to feel really happy at the end of the novel. Although A.O.J. Cochshut comments in "*Hard Times*—Dickens' Masterpiece?" that "The last chapter summarizes in a few hundred words events which might fill a whole novel. Here Dickens's sense of the superiority of life to fact, which is the guiding star of the novel,...seems ironically to have deserted him", the final scenes focus emphatically on Sissy's richness and luster and the Horse-riding's triumphant activity. Dickens keeps his symbolic intentions continuously in hand throughout the moral fable. The flashes of insight are indeed there, and there is also the wonderful capacity for realizing them in language. Dickens is indeed in these respects a poet of almost Shakespearean calibre.

5

Issues

(I) CRITIQUE OF EDUCATION/ UTILITARIANISM

Harvey P. Sucksmith writes in *The Narrative Art of Charles Dickens*: "The autobiography of John Stuart Mill was published in 1874. Dickens can hardly have had direct knowledge about this, but it is possible that he could have learnt about it from Carlyle; part of his novel is a remarkable forecast of Mill's own story, an astonishingly accurate prediction of the psychological consequences of a given philosophical attitude rigorously carried through into an educational system. To any one ignorant of Mill's upbringing, Gradgrind's education of his children may appear a gross and incredible caricature; Mill's early chapters show that it is hardly an exaggeration at all. What is more, Mill experienced a neurotic breakdown in his adolescence and was eventually compelled to acknowledge the claims of the emotions both in his own life and in his philosophical ideas. He gradually modified and softened the harsh and rigid utilitarianism of Bentham and his father" (170-71). Utilitarianism, Dickens saw, led to a special kind of personal and institutional inflexibility, one splendidly suited to his ventriloquistic mimicry, as the opening pages of *Hard Times* testify. But Utilitarianism also argued for a rationally systematic definition of human nature and prescribed a systematic mechanics for the production of social well-being and individual human happiness. Dickens felt a triumphant conviction that he had spotted the fallacy in the Utilitarian reasoning and that he argued effectively against it. The Utilitarian algebra misrepresents human nature by denying the importance of and even the existence of powerful human impulses and needs. The system of education founded on this definition of human nature will therefore fail even in its own terms, since denial of impulses will lead to the repression and eventually to the distortion of those impulses. The result will be social evil, individual human unhappiness, and crime, pronounced enough to be visible even to the eyes of the most convinced Utilitarian.

In *Hard Times* Dickens is unmistakably possessed by a comprehensive vision, one in which the inhumanities of Victorian civilization are seen as fostered and sanctioned by a hard philosophy, the aggressive formulation of an inhumane spirit. The philosophy is represented by Thomas Gradgrind, Esquire, Member of Parliament for Coketown, who has brought up his children on the lines of the experience recorded by John Stuart Mill as carried out on himself. 'Now, what I want is Facts. Teach these boys and girls nothing but Facts' —shouts Mr. Gradgrind. This fact-oriented Benthamite utilitarianism that became the subject of national worship in the Victorian England descended upon the Victorian England like a black demon squeezing the juice of life to the lees. The very title of the novel implies a destitute state of affairs in which lives of those who want to live with love for life for its own sake are inhibited because of their being prevented from giving a free and spontaneous outlet to their natural instinctive feeling and sentiment. In order to develop his theme Dickens has skilfully used the method of contrast between Fact and Fancy—between life and lifelessness—in which the motif for spontaneous life ultimately wins.

Holding that nothing but utility should determine the value of education Mr. Gradgrind sets up a school in which children are considered vessels to be poured to the brim with 'Facts' and the source of their mental pabulum is strangled. Mrs. Gradgrind is always urging her children never to wonder at anything but to go and be 'somethingological' directly. Mr. Bounderby, an embodiment of *laissez-faire*, allows inhumanity in actual practice and he has no sympathy for his workers whom he mechanically calls 'hands'. If Louisa is a helpless victim of the Gradgrindary machinery, Tom is the dangerous product of the Gradgrindary system of education. Bitzer, the most obnoxious offshoot of the fearful factory of 'Facts', refused Gradgrind's request for leaving Tom by saying: 'My schooling was paid for, it was a bargain and when I came away, the bargain ended.' Thus the fundamental principle advocated by Gradgrind 'everything was to be paid for' was boomeranged upon him.

The idea of repression is presented in its most complete and convincing form in *Hard Times*, which contains the fullest exposition of Dickens's general view of human psychology. He tries to show that the conflict between the reason, on the one hand, and the instincts, affections, and imagination, on the other, may be agonizingly real. Such a conflict may be resolved by the conscious acceptance of both 'head' and 'heart' or it may be driven underground through faulty education and result in the stunting of personality, mental breakdown, and even crime. Dickens himself has warned us against this danger which was beginning to assume a sinister shape in his own day and could be seen most clearly in the development of a particular philosophy: "Utilitarian economists, skeletons of schoolmasters, Commissioners of Fact, genteel and used-up infidels, gabblers of many little dog's eared creeds, the poor you will have always with you. Cultivate in them while there is yet time, the utmost graces of the fancies and affections, to adorn their lives so much in need of ornament; or, in the day of your triumph, when romance is utterly driven out of their souls, and they and a bare existence stand face to face, Reality will take a wolfish turn, and make an end of you!" The result of repressing affections, instincts, and imagination in favour of a one-sided rational development is the impoverishment of Bitzer's personality, the nervous collapse of Louisa with its sexual undertones, and the degeneration of Tom Gradgrind into selfishness and thieving.

In sharp contrast to this group of characters, Dickens presents the circus people who are imaginative, fanciful and represents everything humane. Mr. Sleary, owner of the circus party, is the warmhearted exponent of Dickens' philosophy of

Fancy. Unlike Gradgrind, Sleary has formed his philosophy from practice and experience: 'People must be amused somehow...' Sissy, an immaculate angel of love and sympathy, who comes directly from the circus party to save the theorists who seek to mould life to a mistaken theory creates a link between the two worlds—the world of Facts and that of Fancy. Full of vital human impulses and surviving vital human needs, the circus people exhibit a remarkable gentleness, a special inaptitude for any kind of 'sharp practice' and an untiring readiness to 'help and pity' one another.

Sissy has been brought up among horses, and among people whose livelihood depends upon understanding horses, but 'we don't want to know anything about that' and such knowledge isn't knowledge. Bitzer, the model pupil, on the button's being pressed, promptly vomits up the genuine article, 'Quadruped Graminivorous', etc.; and 'Now, girl number twenty, you know what a horse is.' The irony, pungent enough locally, is richly developed in the subsequent action. Bitzer's aptness has its evaluative comment in his career. Sissy's incapacity to acquire this kind of 'fact' or formula, her inaptness for education, is manifest to us, on the other hand, as part and parcel of her sovereign and indefeasible humanity: it is the virtue that makes it impossible for her to understand, or to think of any other human being as a unit for arithmetic. Sissy Jupe, who might be taken here for a merely conventional *persona,* has already, as a matter of fact, been established in a potently symbolic role: she is part of the poetically-creative operation of Dickens's genius in *Hard Times*. Sissy's symbolic significance is bound up with that of Sleary's Horse-riding where human kindness is very insistently associated with vitality. The way in which the Horse-riding takes on its significance illustrates felicitously the poetic-dramatic nature of Dickens's art. From the utilitarian schoolroom Mr. Gradgrind walks towards his utilitarian abode, Stone Lodge, which, as Dickens evokes it, brings home to us concretely the model regime that for the little Gradgrinds (among whom are Malthus and Adam Smith) is an inescapable prison. But before he gets there he passes the back of a circus booth, and is pulled up by the sight of two palpable offenders. Looking more closely, 'what did he behold but his own metallurgical Louisa peeping through a hole in a deal board, and his own mathematical Thomas abasing himself on the ground to catch but a hoof of the graceful equestrian Tyrolean flower act!' Representing human spontaneity, the circus-athletes represent at the same time highly-developed skill and deftness of minds that bring poise, pride and confident ease.

The novelist writers, "Yet there was a remarkable gentleness and childishness about these people, a special inaptitude for any kind of sharp practice, and an untiring readiness to help and pity one another, deserving often of as much respect, and always of as much generous construction, as the everyday virtues of any class of people in the world." Their skills have no value for the Utilitarian calculus, but they express vital human impulse, and they minister to vital human needs. The Horse-riding, frowned upon as frivolous and wasteful by Gradgrind and malignantly scorned by Bounderby, brings the machine-hands of Coketown what they are starved of. It brings to them not merely amusement, but art, and the spectacle of triumphant activity that, seeming to contain its end within itself, is, in its easy mastery, joyously self-justified. In investing a travelling circus with this kind of symbolic value Dickens expresses a profounder reaction to industrialism than might have been expected of him. It is not only pleasure and relaxation the Coketowners stand in need of; he feels the dreadful degradation of life that would remain even if they were to be given a forty-hour week, comfort, security and fun.

The tug of war between Fact and Fancy begins in the beginning of the novel in Gradgrind's school where Sissy 'dark-eyed' and 'dark-haired' cannot describe a horse in the factual terms, but Bitzer 'light-eyed' and 'light-haired' promptly does it—Sissy standing for Fancy and Bitzer for Facts. Sissy came to be taught by Gradgrind that there is only 'One Thing needful' in the world and that is 'Facts', but at the end it is she who taught Gradgrind that there is 'Another thing needful' in life and that is the exercise of fancy, imagination, sympathy and love and that head is to be cared but heart is not to be uncared for. Dickens successfully conveys the message that there is a genuine joy only in the emotions of the heart and humanity, pity, forgiveness and sympathy are the finest things in men and intimacy, tenderness, tears and laughter are the sweetest things in the world. To the question of how the reconciling is done the answer can be given by pointing to the astonishing and irresistible richness of life that characterizes the book everywhere. It meets us everywhere, unstrained and natural, in the prose. Out of such prose a great variety of presentations can arise congenially with equal vividness.

(II) NARRATIVE ART

Quintilian gives his definition of "rhetoric" with the careful proviso that the art should be directed towards an honest and noble end. As late as the time of Dickens, the ablest writer on the subject, Whately, betrays anxiety about this problem. Many writers on rhetoric, including Aristotle, introduce the idea of persuasion into their definition (Quintilian, *Institutes of Oratory*, II. Xv. 23, tr. Revd. John Selby Watson (1856), II. Xv. 33-38, Vol. I, pp. 144-47). Persuasion is a very special anathema of the time when advertising, propaganda, and indoctrination have been pushed to the point of brain washing and mass lunacy. An open study of Dickens as a rhetorical artist has been discouraged not only by the bad sense to which the idea of rhetoric has often been restricted but also by the absence of an adequate positive definition of the term. A bewildering array of meanings is implied in the term. The convenient summary in *SOED* gives the history of the word as follows: (1) The art of using language so as to persuade or influence others; the body of rules to be observed by a speaker or writer in order that he may express himself with eloquence. (2) (a) Elegance or eloquence of language; eloquent speech or writing. (b) Speech or writing expressed in terms calculated to persuade; hence, language characterized by artificial or ostentatious expression. Thus, the technical, pejorative, and figurative senses have survived in the meanings of the word. Possibly the most useful list of meanings is given by the *Dictionary of World Literature*:

> Rhetoric is the art and science of composition in words.... It may denominate: (1) a body of principles concerning the composition of persuasive or otherwise effective public speeches, or (a) the speeches themselves, or (b) the skill of an orator; (2) a body of principles applicable in prose composition in general, whether designed for publication or for oral delivery, or (a) the technique of a master of prose style, or (b) artificial prose of doctrine about artificial prose tinged with insincerity; (3) any classified and systematized body of doctrine about artifices of verbal composition, whether prose or poetry, or (a) the use of such artifices or devices in either prose or verse. (Whitford, 'Rhetoric', *Dictionary of World Literature* 340)

The two most interesting points that emerge from the wide range of definitions are the idea of rhetoric as the art of composition and the stress on the function of rhetoric, which is to produce an effect in the receptor. The use of rhetoric to mean the art of composition, which is found in the United States, was originally current in Great Britain. In *Elements of Rhetoric* (1828), Richard Whately was anxious to establish the meaning of rhetoric as the art of composition. No other word in English covers the senses both of composition as an art or technique and as a function directed towards the specific end of producing effects. Wayne C. Booth has defined 'the rhetoric of fiction' as the technique of non-didactic fiction, viewed as the art of communicating with readers—the rhetorical resources available to the writer of epic, novel, or short story as he tries, consciously or unconsciously, to impose his fictional world upon the reader. And in defending his study as proper one, Booth puts the whole question of rhetoric into a sane perspective: "Regardless of how we define art or artistry, the very concept of writing a story seems to have implicit within it the notion of finding techniques of expression that will make the work accessible in the highest possible degree.... This first defense of rhetoric does not depend on proving that it is indispensable but rather in showing that in fact it has generally been not only tolerated but embraced by competent writers (*The Rhetoric of Fiction*. Chicago: 1961, Preface, 105-06). Dickens's narrative art defines the rhetoric of fiction as the technical means whereby, through structure, effects are created and vision focused.

F.R. Leavis and Q.D. Leavis observe, "In the books and essays on Dickens...it [*Hard Times*] is passed over as a very minor thing; too slight and insignificant to distract us for more than a sentence or two from the works worth critical attention.... Of all Dickens's works it is the one that, having the distinctive strength that makes him a major artist, has it in so compact a way, and with a concentrated significance so immediately clear and penetrating, as, one would have thought, to preclude the reader's failing to recognize that he had before him a completely serious, and, in its originality, a triumphantly successful, work of art" (251). Dickens's art in *Hard Times* differs from Ben Jonson's not in being inconsistent, but in being so very much more flexible and inclusive. In *The Great Tradition* (1950), Leavis's recognition that Dickens's writing shows 'a full critical vision, a stamina, a flexibility combined with consistency, and a depth that he seems to have had little credit for', is just though rather belated. He also surprisingly pays tribute to 'the astonishing and irresistible richness of life that characterizes the book everywhere', and even describes the author as a 'poet dramatist'.

G. Stewart writes in "Escape Artists": "The Dickens novel with the most generic title, *Hard Times* paints the most explicit, the most harrowing picture of the Victorian assault against imagination. The inimical Gradgrind world does indeed represent everything from which the imagination must make its retreat and take its refuge. Otherwise, it is proscribed and exterminated. And more unflinchingly than in any other book, the prose of *Hard Times* displays this chilling alternative where the most pervasive threat to being is that monotony will aggravate it into derangement: a danger latent in the fixated patterns of the style itself. The usual narrative gaiety of Dickens is deliberately minimized for *Hard Times*, where there is considerably less play of mind over the vagaries and private elations of language than in any other of his novels, less unassimilated love of words themselves. The relentless style of the novel is a success precisely...because it scores against the satiric adversary on its own ground: logical argument, tabular reasoning itemization, mensurable considerations only. Nowhere else in Dickens, for so long at a time, is the writing so assiduously paced, the antithetical structure so automatic and tenacious" (Stewart 151-52). One can quote the following words in this context: "Stephen bent over his loom, quiet, watchful, and steady. A special contrast...to the crashing, smashing, tearing piece of mechanism at which he laboured" (I, 11). The contrast of opposed syntactic triads, the quiet and steady adjectives against the grating kinetic participles, has a tightness unfamiliar in Dickens's usual prose. Whereas in *Bleak House* we meet a profusion barely contained by parallelism and repetition, in *Hard Times* Dickens projects a world narrowed to the bounds of a punctual and peremptory antithesis. Yet there are ironies beyond this in the passage selected, for that "special contrast" asserted between hero and machine is partly subverted by the similar three prolonged grammar of their balanced descriptions, and is in fact contradicted by that extra-syntactic parallel throughout the novel which insists that men in this society are slowly being turned into machines.

In the manuscript of *Hard Times*, Dickens revises his first description of Coketown. Structural irony and the irony of understatement combine in an omniscient comment which stresses the theme and hints at possible development in the story: 'A town so sacred to fact, and so triumphant in its assertion, of course got on well? Why no, not quite well.' There is an irony in the town's very architecture in which even the pretensions to spirituality embody themselves in the forms of the materialistic world whose values dominate the life of Coketown. Ironically enough, too, society, which has changed work into a religion and the outward forms of religion into those of work, is indignantly surprised to discover that the working people turn their backs on religion proper. Once more Dickens can be seen, here, deliberately clarifying his vision, making it into a sharper and more specific indictment of the acquisitive values of society:

> ...everything was fact between the lying-in hospital and the cemetery, and what you couldn't state in figures, or show to be purchasable in the cheapest market and salable in the dearest, was not, and never should be, world without end, Amen.

Sucksmith observes in this connection that Dickens inserts into his parody of the doxology from the Prayer Book the phrase, 'or show to be purchasable in the cheapest market and salable in the dearest', thus bringing into collision the most profane of all the economic formulas of *laissez-faire* and the sacred text in the affirmation of Christian faith; the result is to imply ironically that the eternal faith and the gospel according to wealth and work are one, thus exposing more than a social evil—revealing a shocking blasphemy against the Holy Spirit (164-65). Dickens's descriptions of Coketown focus an adverse vision of the ravages made by industrial society through an antipathy created in the reader.

The pattern of structural irony occurs very frequently in Dickens's novels. The following example is much more subtle and complex than might at first appear:

> Thomas Gradgrind took no heed of these trivialities of course, but passed on as a practical man ought to pass on, either brushing the noisy insects from his thoughts, or consigning them to the House of Correction. But, the turning of the road took him by the back of the booth, and at the back of the booth a number of children were congregated in a number of stealthy attitudes, striving to peep in at the hidden glories of the place.
>
> This brought him to a stop. "Now, to think of these vagabonds", said he, "attracting the young rabble from a model school."
>
> A space of stunted grass and dry rubbish being between him and the young rabble, he took his eyeglass out of his waistcoat to look for any child he knew by name, and

> might order off. Phenomenon almost incredible though distinctly seen, what did he then behold but his own metallurgical Louisa, peeping with all her might through a hole in a deal board, and his own mathematical Thomas abasing himself on the ground to catch but a hoof of the graceful equestrian Tyrolean flower-act! (I, III)

The ground for the little catastrophe is carefully prepared by Gradgrind's arrogant dismissal of the circus in the first paragraph; his rejection of the imaginative and affective side of human nature sets in motion against him the machinery of the natural law. The ensuing catastrophe is the kind that Aristotle recommends. It contains both a discovery and a peripety and possesses the proper qualities of surprise and probability. Surprise is not only registered through 'phenomenon almost incredible' but the specific reference to 'his own metallurgical Louisa' and 'his own mathematical Thomas' brings out all the irony in the neat reversal of Gradgrind's expectations as father and educationist. Yet the probability of the incident has been carefully prepared; earlier in the chapter, the education of the Gradgrind children has been described in an ironic tone which culminates in the slight but pregnant hint: '...everything that heart could desire. Everything? Well, I suppose so' (I, III). Harvey P. Sucksmith writes in this connection in *The Narrative Art of Charles Dickens*: "The basic movement of the novel originates in the spiritual blindness of Gradgrind, which is the blindness of a whole philosophy, of a society, of an age. Again, the spiritual myopia of Gradgrind is suggested by the business of the eyeglass which he needs to make out what his children are up to under his very nose; thus the physical action of the passage expresses and underlines the wider spiritual message. Moreover the incident is related organically to the rest of the novel both in form and in content. It foreshadows the major double catastrophe in which daughter and son show so alarmingly the unexpected yet quite inevitable effects of the Gradgrind system of education on their adult lives. The passage is, in fact, the major catastrophe of the novel in miniature. It is more. Since the incident provides an ominous warning, which Gradgrind is to ignore at his peril, it is the act of willful defiance which will trigger off that major catastrophe. Thus, the passage is a tiny model of the whole ironic structure of the novel. As such it is vision as well as structure—a prophetic picture, that is, of the way that an outraged natural law brings about a nemesis in the fullness of time" (157).

The comic world of Dickens, as Middleton Murry has said on Swift, is an orgiastic world, with a dubious relation with the moral hierarchy. It is an alternative world to that of ordinary experience and as valid as the poetic. Dickens is not continually comic; one can, more accurately, call him picturesque, theatrical. We cannot separate the comic from the indignant, sermonizing, melodramatic or revolutionary Dickens, for the comic, in him, was not mere comic relief. The laughter is joined to the hatred and despair Dickens felt about it. In the comic passages we find his poetry and a quality which can be called radiant. In Dickens, the private imagination, comic, poetical and fantastic, was inseparable from the public imagination and the operation of conscience and rebellion. "Humour was his medium; his only way of approaching emotion. Wherever you do not get humour, you get unconscious humour" (Chesterton 185).

Dickens's humour lies in his ability to see through pretence. In *Hard Times* a 'government officer', intended by Dickens as a representative of the newly formed Department of Practical Art, and presented as a monster of pedantry, asks a class of schoolchildren whether they would paper a room with representations of horses.

> After a pause, one half of the children cried in chorus, 'Yes, sir!' Upon which the other half, seeing in the gentleman's face that Yes was wrong, cried out in chorus, 'No, sir!'

Even the children who have given the right answer can't explain why it's right:

'I'll explain to you, then', said the gentleman, after another and a dismal pause, 'why you wouldn't paper a room with representations of horses.... Do you?'

'Yes, sir!' from one half. 'No, sir!' from the other. (I, II)

The arch-hypocrite Bounderby in *Hard Times* wishes it to be believed, despite his perfectly secure childhood, that he fought his way up from the gutter. He employs Mrs. Sparsit, a fellow hypocrite posing as a great lady in reduced circumstances, so that he can feel superior to her fallen grandeur. Bounderby invents elaborate degradations for his own early years, and compares these with the imagined glories of the Sparsit past. In this way both hypocrites can draw satisfaction from completely fictitious accounts of themselves.

> "At a time when", says Bounderby, "to have been a tumbler in the mud of the streets, would have been a godsend to me, a prize in the lottery to me, you were at the Italian Opera. You were coming out of the Italian Opera, ma'am, in white satin and jewels, a blaze of splendour, when I hadn't a penny to buy a link to light you."
>
> "I certainly, sir", returned Mrs. Sparsit, with a dignity serenely mournful, "was familiar with the Italian Opera at a very early age."

Adroitly Mrs. Sparsit embraces the grandeur and rejects the implication of relative seniority. Dickens's hypocrites are the prime beneficiaries of his inventive genius.

In *Hard Times*, Dickens is away from the fantasy and the gothic to the realistic form of humour. Bounderby has the absurd pride of the self-made man. He is proud of his own hard times and he is well-worked out. That is to say "hard times" is an idea added to all the characters and seen, in his case, on the comic level. He is a figure out of social satire and he is not visited by the grace of the comic forgiveness. In *Hard Times*, Dickens reaches very fine point of social irony.

The rigour of a deterministic prose, a stylistic impersonation of the Gradgrind system's own strict sequential logic, is later used to point up the danger more explicitly, as

Dickens warns the oppressors of the poor that "in the day of your triumph, when romance is utterly driven out of their souls, and they and a bare existence stand face to face, Reality will take a wolfish turn, and make an end of you". Here is an explicit danger signal about the revenge of imagination that follows upon its improper cultivation for society at large rather than for the private consciousness. If "romance" is expelled completely, "Reality" itself will turn wolfish: the psychic danger becomes for the industrial society a revolutionary threat. There is a perfect dramatic example of this process when Tom "the whelp" is captured finally and admits his crime to the astonished Mr. Gradgrind. Tom has been treated as a cipher all along, an item in a general statistical theory, and now the statistical "reality" has taken its own whelpish turn: "So many people are employed in situations of trust; so many people, out of so many, will be dishonest. I have you talk, a hundred times, of its being a law. How can I help laws? You have comforted others with such things, father. Comfort yourself!" (III, VII). This pattern of the revenging turn in the case of Tom Gradgrind is even prepared for earlier in the novel, when Tom explains that he has been treated for so long as a mule or donkey that "I should like to kick like one" (I, VIII).

The style in which *Hard Times* is conducted makes a wolfish turn upon itself, a turn into parody and mechanistic simulation. Nothing more light-hearted will do, no risk alternatives by which the healthier tenor of the prose itself becomes a kind of counter argument: the medium as message. "The lights in the great factories, which looked, when they were illuminated, like Fairy palaces—or the travellers by express train said so—were all extinguished" (I, X). The reference to "Fairy palaces" is, in some sense ironic, that these factories are merely temples to fact, not palaces at all but places of toil and the expense of spirit, products of a system which denies the existence both of fairies and of their architecture as absurd castles in the air. Further, though the fancy about "Fairy palaces" seems to be a tribute to the gusto and variety of the narrative voice, it is instead a trenchant parody of the whole romantic sensibility as it becomes an aestheticizing indifference to human pain. G. Stewart writes in "Escape Artists":

> Once more, style is revenging itself on those who value it too cheaply, a facile romanticism turned on its perpetrators. Dickens is not proud of self-display here; rather the world he is drawing for us is so inhuman that even the narrator himself cannot afford the natural and effortless manipulations of his fancy. Too much is at stake for such unearned "poetry of existence" to be anything but a callous fiction. By no means a complacent testament to imagination, the simile here is rather an exposure of fancy as at times a dangerous, an unfeeling indulgence. From a public world that knows only the death of fancy—either by edict and extinction or suicidally, through its own prevarications—there must be some honest means of escape. The chief release for the Gradgrind children, the activity of fire-gazing in the same chapter, is a thought-provoking matter as it is one of the primary romantic employments of Dickens's characters. (Stewart 153-54)

Dr. Leavis's view is that Dickens's art in *Hard Times* is a 'highly conventional art' which is managed with great flexibility and tact, so that many different fictional modes are reconciled with each other in a coherent unity:

> To the question how the reconciling is done...the answer can be given by pointing to the astonishing and irresistible richness of life that characterizes the book everywhere. It meets us everywhere, unstrained and natural, in the prose. Out of such prose a great variety of presentations can arise congenially with equal vividness. There they are, unquestionably 'real'. It goes back to an extraordinary energy of perception and registration in Dickens. (260)

'When people say that Dickens exaggerates', says Mr. Santayana, "it seems to me that they can have no eyes and no ears. They probably have only *notions* of what things and people are; they accept them conventionally, at their diplomatic value." Dickens's flexibility is that of a richly poetic art of the world. He doesn't write 'poetic prose'; he writes with a poetic force of evocation, registering with the responsiveness of a genius of verbal expression what he so sharply sees and feels. In fact, by texture, imaginative mode, symbolic method, and the resulting concentration, *Hard Times* affects us as belonging with formally poetic works.

Dr. Leavis calls Dickens a 'genius of verbal expression'. The great virtue of Dr. Leavis's essay on *Hard Times* is that it points to the qualities in Dickens which make him a genius of verbal expression. One may quote the following passage, for example:

> The square finger, moving here and there, lighted suddenly on Bitzer, perhaps because he had chanced to sit in the same ray of sunlight which, darting in at one of the bare windows of the intensely whitewashed room, irradiated Sissy. For the boys and girls sat on the face of the inclined plane in two compact bodies, divided up the centre by a narrow interval; and Sissy, being at the corner of a row on the sunny side, came in for the beginning of a sunbeam, of which Bitzer, being at the corner of a row on the other side, a few rows in advance, caught the end. But, whereas the girl was so dark-eyed and dark-haired, that she seemed to receive a deeper and more lustrous colour from the sun when it shone upon her, the boy was so light-eyed and light-haired that the selfsame rays appeared to draw out of him what little colour he ever possessed. His cold eyes would hardly have been eyes, but for the short ends of lashes which, by bringing them into immediate contrast with something paler than themselves, expressed their form. His short-cropped hair might have been a mere continuation of the sandy freckles on his forehead and face. His skin was so unwholesomely deficient in the natural tinge, that he looked as though, if he were cut, he would bleed white. (I, II)

The moral and spiritual differences are rendered here in terms of sensation, and the symbolic intention emerges out of metaphor and the vivid evocation of the concrete. There is an essentially Laurentian suggestion about the way in which 'the dark-eyed and dark-haired' girl, contrasting with Bitzer, seemed to receive a 'deeper and more lustrous colour from the sun', so opposing the life that is lived freely and richly from the deep instinctive and emotional springs to the thin-blooded, quasi-mechanical product of Gradgrindery. Dickens is a great poet: his endless resource in felicitously varied expression is an extraordinary responsiveness to life. His senses are charged with emotional energy, and his intelligence plays and flashes in the quickest and sharpest perception. Dickens's metaphorical presentation of Sissy Jupe is a 'flash' of intelligence and insight in another sense too: it flares brilliantly and then goes out. It is one thing to praise *Hard Times* for its economy. We hear nothing more of Sissy Jupe's dark-eyes and dark-hair which 'seemed to receive a deeper and more lustrous colour from the sun'. Though Bitzer is 'colourless' or 'light' at every reappearance, this suggestion is rarely brought to imaginative life after the beginning; but the more important point is that Sissy is never again vividly seen in these or indeed in any 'vivid terms of sensation'. Dickens forgot about Sissy Jupe's lustrous dark-eyes and dark-hair for a good reason—good in terms of the Dickens theatre. What he had in mind as Sissy's further career could not be conveniently adjusted to the earlier, vivid registration of her 'vital impulse'. She shares in the strength of the Horse-riding. She is wholly convincing in the function Dickens assigns to her. The working of her influence in the Utilitarian home is conveyed with a fine tact, and we do really feel her as a growing potency. Sissy's quiet potency makes a significant—and of course effective—contrast with the aggressiveness and bluster of Gradgrind and Bounderby, the tension of Louisa, the sullenness of the whelp. Nor do Sissy's actions—consisting as they do mostly of nursing, receiving confidences, understanding, and being patient—strike us as inept or trivial or sentimental manifestations of what is lacking in the Utilitarian home.

Dickens examines the problem of suffering and of God's nature in a specifically Christian context. Stephen Blackpool, who represents the case of man crucified by the contemporary world, puts the tragic irony of the situation. In his notes, Dickens plans a Christian answer: 'STEPHEN AND RACHAEL Bear and forbear/ The star that leads the way.' Stephen is able to attain a Christian view of forbearance returned for suffering, which transcends his earlier concept of providence, through the star of divine guidance with its strong New Testament associations:

> "It ha' shined upon me", he said reverently, "in my pain and trouble down below. It ha' shined into my mind. I ha' look'n at it an thowt o' thee, Rachael, till the muddle in my mind have cleared awa, above a bit, I hope." (III, VI)

Dickens's compassionate vision is reflected in his rhetoric of sympathy and irony. Dickens's vision is comprehensive and complex enough to take in our equal and contradictory passions for justice and for mercy.

The description of Gradgrind's physical appearance is harsh and grim, and the eyes which 'found commodious cellarage in two dark caves, overshadowed by the wall', seem to promise a really cruel nature. But when the fable requires that Gradgrind be essentially a good man, with kind instincts and loving concern for his children hidden from them and from himself, Dickens's method of rendering this is his old one: Gradgrind is rapidly fitted out with a heart. Robert Garris observes in this connection: "The heart really works, Dickens makes us believe in it, and the rhetorical point is successfully rendered by the theatrical device. The artist is in confident control of his argument, and accordingly when Gradgrind's heart is in full anguished operation, in those last scenes, his grim appearance has become invisible and his strident voice inaudible—they were verbal masks and they have been expertly laid aside" (162).

Dickens embodies in the circus people the kind of gratuitous kindness which derives from spontaneous fellow-feeling and cannot be accounted for by the Utilitarian calculus. This kind of spontaneity is by no means unrelated to the brilliant circus tricks of the performers. The kindness of the

Horse-riding is embodied chiefly in the figure of Sleary, and we are accordingly conscious mostly of the meanings enforced by this character. The scenes in which Sleary helps Gradgrind get Tom out of the country derive their meaning from the eminently theatrical contrast between practical hard-headed Gradgrind, now menaced by his prize pupil Bitzer and sloppy, lisping Sleary. That is, the main accent is on brandy and water; positively 'triumphant activity' comes only in the miniature comic form of the polka-dancing horse. Dickens's point is the surprising practicality of the incompetent-seeming Sleary, and the surprising usefulness of the horse that can dance the polka. This does not in any important way feel inconsistent with Dickens's earlier view of the Horse-riding which emphasizes, as Dr. Leavis points out, the fact that the skills of the Horse-riding contain their end within themselves and are therefore 'wasteful' in terms of Gradgrind's algebra. The broad-hearted circus people offer a contrast to the money-minded brutes like Bounderby. When Gradgrind offers Sleary some money he declines the offer. He accepts only a five-pound note for Mr. Childers who is a family man and asks him to buy a collar for the dog and a belt for the horse. The final scenes focus emphatically on Sissy's richness and lustre and the Horse-riding's triumphant activity. Dickens keeps his symbolic intentions continuously in hand throughout the moral fable. The flashes of insight are indeed there, and there is also the wonderful capacity for realizing them in language. Dickens is indeed in these respects a poet of almost Shakespearean calibre.

The economy of *Hard Times* is a special and brilliant effect in the Dickens theatre, and it is offered as loudly and distinctly, and as proudly, as any of Dickens's other effects. In the very first chapter, Mr. Gradgrind dictates:

> Now, what I want is, Facts. Teach these boys and girls nothing but Facts. Facts alone are wanted in life. Plant nothing else, and root out everything else. You can only form the minds of reasoning animals upon Facts: nothing else will ever be of any service to them. This is the principle on which I bring up these children. Stick to Facts, Sir!

Chapter II ends thus:

> He [Mr. M'Choakumchild] went to work in this preparatory lesson, not unlike Morgiana in the Forty Thieves: looking into all the vessels ranged before him, one after another, to see what they contained. Say, good M'Choakumchild. When from thy boiling store, thou shalt fill each jar brim full by-and-by, dost thou think that thou wilt always kill outright the robber Fancy lurking within—or sometimes only maim him and distort him!

So, the burden of Dickens's moral fable is already before us in outline, and the third chapter begins immediately to show the way the lives of Louisa and Tom Gradgrind have been in fact maimed and distorted. The virtue of this rapidity of demonstration, as a theatrical effect, goes without saying, and the prose in which it is rendered is fully alive. Again, in Chapter V, we see:

> Fact, fact, fact, everywhere in the material aspect of the town; fact, fact, fact, everywhere in the immaterial. The M'Choakumchild school was all fact, and the school of design was all fact, and everything was fact between the lying-in hospital and the cemetery, and what you couldn't state in figures, or show to be purchasable in the cheapest market and saleable in the dearest, was not, and never should be, world without end, Amen.

The primary impression is of the impudent vitality of the performing voice, enjoying its indignation and confident of its power to denounce and banish what makes it so angry. The voice is evoking an image of a kind of death in life. Perhaps when Dickens himself saw the real Coketown, his spirit actually was quenched for a moment, as it never had been by the dense and irregular squalor of the London slums; when he heard the voice of the Utilitarian calculus in action, and learned about its educational theory, perhaps he did indeed realize that so misguided a theory of education, systematically run by well-intentioned technicians, could do serious damage to children.

At its best, *Hard Times* attempts a serious criticism of the problem-plagued Victorian society, and the method of criticism throughout the book is ironical, though the irony is enjoyably fraught with wit. The narrative method is ironical but Dickens maintains detachment and that is why his irony becomes amusing. Behind the wit and fun, Dickens discusses the pathetic aspects of the problems and shows them vividly through the interaction and interplay of characters and situations. His comic method makes us laugh and at the same time makes us think. Fielding writes:

> The novel has...a broad purpose even though it included references to some of Dickens's living contemporaries which most of them were unable to recognize, and satire of specific abuses which was too pointed to be understood by the general reader; and it is only by understanding this broader purpose (which is not so obvious that it can be taken for granted) that one can see how it unifies Dickens's remarks on Stephen Blackpool's marriage, the aesthetic theories of the 'third gentleman' in the second chapter, the problems of Trade Unionism, Louisa's marriage to Bounderby, and her brother's theft from the bank. Dickens once wrote that the ideas took him 'by the throat' and forced him to write. A careful reading shows that he succeeded in giving them a unified purpose, and that *Hard Times* has coherence and power which deserve great respect even though it is not as entertaining as most of the other novels. (133)

F.R. Leavis comments: "The final stress may fall on Dickens's command of word, phrase, rhythm and image: in ease and range there is surely no greater master of English except Shakespeare. This comes back to saying that Dickens is a great poet: his endless resource in felicitously varied expression is an extraordinary responsiveness to life. His senses are charged with emotional energy, and his intelligence plays and flashes in the quickest and sharpest perception. That is, his mastery of 'style' is of the only kind that matters—which is not to say that he hasn't a conscious interest in what can be done with words; many of his felicities could plainly not have come if there had not been, in the background, a habit of such interest" (274-75).

(III) THESIS/SOCIAL/INDUSTRIAL NOVEL

Although F.G. Kitton did not include *Hard Times* in his book *The Novels of Dickens*, and only gave it a short notice in *The Minor Writings of Dickens*, T.J. Jackson calls *Hard Times* 'a frontal attack upon the ethics of capitalism as represented by the Manchester School', adding that it 'shows no confidence in the proletariat'. *Hard Times* is set in a northern industrial town far grimmer than Jack Rouncewell's town in *Bleak House*. *Hard Times* deals with conditions in an industrial town, Coketown, from the point of view both of employer and employee. Coketown takes us back to the nightmare chapters on the Birmingham to Wolverhampton road in *The Old Curiosity Shop*, but in *Hard Times* the horror is seen more analytically than through the eyes of a dying girl. The presiding sensibilities are those of Gradgrind and Bounderby, two gentlemen well calculated to keep fancy and imagination at bay. There is a new ruthlessness of observation on Dickens's part, as befits his setting. It is as if he extinguished his most distinctive gift for poetic resonance and suggestiveness in order to capture a world where the creative powers themselves are in exile. Or rather, as if he drove the resonances of his art inwards, until they acquired a muffled and deadly quality. While there are still evidences of symbolism in Coketown, and it would hardly be Dickens's city without this, the very symbols are oppressive to our minds. Any enchantment in Coketown is claustrophobic and sickening, like the witch's house in *Hansel and Gretel. Hard Times* presents Dickens's theses involving three separate plot sequences Dickens planned for *Hard Times*, each of them presenting opportunities for development and contrast. The plot sequences illustrate Dickens's general plan for revolving his action around his attack on utilitarian economy, since it also encompasses criticism of the educational system, the caste system, and divorce laws. F.R. Leavis comments on *Hard Times*:

> Ordinarily Dickens's criticisms of the world he lives in are causal and incidental—a matter of including among the ingredients of a book some indignant treatment of a particular abuse. But in *Hard Times* he is for once possessed by a comprehensive vision, one in which the inhumanities of Victorian civilization are seen as fostered and sanctioned by a hard philosophy, the aggressive formulation of an inhumane spirit. (*The Great Tradition* 228)

Hard Times is less an imaginative observation than an imaginative judgement. It is a judgement of social attitudes, but again it is something more than *North and South*. It is a thoroughgoing and creative examination of the dominant philosophy of industrialism. In terms of human understanding of the industrial working people Dickens is obviously less successful than Mrs. Gaskell in *Mary Barton*: his Stephen Blackpool, in relation to the people of *Mary Barton*, is little more than a diagrammatic figure. In fact, *Hard Times* is an analysis of Industrialism, rather than experience of it. Josiah Bounderby in *Hard Times* is the embodiment of the aggressive money-making and power-seeking ideal which was a driving force of the Industrial revolution. He is also a braggart, a liar and in general personally repellent. The conjunction of these personal defects with the aggressive ideal is not a necessary conjunction. A large part of the Victorian reader's feelings against Bounderby rests on the older and rather different feeling that trade, as such, is gross. Bounderby is a class-name for the hard Victorian employer. Gradgrind is a Utilitarian seen by Dickens as one of the *feeloosofers* against whom Cobbett thundered, or as one of the *steam-engine intellects* described by Carlyle. Dickens has Mill's *Political Economy* (1849) very much in mind in his general indictment of the ideas which built and maintained Coketown. In condemning Thomas Gradgrind, the representative figure, we condemn the kind of thinking and the methods of enquiry and legislation which in fact promoted a large measure of social and industrial reform. One wonders, for example, what a typical Fabian feels when he is invited to condemn Gradgrind, not as an individual but as a type.

Dickens's understanding of a Victorian civilization is adequate for his purpose; the justice and penetration of his criticism are unaffected. And his moral perception works in alliance with a clear insight into the English social structure. Mr. James Harthouse is necessary for the plot; but he too has his representative function. He has come to Coketown as a prospective parliamentary candidate, for 'the Gradgrind party wanted assistance in cutting the throats of the Graces', and they 'liked fine gentlemen; they pretended that they did not, but they did'. There is Mrs. Sparsit who seems to be there merely for the plot, but her 'husband was a Powler', a fact she reverts to as often as Bounderby to his mythical birth in a ditch; and the two complementary opposites, with Mr. James Harthouse, who in his languid assurance of class-superiority doesn't need to boast, form a trio that suggests the whole system of British snobbery.

Dickens recognizes the industrial working people as objects of pity, and he recognizes the personal devotion in suffering of which they are capable. But the only conclusion he can expect them to draw is Stephen Blackpool's: "Aw a muddle." Stephen, deserted by a drunken wife, desires to be divorced in order to marry the woman he loves who would make a home for him. Divorce he finds is a luxury that the rich alone can afford. Doctor's Commons, Common Law, House of Lords, all have to be invoked, and the fees are never less than £1500. Other incidents in the book go to show that the Law is the prerogative of the well-to-do and of no assistance to the poor. Like the Circumlocution Office, it is 'a device for keeping the snobs off the nobs'. It drove Dickens nearly mad to realize that by treating people as aggregates they could be dehumanized at the whim of an employer. But the hopelessness and passive suffering are set against the attempts of the working people to better their conditions. The trade unions are dismissed by a stock Victorian reaction, with the agitator Slackbridge. Stephen Blackpool is shown to advantage because he will not join them. In Stephen Blackpool Dickens tried to rescue the idea of personality in an individual industrial worker. Stephen's successive defeats by the Law, by the Trade Union, and by his employer might have become the material of genuine tragedy, if Dickens had been prepared to accept his death from the beginning as inevitable and unanswerable; but he was hankering all the time after a way to avoid the proper tragic solution, and the result is nothing but a slow record of inglorious misery and defeat. Humphry House says in "*Hard Times*": "Dickens did not want to admit that Stephen's bargaining power—whether against Bounderby, his marriage, or life itself—was negligible, but wrote as if there might be an unexpected solution at every turn. There is no difficulty about Stephen's relation of the Law or about his relation to Bounderby; the true crux is in the part of the plot that deals with the Trade Union, and in making it so Dickens was apparently trying to work out, in the actual writing of the book, the implications of his old ideal of man to man benevolence in the relations between employers and labour in large-scale industry" (Dyson 1968: 216). Three points may be worthwhile to observe in Dickens's treatment of the Union—Stephen's inexplicable obstinacy in refusing to join it; Dickens's hatred of Slackbridge; and the difference of mood and attitude of the other workers towards Stephen as men and as Union members under Slackbridge's influence. In his article "On Strike" in *Household Words* (II Feb. 1854) Dickens describes the two Union meetings of the cotton strikers that he attended, and they are obviously the foundation for the Union meeting in *Hard Times*. The article stresses the order and courtesy of the strikers, the efficiency of the business and the competence of the local leaders; it decries the influence of an outside orator who is a prototype of Slackbridge; it makes clear that the men fully believed in the justice of their case, but that, at the same time, they had no hatred or resentment for most of the employers. The moral approval seems to be all on the side of the strikers. But the political conclusion is not that the strike is right:

> In any aspect in which it can be viewed, this strike and lockout is a deplorable calamity. In its waste of time, in its waste of a great people's energy, in its waste of wages, in its waste of wealth that seeks to be employed,

> in its encroachment on the means of many thousands who are laboring from day to day, in the gulf of separation it hourly deepens between those whose interests must be understood to be identical or must be destroyed, it is a great national affliction. But, at this pass, anger is of no use, starving out is of no use—for what will that do, five years hence, but overshadow all the mills in England with the growth of a bitter remembrance?—political economy is a mere skeleton unless it has a little human covering and filling out, a little human bloom upon it, and a little human warmth in it.

Dickens accepts the fundamental ethical and political proposition of the political economy he generally so much deplores. The interests of employers and employed must be assumed to be identical or must be destroyed.

Though in *Hard Times* the lives of employer and employed at times intermingle, Dickens realizes that as things are, the interests of both are opposing interests and that because of this all poor people are automatically suspected by all rich people. As Rachael says to Louisa Gradgrind, 'The like of you don't know us, don't care for us, don't belong to us.' While her lover says, 'Life is all a muddle from beginning to end.' When Dickens assures us that "these men (the Coketown workers), through their very delusions, showed great qualities even when they "went astray" by combining or that "every man felt his only hope to be in his allying himself to the comrades by whom he was surrounded; and that in this belief, right or wrong, the whole of that crowd were gravely, deeply, faithfully in earnest", he is speaking with the usual voice of the middle class.

In the manuscript of *Hard Times*, Dickens revises his first description of Coketown as follows (insertions or revisions in bold letters):

> Coketown, to which Messrs. Bounderby and Gradgrind now walked, as a triumph of fact (and figures); it had no greater taint of fancy in it than Mrs. Gradgrind herself.

> Let us strike the keynote, Coketown, before pursuing our tune.
>
> It was a town of red brick or of brick that would have been red if the smoke **and ashes** had allowed it; but, as matters stood it was a town of **unnatural** red and black like the (face of) **painted face of** an ugly savage. It was a town of machinery and tall chimneys, out of which interminable serpents of smoke trailed themselves sluggishly for ever and ever, and never got uncoiled. It had a black canal in it, and a river that ran purple where there was a rattling and a trembling all day long, and where the piston of the steam-engine worked monotonously up and down, like the head of an elephant in a state of melancholy madness. It contained several large streets all very like one another, and many small streets still more like one another, inhabited by people equally like one another, who **all** went in and out at the same hours, **with the same sound upon the pavement**, to do the same work, and to whom every day was the same as yesterday and tomorrow, and every year the counterpart of the last and the next.
>
> These attributes of Coketown were in the main inseparable from the work by which it was sustained; against them were to be set off, comforts of life which found their way all over the world, **and elegances of life which made we will not ask how much of the fine lady, who could scarcely bear to hear the place mentioned.**

The description of Coketown creates a strong antipathy towards the ugly and unnatural nightmare of Coketown. Antipathy is increased by the addition of 'and ashes', 'unnatural', and 'painted'. The effect of antipathy is complicated by irony. Dickens's deliberate rhetoric does not only simply increase the effect of antipathy but draw attention more sharply to the ugly reality behind Gradgrind and Bounderby's delusions. The insertion of 'unnatural' and 'painted' helps to draw attention to the antithesis between natural and unnatural and to the appearance of civilization behind which the ugly reality of a savagery worse than the natural kind is concealing itself. There is an ironical contrast between the town's ugly and uncongenial character and the comforts and elegance it produces through its manufactured goods. Harvey P. Sucksmith observes in this connection in *The Narrative Art of Charles Dickens*: "Through adding the ironic idea of a society which is glad to adorn itself with the products of a place which it is too snobbish to name, Dickens intensifies the power of his satirical vision" (164).

Dickens presents another revised description of Coketown:

> In the hardest working part of Coketown; (where) **in the innermost fortifications of that ugly citadel, where** Nature was as strongly bricked out as killing airs and gases were bricked in: at the heart of the labyrinth of narrow courts upon courts, and close streets upon streets, which had come into existence piecemeal, every piece in a violent hurry for some one man's purpose, and the whole an unnatural family, shouldering, and (jostling) **trampling,** and pressing one another to death; in the last close nook of this great exhausted receiver, where the chimneys, for want of air to make a draught, were **built in an immense variety of** stunted and crooked shapes, as though every house put out a sign of the kind of people who might be expected to be born in it; among the multitude of Coketown, generically called "the Hands",—a race who would have found more favour with some people, if Providence had seen fit to make them only hands, or like the lower creatures of the seashore, only hands and stomachs—lived a certain Stephen Blackpool.

A pure, antipathy is created towards the unnatural industrial horror of Coketown which stifles and cripples its inhabitants. He intensifies the repelling claustrophobic atmosphere of Coketown by the insertion of 'in the innermost fortifications of that ugly citadel'. By emending 'jostling' to 'trampling', he makes a smoother transition from 'shouldering' to the climax, 'pressing one another to death', and this emphasizes the cramping and stifling results of industrial haste and anarchy. Finally, he adds to the horror of a crippling environment by calling attention to 'an immense variety' of deformed shapes.

There is an irony in the town's very architecture in which even the pretensions to spirituality embody themselves in the forms of the materialistic world whose values dominate the life of Coketown. Ironically enough, too, society, which has changed work into a religion and the outward forms of religion into those of work, is indignantly surprised to discover that the working people turn their backs on religion proper. Once more Dickens can be seen, here, deliberately clarifying his vision, making it into a sharper and more specific indictment of the acquisitive values of society:

> everything was fact between the lying-in hospital and the cemetery, and what you couldn't state in figures, **or show to be purchasable in the cheapest market and saleable in the dearest**, was not, and never should be, world without end, Amen.

Sucksmith observes in this connection that Dickens inserts into his parody of the doxology from the Prayer Book the phrase, 'or show to be purchasable in the cheapest market and saleable in the dearest', thus bringing into collision the most profane of all the economic formulas of *laissez-faire* and the sacred text in the affirmation of Christian faith; the result is to imply ironically that the eternal faith and the gospel according to wealth and work are one, thus exposing more than a social evil—revealing a shocking blasphemy against the Holy Spirit (164-65). Dickens's descriptions of Coketown focus an adverse vision of the ravages made by industrial society through an antipathy created in the reader.

Dickens's main intention, as Leavis says, was 'to comment on certain key characteristics of Victorian civilization'. Dickens was concerned about the difference between Fact and Fancy. The novel emphasizes, with all his power and skill, the concern that this was not just a rhetorical antithesis: that mere fact, or logic, that leaves half of our lives out of account is not merely sterile, but bitterly destructive of all the moral virtues, beauty, and everything that is best; that a sound life cannot exist without happiness; and that the proper education of children must take into account their moral development, which it should foster through their fancy and love of life. K.J. Fielding writes:

> The government of a country, he maintained, cannot safely be left to be administered from self-interest, nor trusted to a single class certain to look after itself first and last. He held that the relations between Capital and Labour, or (as he preferred to call them) between Masters and Men, can never be properly managed or understood if it is assumed that they must be in a perpetual state of conflict, or that the men must inevitably be subject to the paternal rule of the masters. Above all, he believed that the relations between men and women; between father and children, mother and child, or brother and sister; between friends, or any persons in almost any permanent association, must originate and be rooted in liking, affection, or love. (132)

Hard Times protests not merely against certain characteristics of Victorian society, but against certain tendencies to be found in any industrial civilization. It protests against all repression of the human spirit by the letter of the classroom, the constitution, the law, and the so-called principles of political economy. As Fielding puts it,

> Dickens's purpose was not just to strike at utilitarianism, but at all kinds of social abuses which he thought ran counter to human life and happiness because they were framed according to supposed 'facts' while they ignored obvious human needs. That is why even the sawdust ring of the circus was preferable to the cinders of Coketown or the dust and ashes of the political arena. The novel has such a broad purpose even though it included references to some of Dickens's living contemporaries which most of them were unable to recognize, and satire of specific abuses which was too pointed to be understood by the general reader; and it is only by understanding this broader purpose (which is not so obvious that it can be taken for granted) that one

> can see how it unifies Dickens's remarks on Stephen Blackpool's marriage, the aesthetic theories of the 'third gentleman' in the second chapter, the problems of Trade Unionism, Louisa's marriage to Bounderby, and her brother's theft from the bank. Dickens once wrote that the ideas took him 'by the throat' and forced him to write...that he succeeded in giving them a unified purpose, and that *Hard Times* has coherence and power which deserve great respect even though it is not as entertaining as most of the other novels. (133)

Dickens thought that there should be the right to strike, but almost always wrong to use it. He disliked the extremists on both sides. He hated employers like Bounderby, and he distrusted trade union organizers such as Slackbridge. He was in favour of all attempts to encourage better industrial relations and for conciliation on both sides; and he considered that the government should take action by setting up an independent body to arbitrate between them. Lionel Stevenson, writing on "Dickens's Dark Novels" (*Sewanee Review*, LI, 1943), has thought that Dickens watched 'the beginnings of a sounder structure of Trade Unions, initiated in 1851, by...the Amalgamated Society of Engineers', with interested approval. When they struck, next year, he wrote to a friend:

> As to the Engineers.... I believe the difficulty in the way of compromise, from the very beginning, is not so much with the masters as with the men. Honorable, generous, and spirited themselves, they have fallen into an unlucky way of trusting their affairs to contentious men, who work them up into a state of conglomeration and irritation, and are the greatest Pests that their own employers can encounter upon earth. I am much mistaken if this be not the case.

It is central to an understanding of what Dickens thought of his own times and how he commented on them in the novels like *Hard Times*. In reality Dickens believed in 'independent self-reliance'. It has caused some surprise considering the picture of industrialism presented in *Hard Times*, that Dickens should have paid tribute at a public banquet the year before the novel appeared to:

> ...the great compact phalanx of the people, by whose industry, perseverance, and intelligence, and their result in money-wealth such places as Birmingham, and many others like it, have arisen.

Hard Times is concerned with the conflict between two forms of relationship: relation to society, and direct, intimate relation to other individuals. In the novel, the choice of the relation to society as a source of selfhood is shown to fail, and to lead rather to the loss of identity. Society turns out to be a fraud (like the Merdle enterprises in *Little Dorrit*). It breaks beneath the pressure put on it by the individual, and reveals its non-entity. As J. Hillis Miller puts it, "Society is only a projection of the selfish desires of individuals; it is all too human. Society is fictive, a game of false appearances, and he who puts confidence in it is absorbed into its unreality. But this brittle facade has power too, and the elaborate machinery of a false civilization can enslave the individual, turn him into an object. Against this destructive relation Dickens sets an increasingly profound analysis of the mystery of a direct relation between two people without intermediary: the relation of love" (226). The caste system finds satiric emphasis through the story of Mrs. Sparsit, whose ambition and position in the social scheme are at variance. Mr. Harthouse shows the decay which comes from rank without character. The criticism of the divorce law is quite modern, because it is obvious that one cannot get a divorce in England without luck, influence, or money. Since Stephen's wife is an impossible matrimonial companion, since she has not even enough personality to give him reason for divorcing her according to the law which fixes adultery as the only legal excuse, and since Stephen has not enough money to circumvent the law, happiness is out of reach. Dickens had some feelings about his own marital unhappiness which related to the opinions expressed in the novel.

In *Hard Times*, Dickens dramatizes in strikingly symbolic terms the opposition between a soul-destroying relation to a utilitarian, industrial civilization, and the reciprocal interchange of love. If the perpetually clanking machinery of the Coketown mills, which turns men into "hands", is the symbol of one, the "horse-riding", as in Picasso's *Saltimbanques*, is the dominant symbol of the other: "The father of one of the families was in the habit of balancing the father of another of the families on the top of a great pole; the father of a third family often made a pyramid of both those fathers, with Master Kidderminster for the apex, and himself for the base.... They all assumed to be mighty rakish and knowing, they were not very tidy in their private dresses, they were not at all orderly in their domestic arrangements, and the combined literature of the whole company would have produced but a poor letter on any subject. Yet there was a remarkable gentleness and childishness about these people, a special inaptitude for any kind of sharp practice, and an untiring readiness to help and pity one another..." (I, VI). J. Hillis Miller writes:

> ...the circus here is still only a symbol of a good *society*, that is, of communion around a third thing, the "act". In this relation contact with others is still in a way impersonal, and the individual is still defined by his role, by his cooperative submission to a common activity and goal. In the circus act, as in even the best society, the otherness of other people tends to be submerged. (226)

Raymond Williams observes in "The Industrial Novels":

> *Hard Times*, in tone and structure, is the work of a man who has "been through" society, who has found them all out. The only reservation is for the passive and the suffering, for the meek who shall inherit the earth but not Coketown, not industrial society. This primitive feeling, when joined by the aggressive conviction of having found everyone else out, is the retained position of an adolescent. The innocence shames the adult world, but also essentially rejects it. As a whole response, *Hard Times* is more a symptom of the confusion of industrial

> society than an understanding of it, but it is a symptom that is significant and continuing. (Watt 151)

Dickens' *Hard Times* is no doubt a realistic novel in that it deals with some hard facts of life of the Victorian age in sharp contrast with novels dealing with situations and incidents. The said hard facts consist in evils dominating the various aspects of social life—education, industry, marriage, etc. The Victorian age was a victim to the unwholesome principles of Utilitarianism and 'Laissez-faire' or materialism which laid stress on happiness, philosophy and self-interest, facts and figures, greed for money, snobbery, hypocrisies rather than old moral upliftment and personal feelings and imaginations. Through playful humours, Dickens lays bare some of the social evils of his age in a very apt manner in this novel. In the beginning of the novel Dickens launches a scathing attack on the educational system of his age. This description of the pragmatic system of education based on facts and figures smacks of the evil consequences of materialism. He describes through symbol, represented by Mr. Gradgrind. We may say that the Circus is set against Coketown. The schoolroom contrast of Sissy Jupe and Bitzer is a contrast between the education, practical but often inarticulate which is gained by living and doing, and the education, highly articulated, which is gained by systemization and abstraction. The instinctive, un-intellectual, unorganized life is the ground of genuine feeling and of all good relationships. The Circus is one of the very few ways in which Dickens has dramatized this through the experience described by Sleary:

> ...that there ith a love in the world, not all Thelf-interetht after all, but thomething very different...it hath a way of ith own of calculating or not calculating, which thomehow or another ith at leatht ath hard to give a name to, ath the wayth of the dogth ith.

It is a characteristic conclusion, in a vitally important tradition which based its values on such grounds. It is the major criticism of Industrialism as a whole way of life, and its grounds in experience have been firm. What is essential is to recognize that Dickens saw no social expression of it, or at least nothing that could be "given a name to". Almost the whole organization of society, as Dickens judges, is against it. The Circus can express it because it is not part of the industrial organization. The Circus is an end in itself, a pleasurable end, which is instinctive and (in certain respects) anarchic. It is significant that Dickens has thus to go outside the industrial situation to find any expression of his values. This going outside is similar to the Canada in which *Mary Barton* ends, or the legacy of Margaret Hale. But it is also more than these, in so far as it is not only an escape but a positive assertion of a certain kind of experience, the denial of which was the real basis of the hard times. Ruskin's reservations about Dickens in his "A Note on *Hard Times*" are worth considering:

> Allowing for his manner of telling them, the things he tells us are always true. I wish that he could think it right to limit his brilliant exaggeration to works written only for public amusement; and when he takes up a subject of high national importance, such as that which he handled in *Hard Times*, that he would use severer and more accurate analysis. The usefulness of that work (to my mind, in several respects, the greatest he has written) is with many persons seriously diminished because Mr. Bounderby is a dramatic monster, instead of a characteristic example of a worldly master; and Stephen Blackpool a dramatic perfection, instead of a characteristic example of an honest workman. But let us not lose the use of Dickens's wit and insight, because he chooses to speak in a circle of stage fire. He is entirely right in his main drift and purpose in every book he has written; and all of them, but especially *Hard Times*, should be studied with close and earnest care by persons interested in social questions. (Ford 47-48)

Like Blake, Dickens finds the really dangerous social evils in those which have achieved some acceptance by being rationalized. In *Oliver Twist* the word "experience" stands as a contrast to the words "experimental" and "philosophical". In *Hard Times*, the pedantry of the obstructing society is associated with a utilitarian philosophy and an infantile trust in facts, statistics, and all impersonal and generalized forms of knowledge. We may wonder why Dickens denounces this philosophy so earnestly and caricatures it so crudely, instead of letting its absurdities speak for themselves. It is clear that *Hard Times* comes nearest to being what is sometimes called dystopia. Like *Brave New World* or *1984*, it shows the nightmare world that results from certain perverse tendencies inherent in society getting free play. Dickens sees in the cult of facts and statistics a threat to the unfettered imagination, the mind that can respond to fairy tales and fantasy and understand their relevance to reality. The insistence is on the importance of fairy tales, nursery rhymes, and similar genres in education. *Hard Times* "stamps and records the reality of Dickens's emotion on a great many things that were then considered unphilosophical grumblings, but which since have swelled into the immense phenomena of the socialist philosophy. To call Dickens a Socialist is a wild exaggeration; but the truth and peculiarity of his position might be expressed thus: that even when everybody thought that Liberalism meant individualism he was emphatically a Liberal and emphatically not an individualist. Or the truth might be better still stated in this manner: that he saw that there was a secret thing, called humanity, to which both extreme socialism and extreme individualism were profoundly and inexpressibly indifferent, and that this permanent and presiding humanity was the thing he happened to understand; he knew that individualism is nothing and non-individualism is nothing but the keeping of the commandment of man. He felt, as a novelist should, that the question is too much discussed as to whether a man is in favour of this or that scientific philosophy; that there is another question, whether the scientific philosophy is in favour of the man. That is why such books as "Hard Times" will remain always a part of the power and tradition of Dickens. He saw that economic systems are not things like the stars, but things like the lamp posts, manifestations of the human mind, and things to be judged by the human heart" (Chesterton 171-72). Una Pope-Hennessy wrote in *Charles Dickens*: "If Dickens's intention in this book was to make readers understand that the tendency of industrialism was to kill the imagination, suppress all spontaneous life, and force men and women to lead utilitarian existences in 'Hellhole' surroundings, *Hard Times* may have fulfilled its purpose" (487).

(IV) PLOT

The name of Charles Dickens is associated with the construction of extremely complicated novelistic plots which accommodate innumerable threads or strands of stories within their vast canvas. Since *Hard Times* promises to convey the strains of contemporary time, its plot may be expected to be comprehensive with the social and domestic extensions handled with skilful neediness and precision. Love of melodrama and emotional excess often set a Dickens's novel chaotic but *Hard Times* shows signs of maturity not only in the theme of social criticism but also in the accomplished neatness of its structure. The novel is constructed on a broad design of sowing, reaping and garnering—which is a general approach to any moral theme.

It is interesting to know that the novel begins with Mr. Gradgrind, the enthusiastic and vociferous exponent of Utilitarianism, and ends with him. The central division of the plot of the novel fits in with the beginning, middle and end of his utilitarianistic career. Criticism of Benthamite Utilitarianism which pervaded the Victorian society is the conspicuous theme of the novel. So Mr. Gradgrind's school has been presented in a dramatic setting. Bitzer bids fare by the side of Sissy with his brilliant off-handed materialistic and scientifically accurate definition of a horse. Mr. Gradgrind who is satisfied to bring up his children in his own system of utilitarian education cannot believe his own eyes finding Louisa and Tom peeping through the circus tent. To trace the root of such indulgence in fancy on the part of his children, Mr. Gradgrind in company with Mr. Bounderby reaches the circle of Sissy's home which is dominated by an essentially instinctive mode of life—where every individual is guided by instinct or 'fancy' rather than by 'fact'. There finding Sissy deserted by her father Mr. Gradgrind adopts her. As a learner

Sissy cuts a miserable figure, proves hopeless and Louisa's former intimacy with her comes to a break.

The second division of the plot centres round Mr. Bounderby. He is the epitome, the summation and the visible monstrous manifestation of the Gradgrind formula. He boasts of being 'self made' and blackens his mother and grandmother in his daily routine. Mrs. Sparsit with her dimmed aristocracy is a foil to throw Mr. Bounderby's economic height into relief. The effect of Gradgrind's system-education begins to surface very soon when Tom tries to instrumentalise Louisa to gratify his own rapacity. Being over-powered by her father's Utilitarian arguments and also being already won over by Tom, Louisa accepts Mr. Bounderby, her father's friend, as her husband. This loveless marriage thus unifies the Gradgrind and Bounderby threads of the plot quite organically. The emergence of Mr. Harthouse becomes credible because through him Bounderby impresses his vanity of urbanity. Characteristic cynicism in league with Louisa's emotional unfulfilment naturally draws Louisa and Harthouse together. As the latter is a villain, he already collects materials about her bribing Tom.

Stephen Blackpool the good workman and Slackbridge the Union agitator form a separate story line which has been generally condemned as fairly thin and crude in itself and not very well adjusted to the central fable. The episode of Stephen Blackpool seems to be superfluous because Stephen is nothing more than a mere Coketown hand. His complication with his wife and his admiration for Rachael have a weak ex nihilo origin. Louisa's sudden offer of help to Stephen seems not only unconvincing but also sentimental. Stephen's reluctance to join the worker's strike and his resistance against playing the role of Bounderby's informer make him a dreamy idealistic figure. Tom's instruction to Stephen for waiting near the Bank intensifies the suspicion in connection with the bank robbery. The tender goodness and suffering of Stephen help a lot to darken the character of Tom. But over-sentimentalisation of Stephen's death remains unintegrated with the plot, although it should be admitted all fairness to Dickens's craftsmanship, that the Stephen episode itself is not totally unnecessary or extraneous in the plot. Through this episode Dickens shows how a bad wedlock may imprison a good heart. It also enables him to cavil at the rigidity of the contemporary marriage-laws and their expensiveness which renders a poor man like Stephen incapable of getting a divorce that might save him from a veritable hell. In a sense Stephen is the worst sufferer of the *Hard Times* because he is misunderstood by everybody. Besides, the functional importance of the Stephen episode in the scheme of the novel lies in the fact that it offers a breathing space for the development of the relation between Louisa and Mr. Harthouse. The role of Mr. Harthouse is quite integral to the plot because he exposes the abject hollowness of the conjugal relationship between Louisa and Mr. Bounderby.

The third section of the novel is dominated by the circus people and all that they stand for. The circus people are headed by the asthmatic Sleary and represented perfectly by Sissy, a naïve, immaculate angel of love, affection, fellow feeling and tenderness. Like Rachael in the Stephen episode, Sissy in the main plot upholds the values of respect for tender human emotions and of dedicated sincerity over the inhuman mechanical formula of life enforced by Gradgrind. When Louisa feels emotionally lost and degraded the role of Sissy assumes a special significance. Gradgrind in this section begins to reap the harvest of his own sowing. Tom turns out to be thief and Louisa, whose life had been utterly shattered, runs away from her husband's house to throw in to her father's face the truth that his philosophy and his teaching did not save her. And at this crucial juncture of the plot of the novel Sissy begins to be foregrounded. Sissy's role really assumes a special significance when Louisa feels emotional, lost and degraded. This Sissy was always a dull hopeless student in Gradgrind's School. But now with remarkable firmness she makes the urban gentleman Mr. Harthouse stoop to her position and compel him to leave the place. Mr. Gradgrind finding no way out about Tom falls back upon the co-operation of Sleary and his team. From the very beginning, Gradgrind has been proud of Bitzer for his easy adjustment with the utilitarian principle and the education of 'facts'. On the other hand, he has always treated the circus people as worthless. But when the ungrateful and selfish Bitzer, the most abominable offshoot of Gradgrindian education system, uncompromising in his determination to arrest Tom and thereby pave the way for his own promotion, it is Sleary who employs his horses and the dog to do the impossible task of helping Tom slip away from Bitzer's clutches. Thus, the Coketown plot is nicely rounded off by the circus people.

In most of the novels Dickens quite freely moves along with a lot of loose stags. But in this novel, he seems to be wonderfully controlled. Mrs. Pegler, who in the first few appearances seems to have no *locus standi* in the Coketown area, is ultimately proved to be Bounderby's mother. She carries the bombshell of proof that Bounderby's confession about his inglorious ancestry is a blatant lie and thus becomes the instrument of *Nemesis* for Bounderby. So Dickens knows the novelistic trick of utilizing a minor character and an apparently insignificant situation as an integral part of the broad design of his plot. It is true that with greater insight and care Dickens could have achieved much more artistic effect in his handling of the characters like Mrs. Sparsit and Stephen Blackpool. But, his not doing what he could have done detracts little from the merit or strength of his meticulous craftsmanship as exhibited in this novel. F.R. Leavis has agreed that in *Hard Times* Dickens has evinced immense restraint in the plot construction and that its structuration is simplified into a form of fable based on clearly conceived morality.

The novel has the clear, strong, and rapid forward movement, the succinct rendition of episode and character, above all the emphasis with which logical refutation is announced as Dickens's object and the success with which it is accomplished.

(V) COKETOWN

Hard Times is set in a northern industrial town far grimmer than Jack Rouncewell's town in *Bleak House*. Dickens gives it the name of Coketown which takes us back to the nightmare chapters on the Birmingham to Wolverhampton road in *The Old Curiosity Shop*, but in *Hard Times* the horror is seen more analytically than through the eyes of a dying girl. The presiding sensibilities are those of Gradgrind and Bounderby, two gentlemen well calculated to keep fancy and imagination at bay. There is a new ruthlessness of observation on Dickens's part, as befits his setting. It is as if he extinguished his most distinctive gift for poetic resonance and suggestiveness in order to capture a world where the creative powers themselves are in exile. Or rather, as if he drove the resonances of his art inwards, until they acquired a muffled and deadly quality. While there are still evidences of symbolism in Coketown, and it would hardly be Dickens's city without this, the very symbols are oppressive to our minds. Coketown's 'fairy palaces' seen by travellers on the railway in early evening are pure illusion, its 'melancholy mad elephants' conjure no jungle freedom to our eyes. Any enchantment in Coketown is claustrophobic and sickening, like the witch's house in *Hansel and Gretel*. *Hard Times* indeed is a symbol of the world without creativity where the 'robber Fancy' is left, depraved by neglect, to seek revenge.

Coketown is described by Dickens as a town of machinery and tall chimneys out of which unending columns of smoke rose upwards forever and ever. The streets are exactly like one another, the people are also the same: they all go in and out at the same hours, with same sound upon the same pavements, to do the same work. Thus, the monotony of the workmen's life is fully conveyed to us. The need for any relaxation or physical relief is never realized by the employees. The workmen are reduced to mere 'hands', "so many hundred horse steam powers". These men are not supposed to have any souls; they are hands who have to work upon "the crashing, smashing, tearing machines day in and day out". Speaking to Harthouse, Bounderby describes Coketown's smoke as "the healthiest thing in the world in all respects and particularly for the lungs". The point for *Hard Times* is that people have become less a law unto themselves, the stuff of their lives less variegated, and it is this sense of lives clamped under a grid that haunts Dickens throughout his work. Coketown in the darkness and cold of winter is bad, but Coketown in the summer is almost worse. God's sunshine falls faintly through the dusty vapour that hangs in the sky. Down on the dusty streets it shines where men toil, as in a desert, at fiery furnaces amid steam engines that drone on and on, emitting hot oil gusts like the breath of a simoon. The great pistons and hammers dominate all. "No sun, no temperature, made the melancholy, mad elephants more mad or more sane.... Their wearisome heads went up and down at the same rate.... The measured motion of their shadows on the walls, was the substitute Coketown had to show for the shadows of rustling woods." The employers do not understand that industrialism is as bad for them as it is for the employees, for it forces them equally to be people of fact undiluted by fancy. Mr. Gradgrind had built himself a fine modern house in which to keep his family:

> Gas and ventilation, drainage and water service all of the primest quality. Iron clamps and girders, fireproof from top to bottom; mechanical lifts for the housemaids with all their brushes and brooms; everything that heart could desire.

The rich little Gradgrinds 'had never seen a face in the moon':

> No little Gradgrinds had ever learnt the silly jingle, Twinkle twinkle little star; how I wonder what you are! No little Gradgrind had ever known wonder on the subject, each little Gradgrind having at five years old dissected the Great Bear like a Professor Owen, and driven Charles's Wain like a locomotive engine driver.

In the manuscript of *Hard Times*, Dickens revises his first description of Coketown as follows (insertions or revisions in bold letters):

> Coketown, to which Messrs. Bounderby and Gradgrind now walked, as a triumph of fact (and figures); it had no greater taint of fancy in it than Mrs. Gradgrind herself. Let us strike the keynote, Coketown, before pursuing our tune.

> It was a town of red brick or of brick that would have been red if the smoke **and ashes** had allowed it; but, as matters stood it was a town of **unnatural** red and black like the (face of) **painted face of** an ugly savage. It was a town of machinery and tall chimneys, out of which interminable serpents of smoke trailed themselves sluggishly for ever and ever, and never got uncoiled. It had a black canal in it, and a river that ran purple where there was a rattling and a trembling all day long, and where the piston of the steam-engine worked monotonously up and down, like the head of an elephant in a state of melancholy madness. It contained several large streets all very like one another, and many small streets still more like one another, inhabited by people equally like one another, who **all** went in and out at the same hours, **with the same sound upon the pavement**, to do the same work, and to whom every day was the same as yesterday and tomorrow, and every year the counterpart of the last and the next.
>
> These attributes of Coketown were in the main inseparable from the work by which it was sustained; against them were to be set off, comforts of life which found their way all over the world, **and elegances of life which made we will not ask how much of the fine lady, who could scarcely bear to hear the place mentioned.**

The description of Coketown creates a strong antipathy towards the ugly and unnatural nightmare of Coketown. Antipathy is increased by the addition of 'and ashes', 'unnatural', and 'painted'. The effect of antipathy is complicated by irony. Dickens's deliberate rhetoric does not only simply increase the effect of antipathy but draw attention more sharply to the ugly reality behind Gradgrind and Bounderby's delusions. There is irony in the imagery. The unnatural apparatus of industry is described through images drawn from the natural world of animals and savages; an ironic contrast is obviously implied in the comparison, here, but a further irony is suggested in the paradoxical, jungle-like character of industrial civilization. The insertion of 'unnatural' and 'painted' helps to draw attention to the antithesis between natural and unnatural and to the appearance of civilization behind which the ugly reality of a savagery worse than the natural kind is concealing itself. There is an ironical contrast between the town's ugly and uncongenial character and the comforts and elegance it produces through its manufactured goods. Harvey P. Sucksmith observes in this connection in *The Narrative Art of Charles Dickens*: "Through adding the ironic idea of a society which is glad to adorn itself with the products of a place which it is too snobbish to name, Dickens intensifies the power of his satirical vision" (164).

Dickens presents another revised description of Coketown (insertions or revisions in bold letters):

> In the hardest working part of Coketown; (where) **in the innermost fortifications of that ugly citadel, where** Nature was as strongly bricked out as killing airs and gases were bricked in: at the heart of the labyrinth of narrow courts upon courts, and close streets upon streets, which had come into existence piecemeal, every piece in a violent hurry for some one man's purpose, and the whole an unnatural family, shouldering, and (jostling) **trampling**, and pressing one another to death; in the last close nook of this great exhausted receiver, where the chimneys, for want of air to make a draught, were **built in an immense variety of** stunted and crooked shapes, as though every house put out a sign of the kind of people who might be expected to be born in it; among the multitude of Coketown, generically called "the Hands",—a race who would have found more favour with some people, if Providence had seen fit to make them only hands, or like the lower creatures of the seashore, only hands and stomachs—lived a certain Stephen Blackpool.

The description of Coketown is organized around a single theme which contributes to it a unity of feeling-tone. A pure, antipathy is created towards the unnatural industrial horror of Coketown which stifles and cripples its inhabitants. The conscious artistry here can be seen in the revisions through which Dickens intensifies the effect of antipathy. He intensifies the repelling claustrophobic atmosphere of Coketown by the insertion of 'in the innermost fortifications of that ugly citadel'. By emending 'jostling' to 'trampling', he makes a smoother transition from 'shouldering' to the climax, 'pressing one another to death', and this emphasizes the cramping and stifling results of industrial haste and anarchy. Finally, he adds to the horror of a crippling environment by calling attention to 'an immense variety' of deformed shapes. Sucksmith writes in this connection in *The Narrative Art of Charles Dickens*: "There are, however, two basic weaknesses in this passage. First, there is an unsuccessful kind of 'distancing'—if we can properly call it that. To represent the stifled and crippled people of Coketown symbolically through their cramped and misshapen houses is imaginative and it is certainly an instance of that vision of 'correspondence' and oneness in the Dickens world referred to earlier. But, unfortunately, while Dickens consciously strives to intensify the horror of industrialization and while the ultimate horror is rightly seen to be the stunting of human beings, the indirect manner of realizing this ultimate horror, its whimsical displacement from people on to things, weakens the final impression. Secondly, without a successful kind of distancing, any intensification of effect only focuses a simple vision more sharply" (163).

Structural irony and the irony of understatement combine in an omniscient comment which stresses the theme and hints at possible development in the story: "A town so sacred to fact, and so triumphant in its assertion, of course got on well? Why no, not quite well." There is an irony in the town's very architecture in which even the pretensions to spirituality embody themselves in the forms of the materialistic world whose values dominate the life of Coketown. Ironically enough, too, society, which has changed work into a religion and the outward forms of religion into those of work, is indignantly surprised to discover that the working people turn their backs on religion proper. Once more Dickens can be seen, here, deliberately clarifying his vision, making it into a sharper and more specific indictment of the acquisitive values of society:

> everything was fact between the lying-in hospital and the cemetery, and what you couldn't state in figures, or **show to be purchasable in the cheapest market and saleable in the dearest,** was not, and never should be, world without end, Amen.

Sucksmith observes that Dickens inserts into his parody of the doxology from the Prayer Book the phrase, 'or show to be purchasable in the cheapest market and saleable in the dearest,' thus bringing into collision the most profane of all the economic formulas of *laissez-faire* and the sacred text in the affirmation of Christian faith; the result is to imply ironically that the eternal faith and the gospel according to wealth and work are one, thus exposing more than a social evil—revealing a shocking blasphemy against the Holy Spirit (164-65). Dickens's descriptions of Coketown focus an adverse vision of the ravages made by industrial society through an antipathy created in the reader. Dorothy Van Ghent comments on Dickens's description of Coketown in "The Dickens World: A View from Todgers's":

> The animation of inanimate objects suggests both the quaint gaiety of a forbidden life, and an aggressiveness that has got out of control.... The animate is treated as if it is a thing. It is as if the life absorbed by things had been drained out of people who have become incapable of their humanity. (Ford 214)

Dickens's social analysis is of two nations, the rich and the poor. But Coketown is a prison for both, the masters as much as the men. It is a society based on slavery, where Gradgrind, far from counteracting Bounderby's crude savagery by his own natural kindliness, provides the intellectual sanctions which such cruelty needs. Malthusian *laissez-faire* becomes universe in the novel. We never get out of Coketown, and the nearest approach to escape—the journeys to Bounderby's house, and to the mineshaft where Stephen dies—merely emphasise the claustrophobia. The twin influences of Malthus and utilitarianism, caught up in the triumphant *laissez-faire* of the mid-1850 and unblushingly equated by many Victorians with Christianity, have led to the Coketown world. A.E. Dyson says in *The Inimitable Dickens*: "Coketown must be seen and felt as a town without art. All myths and fairy tales, all imaginative writing and creation, all fancies strange or consoling, and all mediators of such wares, Dickens included, are exiled from the Gradgrind and Bounderby world. In their place we have Coketown, a Fact complete and sufficient in its streets and chapels, its suspended smoke serpents, its 'melancholy mad elephants', as in the enslaved and destroyed consciousness of its children, its confines where Stephen Blackpool will live and die" (187).

In *Hard Times*, the myth is Coketown, the imprisoning streets and stifling air, a total image of the spiritual malaise engendered there: "The jail might have been the infirmary, the infirmary might have been the jail, the town-hall might have been either, or both, or anything else, for anything that appeared to the contrary in the graces of their construction. Fact, fact, fact, everywhere in the material aspect of the town; fact, fact, fact everywhere in the immaterial." Dickens is able, even though he has sacrificed his habitual resonance, to retain and even concentrate that element in his work now widely referred to as projective fiction: the creation of a world when the houses and streets, the urban environs, the very feel of the air initiate us into the psychology of living and suffering people. It is not through formal description or analysis of character but through every detail of Coketown that we see into the human heart. Coketown is the innermost dereliction and despair of Louisa and Stephen, the environment which has shaped them, the prison where they will die. Despite the social realism, it is tinged with nightmare, akin to the delirium of a fever running its course. Everything seems fated and unalterable. As we see Mr. Gradgrind's 'metallurgical Louisa' handed over in marriage to Bounderby, a 'big, loud man, with a stare, and a metallic laugh', it is as though the moment had always been predestined. There is the same sense of profound irrationality and evil that we find in Dickens's other, more characteristic, books. At the same time, the thematic imagery of *Hard Times* greatly reinforces the effect of proliferating evil. The novel is divided into three books, "Sowing", "Reaping" and "Garnering", where these natural processes, sufficiently ironic in Coketown, chart the logic of stunted and withered lives.

In fine, one may quote what A.E. Dyson said in *The Inimitable Dickens*: "*Hard Times* is a successful novel because it is a uniquely un-Dickensian novel—except in so far as the triumph of tone and texture is, after all, so Dickensian, while Coketown, by so totally excluding myth, becomes a myth" (187).

(VI) CIRCUS PARTY

The intellectual with his hard-won freedom of thought and sense of discrimination should fear the contagion of the rabble, should dread an almost bodily possession by emotions sympathetically induced in him by others. We have only to read Le Bon on the crowd or Freud on group psychology to appreciate how and why this is so. Nevertheless, there are already certain indications by the time of Dickens of an uneasy victory for the intellectual standpoint. Dickens himself has warned us against this danger which was beginning to assume a sinister shape in his own day and could be seen most clearly in the development of a particular philosophy: "Utilitarian economists, skeletons of schoolmasters, Commissioners of Fact, genteel and used-up infidels, gabblers of many little dog's-eared creeds, the poor you will have always with you. Cultivate in them, while there is yet time, the utmost graces of the fancies and affections, to adorn their lives so much in need of ornament; or, in the day of your triumph, when romance is utterly driven out of their souls, and they and a bare existence stand face to face, Reality will take a wolfish turn, and make an end of you" (*HT*. II, VI). Special attention should be given to that ominous phrase 'while there is yet time', yet it has less dramatic manifestations. Harvey P. Sucksmith observed in *The Narrative Art of Charles Dickens*: "If the thesis of Dickens in *Hard Times* is a valid one, if any abstract study of problems which bear upon human life and human values ignores the affections at its peril, then this holds good also for the study of fiction which is much closer than either economics or philosophy to the very stuff of life, to living in all its concreteness and immediacy" (5).

At the outset Dickens opens *Hard Times* with Sleary's Circus in which the natural goodness and generosity of members of the troupe are displayed; he closes the novel with an act of kindness shown by Sleary to the very magnates who regard his troupe as vagabonds and their entertainment as a time-and-money-wasting opportunity for their operatives. In *Hard Times*, the readers are first acquainted with the world of fancy through Cecelia Jupe, the daughter of the circus clown, Signor Jupe. The tent of the circus people is established safely in a neutral ground upon the outskirts of Coketown, the citadel of Fact. The circus party always makes a contrast between the fact world and the fancy world. Fancy is cultivated by them. The name of their public house is 'Pegasus' Arms' which is the symbol of imagination. Sissy read fairy tales to her father and her father had a weakness for reciting Shakespeare. Mr. Sleary, the circus manager, is undoubtedly an able organizer and a kind-hearted man. Dickens's letter to Charles Knight when he was writing *Hard Times* is worth quoting:

> I earnestly entreat your attention to the point (I have been working upon it, weeks past, in *Hard Times*)...the English are, as far I know, the hardest-worked people on whom the sun shines. Be content if, in their intervals of pleasure, they read for amusement and do no worse. They are born at the oar, and they live and die at it. Good God, what would you have of them! (Letter, 17 March 1854)

In *Hard Times,* this turns out to have simply been reworded:

> I entertain a weak idea that the English people are as hard-worked as any people upon whom the sun shines. I acknowledge to this ridiculous idiosyncrasy, as a reason why I would give them a little more play. (I, IX)

With this one may usefully compare Mr. Gradgrind's 'annihilating the flowers of existence' with his excise-rod and compasses, and Louisa's lament to her brother:

> I don't know what other girls know. I can't play to you, or sing to you. I can't talk to you so as to enlighten your mind, for I never see any amusing sights or read any amusing books that it would be a pleasure or a relief to you to talk about, when you are tired. (I, VIII)

One may compare also the decisive closing paragraph of the novel, about the main survivor of the book, Sissy Jupe:

> ...thinking no innocent and pretty fancy ever to be despised; trying hard to...beautify...lives of machinery and reality with...imaginative graces and delights. (III, VIII)

and the concluding words of Mr. Sleary, with their emphasis on amusement:

> ...Don't be croth with uth poor vagabondth. People mutht be amuthed. They can't alwayth be a learning, nor yet they can't be alwayth a working, they an't made for it. You *mutht* have uth, Thquire. Do the withe thing and the kind thing too, and make the betht of uth; not the wurtht! (III, VIII)

The *Household Words* article on the Preston lockout makes the same point, and one must bear in mind that it is one entirely characteristic of Dickens from Mr. Pickwick on:

> ...there must enter something of feeling and sentiment, something which is not to be found in Mr. McCulloch's Dictionary...political economy is a mere skeleton unless it has a little human covering and fitting out, a little human bloom on it, and a little human warmth in it. (*Household Words*, 11 Feb. 1654)

Dickens was a life-long champion of amusement. Many of the issues on which his voice is clearest, his opposition to teetotalism and Sabbath laws, became clear to him precisely because of his Sleary philosophy: "People must be amused somehow...." F.R. Leavis observes in *Dickens: The Novelist*:

> Their skills have no value for the Utilitarian calculus, but they express vital human impulse, and they minister to vital human needs. The horse-riding, frowned upon as frivolous and wasteful by Gradgrind and malignantly

> scorned by Bounderby, brings the machine-hands of Coketown (the spirit-quenching hideousness of which is hauntingly evoked) what they are starved of. It brings to them, not merely amusement, but art, and the spectacle of triumphant activity that, seeming to contain its end within itself, is, in its easy mastery, joyously self-justified. In investing a travelling circus with this kind of symbolic value Dickens expresses a profounder reaction to industrialism than might have been expected of him. It is not only pleasure and relaxation the Coketowners stand in need of; he feels the dreadful degradation of life that would remain even if they were to be given a forty-four-hour week, comfort, security and fun. (257-58)

F.R. Leavis further comments,

> There is, however, more to be said about the success that attends Dickens's symbolic intention in the Horse-riding; there is an essential quality of his genius to be emphasized. There is no Hamlet in him, and he is quite unlike T.S. Eliot.
>
> The red-eyed scavengers are creeping
> From Kentish Town and Golders Green
>
> ...He observes with gusto the humanness of humanity as exhibited in the urban (and suburban) scene. When he sees, as he sees so readily, the common manifestations of human kindness, and the essential virtues, asserting themselves in the midst of ugliness, squalor and banality, his warmly sympathetic response has no disgust to overcome. There is no suggestion, for instance, of recoil —or of distance-keeping—from the game-eyed, brandy-soaked, flabby-surfaced Mr. Sleary, who is successfully made to figure for us a humane, anti-Utilitarian positive. This is not sentimentality in Dickens, but genius. (261)

The world of the circus party is marked by fellow-feeling and there is an untiring readiness to help and pity one another. Mr. Sleary really feels a paternal interest in Sissy and this attitude is to be contrasted with Bounderby's contemptuous attitude. Sissy's father who finds himself unable any longer to amuse the audience, runs away, leaving his daughter to an uncertain fate. All the circus athletes came to console Sissy: "Meanwhile, the various members of Sleary's company gradually gathered together from the upper regions, where they were quartered, and, from standing about, talking in low voices to one another and to Mr. Childers, gradually insinuated themselves and him into the room. There were two or three handsome young women among them, with their two or three husbands, and their two or three mothers, and their eight or nine little children, who did the fairy business when required" (I, VI). The dignity and wit and finesse with which the sexual freedom of these women is described needs no exegesis—we are reminded that the limited Dickens was also the rebellious Dickens. The action of Sissy's father is, apparently, unpardonable. But as we know more of the circus people we guess that he was confident that his circus comrades would take due-care of his daughter. They are the embodiment of these simple virtues like sympathy and camaraderie for which the utilitarian educationist Gradgrind has no respect and the utilitarian industrialist Bounderby has no love. When Bounderby sharply says to Sissy that her father has absconded and deserted her, some of the members of the circus troupe mutter words like 'shame' 'brute' as a protest against Bounderby's way of talking to an unhappy girl. The circus people "...all assumed to be mighty rakish and knowing, they were not very tidy in their private dresses, they were not at all orderly in their domestic arrangements, and the combined literature of the whole company would have produced but a poor letter on any subject. Yet there was a remarkable gentleness and childishness about these people, a special inaptitude for any kind of sharp practice, and an untiring readiness to help and pity one another, deserving often of as much respect, and always of as much generous construction, as the every-day virtues of any class of people in the world" (I, VI). The circus athletes represent human spontaneity and at the same time highly developed skill: "The father of one of the families was in the habit of balancing the father of another of the families on the top of a great pole; the father of a third family often made a pyramid of both these fathers, with

Master Kidderminster for the apex, and himself for the base; all the fathers could dance upon rolling casks, stand upon bottles, catch knives and balls, twirl hand-basins, ride upon anything, jump over everything, and stick at nothing. All the mothers could (and did) dance, upon the slack wire and the tight rope, and perform rapid acts on bare-backed steeds; none of them were at all particular in respect of showing their legs; and one of them, alone in a Greek chariot, drove six in hand into every town they came to" (I, VI). It brings to them, not merely amusement, but art, and the spectacle of triumphant activity that, seeming to contain its end within itself, is, in its easy mastery, joyously self-justified. In investing a travelling circus with this kind of symbolic value Dickens expresses a profounder reaction to industrialism than might have been expected of him. One understands that though the skills of the circus athletes have no value to the utilitarians but they express vital human impulse and they minister to vital human needs.

The vitality of the circus people has nicely been conveyed through their association with animals like dog and horse. Mr. Sleary has a simple philosophy of life. He says that people must be amused, that they are not machines to do work all the time. In his lisping manner what he says is that circus-shows make life worthwhile by creating fun and entertainment. In addition to learning and working, common people need some diversion also. It has been alleged that the picture of circus life is fanciful and gives a misleading representation of human nature. Raymond Williams, for example, argues that the circus is less an alternative social vision to industrial capitalism. It is a regressive image, a nostalgic throw-back to a pre-industrial era of artisans, nomadic men and women in touch with Nature and the body free of all social restraint. But it should never be forgotten that the circus party is a symbol in the scheme of this moral fable. The circus people symbolize not only art but humanity. They add to the variety of Dickensian characterization and are a main source of humour in this novel.

The kindness of the Horse-riding is embodied chiefly in the figure of Sleary, and we are accordingly conscious mostly of the meanings enforced by this character. The scenes in which Sleary helps Gradgrind get Tom out of the country derive their meaning from the eminently theatrical contrast between practical hard-headed Gradgrind, now menaced by his prize pupil Bitzer and sloppy, lisping Sleary. That is, the main accent is on brandy and water; positively 'triumphant activity' comes only in the miniature comic form of the polka-dancing horse. Dickens's point is the surprising *practicality* of the incompetent-seeming Sleary, and the surprising *usefulness* of the horse that can dance the polka. This does not in any important way *feel* inconsistent with Dickens's earlier view of the Horse-riding which emphasizes, as Dr. Leavis points out, the fact that the skills of the Horse-riding contain their end within themselves and are therefore 'wasteful' in terms of Gradgrind's algebra. The broad-hearted circus people offer a contrast to the money-minded brutes like Bounderby. When Gradgrind offers Sleary some money he declines the offer. He accepts only a five-pound note for Mr. Childers who is a family man and asks him to buy a collar for the dog and a belt for the horse. The final scenes focus emphatically on Sissy's richness and luster and the Horse-riding's triumphant activity. Dickens keeps his symbolic intentions continuously in hand throughout the moral fable.

(VII) IMAGES, METAPHORS, AND SYMBOLS, ETC.

'It is my infirmity', wrote Dickens, 'to fancy or perceive relations in things which are not apparent generally.' The infirmity is indispensable to poets. Dickens's similes remake the world—his similes, and the symbols that work through similitude. His *Hard Times* is set in a northern industrial town far grimmer than Jack Rouncewell's town in *Bleak House*. Coketown takes us back to the nightmare chapters on the Birmingham to Wolverhampton road in *The Old Curiosity Shop*, but in *Hard Times* the horror is seen more analytically than through the eyes of a dying girl. The presiding sensibilities are those of Gradgrind and Bounderby, two gentlemen well calculated to keep fancy and imagination at bay. There is a new ruthlessness of observation on Dickens's part, as befits his setting. It is as if he extinguished his most distinctive gift for poetic resonance and suggestiveness in order to capture a world where the creative powers themselves are in exile. Or rather, as if he drove the resonances of his art inwards, until they acquired a muffled and deadly quality. While there are still evidences of symbolism in Coketown, and it would hardly be Dickens's city without this, the very symbols are oppressive to our minds. Coketown's 'fairy palaces' seen by travellers on the railway in early evening are pure illusion, its 'melancholy mad elephants' conjure no jungle freedom to our eyes. Any enchantment in Coketown is claustrophobic and sickening, like the witch's house in *Hansel and Gretel. Hard Times* indeed is a symbol of the world without creativity where the 'robber Fancy' is left, depraved by neglect, to seek revenge.

The thematic imagery of *Hard Times* greatly reinforces the effect of proliferating evil. Its angry insistence on organic images needs little comment. The novel is divided into three books, 'Sowing', 'Reaping' and 'Garnering', where these natural processes, sufficiently ironic in Coketown, chart the logic of stunted and withered lives. The three books—'Sowing', 'Reaping' and 'Garnering'—symbolize the triadic structure of the novel. Taken from the world of cultivation, these represent the thesis, antithesis and synthesis of logic. In the first book Gradgrind and Bounderby assiduously cultivate utilitarianism in education and industry respectively. Gradgrind would extirpate everything but fact: "In this life, we want nothing but Facts, Sir." He would bring up even his own children on the philosophy of 'somethingology' all the hours of their waking life, and exclude, fancy and entertainment. As a consequence he will 'reap' a dissatisfied daughter who would barely escape being reduced, though she would not escape ruining her marriage. The son would be turned into a criminal who would rob a bank and then be compelled to flee his country. What will ultimately be 'garnered' is the wisdom that one must make 'facts and figures subservient to Faith, Hope and Charity' ('Final'). In industrial life, Bounderby sows greater production out of the expenses of the basic comforts of the workers, and the consequence is not only a clash between the workers and the employer, but ultimately even death as in the case of

Stephen. The chapter titles such as 'Murdering the Innocents', 'A Loophole' and 'Never Wonder' successfully suggest this thematic preoccupation.

The characters, too, are symbolic. Mr. Gradgrind has a 'square forefinger', a 'square wall of a forehead', a 'square coat', and all these indicate Gradgrind's rigid, inflexible nature. As his name suggests he is infamous for grinding—although gradually—the triad of 'Faith, Hope and Mercy' to dust. A large part of the Victorian readers' feelings against Bounderby rests on the older and rather different feeling that trade, as such, is gross. The very name—and Dickens uses his names with conscious and obvious effect—incorporating *bounder*, incorporates this typical feeling. Bounderby has 'a metallic laugh', and is 'inflated like a balloon', and his inflation of self-made bullying will be deflated with the disclosure of his protected childhood. If Louisa is a symbol of suffering as a consequence of wrong upbringing, Tom symbolizes the dangerous consequences of it. Mrs. Sparsit represents the snobbery and hypocrisy of the upper class people, and her staircase is a symbol of illness of the heart to enjoy somebody's fall. The moral and spiritual differences of Sissy and Bitzer are rendered in the following passage in terms of sensation, and the symbolic intention emerges out of metaphor and the vivid evocation of the concrete:

> The square finger, moving here and there, lighted suddenly on Bitzer, perhaps because he chanced to sit in the same ray of sunlight which, darting in at one of the bare windows of the intensely whitewashed room, irradiated Sissy. For, the boys and girls sat on the face of the inclined plane in two compact bodies, divided up the centre by a narrow interval; and Sissy, being at the corner of a row on the sunny side, came in for the beginning of a sunbeam, of which Bitzer, being at the corner of a row on the other side, a few rows in advance, caught the end. But, whereas the girl was so dark-eyed and dark-haired, that she seemed to receive a deeper and more lustrous colour from the sun, when it shone upon her, the boy was so light-eyed and light-

> haired that the self-same rays appeared to draw out of him what little colour he ever possessed. His cold eyes would hardly have been eyes, but for the short ends of lashes which, by bringing them into immediate contrast with something paler than themselves, expressed their form. His short-cropped hair might have been a mere continuation of the sandy freckles on his forehead and face. His skin was so unwholesomely deficient in the natural tinge, that he looked as though, if he were cut, he would bleed white. (I, II)

What may, perhaps, be emphasized is that Sissy stands for vitality as well as goodness—they are seen, in fact, as one; she is generous, impulsive life, finding self-fulfilment in self-forgetfulness—all that is the antithesis of calculating self-interest. There is an essentially Laurentian suggestion about the way in which 'the dark-eyed and dark-haired' girl, contrasting with Bitzer, seemed to receive a 'deeper and more lustrous colour from the sun', so opposing the life that is lived freely and richly from the deep instinctive and emotional springs to the thin-blooded, quasi-mechanical product of Gradgrindery. Sissy Jupe, who might be taken here for a merely conventional *persona,* has already, as a matter of fact, been established in a potently symbolic role: she is part of the poetically-creative operation of Dickens's genius in *Hard Times*. Sissy's symbolic significance is bound up with that of Sleary's Horse-riding where human kindness is very insistently associated with vitality. The way in which the Horse-riding takes on its significance illustrates felicitously the poetic-dramatic nature of Dickens's art.

In *Hard Times*, Dickens dramatizes in strikingly symbolic terms the opposition between a soul-destroying relation to a utilitarian, industrial civilization, in which everything is weighed, measured, has its price, and in which emotion is banished. If the perpetually clanking machinery of the Coketown mills, which turns men into "hands", is the symbol of one, the "horse-riding", as in Picasso's *Saltimbanques*, is the dominant symbol of the other: "The father of one of the families was in the habit of balancing the father of another of the families on the top of a great pole; the father of a third family often made a pyramid of both those fathers, with Master Kidderminster for the apex, and himself for the base.... They all assumed to be mighty rakish and knowing, they were not very tidy in their private dresses, they were not at all orderly in their domestic arrangements, and the combined literature of the whole company would have produced but a poor letter on any subject. Yet there was a remarkable gentleness and childishness about these people, a special inaptitude for any kind of sharp practice, and an untiring readiness to help and pity one another..." (I, 6). J. Hillis Miller writes:

> ...the circus here is still only a symbol of a good *society*, that is, of communion around a third thing, the "act". In this relation contact with others is still in a way impersonal, and the individual is still defined by his role, by his cooperative submission to a common activity and goal. In the circus act, as in even the best society, the otherness of other people tends to be submerged. (226)

Coketown is myth in *Hard Times*. The imprisoning streets and stifling air of Coketown impresses a total image of the spiritual malaise engendered there. It is a world where the houses and streets, the urban environs, the very feel of the air initiate us into the psychology of living and suffering people. It is not through formal description or analysis of character but through every detail of Coketown that we see into the human heart. Coketown is the innermost dereliction and despair of Louisa and Stephen, the environment which has shaped them, the prison where they will die. Despite the social realism it is tinged with nightmare, akin to the delirium of a fever running its course. Everything seems fated and unalterable. As we see Mr. Gradgrind's 'metallurgical Louisa' handed over in marriage to Bounderby, a 'big, loud man, with a stare, and a metallic laugh', it is as though the moment had always been predestined.

This is a crucial seene in which from the utilitarian schoolroom Mr. Gradgrind walks, towards his utilitarian abode, Stone Lodge, which, as Dickens evokes it, brings home to us concretely the model regime that for the little Gradgrinds (among whom are Malthus and Adam Smith) is an inescapable prison. But before he gets there he passes the back of a circus booth, and is pulled up by the sight of two palpable offenders. Looking more closely, 'what did he behold but his own metallurgical Louisa peeping through a hole in a deal board, and his own mathematical Thomas abasing himself on the ground to catch but a hoof of the graceful equestrian Tyrolean flower act'! It contains both a discovery and a peripety and possesses the proper qualities of surprise and probability. Surprise is not only registered through 'phenomenon almost incredible' but the specific reference to 'his own metallurgical Louisa' and 'his own mathematical Thomas' brings out all the irony in the neat reversal of Gradgrind's expectations as father and educationist. Harvey P. Sucksmith writes in this connection in *The Narrative Art of Charles Dickens*: "The basic movement of the novel originates in the spiritual blindness of Gradgrind, which is the blindness of a whole philosophy, of a society, of an age. Again, the spiritual myopia of Gradgrind is suggested by the business of the eyeglass which he needs to make out what his children are up to under his very nose; thus the physical action of the passage expresses and underlines the wider spiritual message. Moreover, the incident is related organically to the rest of the novel both in form and in content. It foreshadows the major double catastrophe in which daughter and son show so alarmingly the unexpected yet quite inevitable effects of the Gradgrind system of education on their adult lives" (157). The discovery is the major catastrophe of the novel in miniature. It is vision as well as structure—a prophetic picture, that is, of the way that an outraged natural law brings about a *nemesis* in the fullness of time.

The passage in which Sissy describes her father's failure and the beating of Merrylegs is replete with symbolic overtones:

> Father, soon after they came home from performing, told Merrylegs to jump up on the backs of the two chairs and stand across them—which is one of his tricks.

> He looked at father and didn't do it at once. Everything of father's had gone wrong that night, and he hadn't pleased the public at all. He cried out that the very dog knew he was failing, and had no compassion on him. Then he beat the dog, and I was frightened, and said, 'Father, father! Pray don't hurt the creature who is so fond of you! O Heaven forgive you, father, stop!' And he stopped, and the dog was bloody, and father lay down crying on the floor with the dog in his arms, and the dog licked his face.
>
> Louisa saw that she was sobbing; and going to her, kissed her, took her hand, and sat down beside her. (*HT*. I, IX)

Dickens examines the problem of suffering and of God's nature in a specifically Christian context. Stephen Blackpool represents the case of a man crucified by the contemporary world.

> "It ha' shined upon me", he said reverently, "in my pain and trouble down below. It ha' shined into my mind. I ha' look'n at it and thowt o' thee, Rachael, till the muddle in my mind have cleared awa, above a bit, I hope." (III, VI)

The muddle turns out to have been only in Stephen's mind, a paranoid delusion of a persecuting fate. It is dispelled by a compassionate Christian love which is also enlightenment.

A horse figures prominently in the classroom scene at the start when the tyranny of fact is being demonstrated. Sissy Jupe can't define a horse, though she belongs to Sleary's horse-riders, whereas Bitzer knows it's a graminivorous quadruped with forty teeth. But in the end a dancing horse of Sleary's is instrumental in defeating Bitzer and rescuing Tom Gradgrind from justice. More in the tradition of Cracker's parrot is the scene where Tom Gradgrind sits on the terrace with Harthouse, picking roses and tearing them to pieces with his teeth. The sorry state of Tom's soul, implied by such a behaviour, is fully explained in the later interview between Louisa Gradgrind and her father, when she strikes herself on the bosom and asks 'what have you done, O father, what have you done, with the garden that should have bloomed once, in this great wilderness here!'

The fire gazing scene in the chapter (I, VIII) when Louisa and Tom are at their father's hearth, a place where the 'fanciful imagination' is a 'treason', is very significant. Louisa seems transfixed by the flames, and she speaks slowly, and in a curious tone, as if she were reading what she asked in the fire, and it were not quite plainly written there. When Tom looks into the fire to see what engrosses his sister, he finds nothing; to him it looks "as stupid and blank as everything else looks". Their exchange of words shows that the fire brings on wonder. Tom is looking for some substantial relief from the mulish drudgery of his life. But as Louisa's response shows, the fire-gazing reaches deeper into the psychic life, inducing the very wonder upon which circus-going and all imaginative enterprise are founded. The metaphor of fire appears often in the novel. Louisa's "starved imagination" is described as "a fire with nothing to burn" (I, III). Her repressed energies are described as "smouldered within her like an unwholesome fire" (III, I), and this opens out into a vision of reality turning back on itself in destructive reprisal, the imagination's revenge when denied a refuge in fancy: "All closely imprisoned forces rend and destroy. The air that would be healthful to the earth, the water that would enrich it, the heat that would ripen it, tear it when caged up. So in her bosom even now; the strongest qualities she possessed, long turned upon themselves, became a heap of obduracy, that rose against a friend." For Dickens this psychic retaliation is a kind of natural law, and part of Louisa's tragedy is that only she seems to sense this. When discussing with her father her proposed loveless marriage to Bounderby, she looks hopelessly into the distance, and Gradgrind asks if she is "consulting with the chimneys of the Coketown works" (I, XV). Louisa's hours of fire-gazing drew her to a sense of wonder and provided Dickens with an icon for her constrained but vital energies. But these energies have stagnated, and she can now find symbolic expression for them only in the smouldering, incendiary nature of the Coketown furnaces waiting for their violent discharge.

In the final chapter of the novel Louisa is "watching the fire as in the days of yore, though with a gentler and a humbler face". The question "How much of the future might arise before her vision?" is answered in a long series of noun fragments and participles in an overall present tense of anticipated futurity, which foresees in the fire, among other things, Louisa "grown learned in childish lore" and dedicating herself, on behalf of Sissy's children, to "those imaginative graces and delights, without which the heart of infancy will wither up". Much like the way the coda of *Pickwick* widened to the scope of the author's whole creative imagination bidding farewell to the characters of his own brain, in *Hard Times* the chronicler's expected resume of the future and of the fate of his characters is internalized as Louisa's private and habitual fire-gazing raised finally to a visionary power.

John Holloway in "*Hard Times*: A History and a Criticism" writes, "Perhaps the most vividly memorable part of the whole novel is that of Mrs. Sparsit spying on Louisa and Harthouse, and following the fleeing Louisa, through the thunderstorm, to the railway station and to Coketown. It is the culmination of one of the great imaginative strokes of the book, Dickens's likening of her temptation to the descent of a great staircase, into chaos at its foot. He extracts the image, with great skill and economy, from Louisa's own 'what does it matter?', then imposes it on Mrs. Sparsit, and modulates it, with a truly poetic movement, into the 'deep water' and universal deluge of the railway scene. This whole scene of the flight, in its fluent modulation of imagery and its melodrama charged with human weight, is Dickens at his most characteristic and his best" (Gross 173-74).

In fact, by texture, imaginative mode, symbolic method, and the resulting concentration, *Hard Times* affects us as belonging with formally poetic works.

(VIII) MORAL FABLE/FAIRY WORLD

Dr. Leavis's illuminating classification of *Hard Times* is that it is a 'moral fable'—that is, a fictional story with a clear intellectual purpose:

> I need say no more by way of defining the moral fable than that in it the intention is peculiarly insistent, so that the representative significance of everything in the fable—character, episode, and so on—is immediately apparent as we read. (*The Great Tradition* 227)

This is a fine account of that central quality in Dickens's art which one may call 'theatrical'. Intention might seem to be insistent enough in the opening of *Hard Times,* in that scene in Mr. Gradgrind's school. But then, intention is in some well-known places in Dickens's work—and this has been generally thought of as a Dickensian characteristic—notably insistent without its being taken up in any inclusive significance that informs and organizes a coherent whole. In a semi-realistic work like *Hard Times*, we can hardly be satisfied with the circus as a simple undifferentiated alpha and omega, like Kafka's castle or the lake from which Arthur's sword appeared and to which it returned. Dr. Leavis sounds too enthusiastic when he speaks of "the solemn moral of the whole fable, put with the rightness of genius in Mr. Sleary's asthmatic mouth", as Sleary belongs to a long tradition of the wise or holy fool. To speak of his genius is surely to place Sleary among the finest representatives of this tradition, to put him in the company of the Fool in *King Lear* and Dostoevsky's *Myshkin*.

Dickens marks out the enemies, Gradgrind and Bounderby, and he makes of them mere ciphers, predictable, hateful and readily condemned. But between them they represent a way of life which is meant to be powerful enough to squeeze out all hope for human decency. What Gradgrind stands for, is, though repellent, nevertheless respectable. His utilitarianism is a theory sincerely held and there is intellectual disinterestedness in its application. But Gradgrind marries his eldest daughter Louisa to Bounderby, banker, merchant, manufacturer about whom there is no disinterestedness whatever, and nothing to be respected. Bounderby embodies the rugged individualism of the Victorian period in its grossest and most intransigent form. Concerned with nothing but material power and material success, he has no interest in ideals as ideas—expect the idea of being the completely self-made man which he is not in fact, despite all his brag. But the impulse which produced 'Facts, facts, facts' is not brought into harmony with Gradgrind's love for his children. It is simply condemned, and we are satisfied, for we know—and willingly accept the fact—that the mind behind those brilliant last scenes, in which Bitzer's bloodless arguments menace the broken Gradgrind, is not a mind interested in or capable of such mediation.

Gradgrind seems to belong to the world of pure moral fable. So the readers may feel uneasy whenever Gradgrind has dealings with Bounderby and Harthouse. They are not the same kind of creature at all, and so can only communicate, as it were, through the author's mind. And so there is no reserve of dramatic force to play with at the time of Gradgrind's conversion. Of course, the atmosphere of the moral fable, or even of the fairy tale is introduced deliberately at times. We cannot doubt that when we read a sentence like this: "Stephen, whose way had been in a contrary direction, turned about, and betook himself as in duty bound to the red brick castle of the giant Bounderby." Neither Bounderby nor Stephen really deserves the aura of fairy tale. Each has his own psychological truth; and each has characteristics which could not occur in any pre-industrial society.

Since the moral message communicated by Dickens in *Hard Times* is that of the confutation of utilitarianism by life, Gradgrind and Bounderby have confronted their opponents in the world of moral values. What may be emphasized is that Sissy Jupe—"Girl number twenty"—who fails to give the definition of a horse in the Gradgrind's elementary school stands for vitality as well as goodness—they are seen, in fact, as one. Sissy's symbolic significance is bound up with that of Sleary's horse-riding where human kindness is most insistently associated with vitality. The circus owner who remarks to Grandgrind that 'People must be amused...' is undoubtedly seen as embodying the novel's positive values. Sleary is made to represent the anti-utilitarian, positive and the jovial circus athletes, at the same time human spontaneity and the warmth of the creative impulse. Their skills have no value for the utilitarian calculus but they minister to vital human needs. The horse-riding, frowned by Gradgrind and scorned by Bounderby, brings upon the machine hands of Coketown what they are starved of. It brings them not merely amusement but art that springs from the joy and woe of life. Mr. Sleary's decision to stand by Tom, and compound the felony which Bitzer will not compound, is a major landmark in the whole fable. For, after all, it is the key point, along with the 'discovery' of Bounderby's mother and her devotion, at which the fable creates its picture of the lengths to which untutored kindness and unreasoned feeling can go, and how they look as they go to these lengths. Dr. Leavis writes of the scene where Sleary finally points the book's moral: "Reading it there we have to stand off and reflect at a distance to recognize potentialities that might have been realized elsewhere as Dickensian sentimentality. There is nothing sentimental in the actual fact." The circus is at the beginning and the end. From it comes Sissy Jupe to save the Gradgrind family; and Tom, the disgraced product of a politico-economical education returns to it to make his escape. The members of Mr. Sleary's circus party are fanciful and imaginative and become a part of the fairy world. The words 'fairy business' has been repeatedly used in the novel. Sissy is also acquainted with the fairy story. In answer to the questions of Mr. Gradgrind Sissy says that she reads only the fairy tales. She forces Mr. Harthouse to go from Coketown without delay and stops bothering Louisa with his attentions. In this way she rescues Louisa from the grip of Harthouse. The life of Coketown is drab, dreary, monotonous and its people are sinful, heartless. On the contrary, the members of the circus party are involved in disinterested activities. They have love, fellow-feeling, tenderness, sympathy. This contrast has an ironic implication to the people of Coketown. The people of the circus act as good fairies. Sleary saves Tom from arrest. Moreover the people of the circus are without 'sharp practices'. These qualities relate the circus party to the fairy world of the novel.

Mr. Bounderby's mother, Mrs. Pegler has been described as 'a mysterious old woman'. Mr. Bounderby deserted her taking all her money and forbade her to come again. But Mrs. Pegler occasionally comes in dark night to see her son Bounderby. Thus her visit to see her son in such a ghostly manner is a part of the fairy story. Mrs. Sparsit has been described as 'bank fairy'. Mr. Bounderby describes her as a 'devilishly sensible woman'. She is a witchy character in the story and she moves with her 'cat like' observation of the people around her. The fairy-tale world is dominated by innocence. This world is the product of fancy and imagination, which are not to be found in the materialistic Victorian society. Dickens is pleading for the fairy-tale world. And in order to bring into focus the negative side of the existing Victorian society he introduces the fairy world in the texture of the novel with his invested moral intention.

Apparently the fairy world has no importance in the novel and may be regarded as a subsidiary element. But it acts as a commentary to the major theme of the novel. Dickens satirises the materialistic tendency of the Victorian society through this device. It shows the hollowness of the life of Coketown as well as of England. Therefore, the introduction of the fairy-tale elements in the novel has proper moral and artistic justification.

Hard Times may even be called a morality drama, which is Johnson's term. But, like the Christmas books and the other novels serialized in *Household Words* and *All the Year Round*, it is based on a Christian morality. In many ways, even, the story is to be read less as a fable than as a parable, or a tract for the times. If it is not read thus, Stephen's fall down Old Hell Shaft, at the end of the book, and the star he thought, he could see as he lay there dying, is as trite and tasteless a piece of false piety as an author has ever committed:

> I ha' fell into a pit that ha' been wi' th' Fire-damp crueller than battle. I ha' read on't in the public petition, as onny one may read, fro' the men that works in pits, in which they ha' pray'n an pray'n the lawmakers for

> Christ's sake not to let their work be murder to 'em [....] But look up yonder, Rachel! Look above!'

Following his eyes, Rachael saw that he was gazing at a star. 'It ha' shined upon me', he said reverently, 'in my pain and trouble down below. It ha' shined into my mind [....]' 'Often as I coom to myself and found it shining on me down there in my trouble, I thowt it were the star as guided to Our Saviour's home. I awmost think it be the very star!'

> They lifted him up, and he was overjoyed to find that they were about to take him in the direction whither the star seemed to him to lead....
>
> They carried him very gently along the fields, and down the lanes, and over the wide landscape.... It was soon a funeral procession. The star had shown him where to find the God of the poor; and through humility, and sorrow, and forgiveness, he had gone to his Redeemer's rest.

K.J. Fielding comments in "*Bleak House* and *Hard Times*": "Of course Dickens was attacking society, but not—as Shaw would have it—in company with Karl Marx in order to arouse revolution, but in the hope that all who were part of it would act with greater Christian humility and charity" (138).

John Holloway in "*Hard Times*: A History and a Criticism" writes: "As a 'moral fable' *Hard Times* is a vigorous and good-hearted book, but if 'shallow' is unduly severe with regard to the level of insight with which it proceeds, Dr. Leavis, in writing that here 'the creative exuberance is controlled by a profound inspiration' has conceded just the word which requires to be withheld" (Gross 172). *Hard Times* should be interpreted as a moral fable, in the everyday sense. Henry James, like F.R. Leavis, called *Hard Times* a 'moral fable' and Henry James's *The Europeans* may be classed with *Hard Times* as a moral fable. Henry James has made the point in "The Art of Fiction": 'The essence of moral energy is to survey the whole field...try to catch the colour of life itself.'

Although Dr. Leavis speaks of its peculiarly insistent moral intention, the complexity of the issues that Dickens takes up in the novel cannot be reduced to the formulae by calling it a moral fable. As John Holloway puts it:

> Perhaps we are too much inclined to demand the all-embracing moral structure in fiction, to take its mere presence as its success, to forget that what is all-embracing may also be all-consuming, and in some measure to forgo the free life, the unconstrained movement, the inexhaustible wealth of fiction, for the chiaroscuro of moralism and tyranny of theme. (Gross 174)

Dr. Leavis praises the success with which Dickens 'reconciles' his various characteristic modes in this novel, and one agrees that the reconciling is done with great finesse.

(IX) MOST MOVING AND AMUSING SCENES

The most distinguishing elements of Dickens's artistry, and also the most remarkable quality contributing significantly to his popularity as a novelist are pathos and humour. That he was a master artist in handling pathetic and humorous situations in his novels is established beyond doubts. And what is more, he has rendered them in the popular way. In *Hard Times*, however, there is hardly any pathetic scene in the strictest sense of the term. But there are certainly some scenes which are highly moving. We may instance the scene depicting the death of Stephen Blackpool. The scene is moving because a righteous man like Stephen is so misunderstood that he is compelled to leave Coketown and when he is pulled out of a pit—more dead than alive—he impresses us as a really pathetic figure. His last interview with Rachael attains something of poetic justice. This seems to be the most longing for his union with Rachael and his honesty to represent the truthful courage and righteousness both to the workers of the union and to the master. But, strictly speaking and dispassionately analyzed, the effect of the scene is pathetic only when it is viewed sentimentally. The Stephen episode is not central in the thematic design of the novel; in fact, Dickens has not taken care in investing the character of Stephen with the potential and lively complexities. The result is that the reader may pity his plight but finds it difficult to identify himself or herself with him. Dickens wrote to Forster, "I have done what I hope is a good thing with Stephen, taking his story as a whole." In this connection S. Monod observes: "Perhaps he had done a good thing in the sense of a well meant and virtuous attempt, but not in the sense of a successful artistic creation." So, for a most moving organic scene, we have to look elsewhere in the novel.

One may choose the scene of Louisa's return to her father after her mishap with Mr. Harthouse as the most moving. Mr. Gradgrind is in a mood of contemplation at home during the vacation. After the rains he looks fresh. Thunder is still roaring at a distance. And from the midst of darkness and rain comes Louisa, disheveled and frantic. She looks colourless, despairing and defined. Without any introduction she accuses her father of imparting wrong education to her. Louisa curses the hour in which she was born. She says that her father's education through which she had been brought up has taken away the graces of her soul, the sentiments of her heart and the bliss of life: "What have you done, O father, what have you done, with the garden that should have bloomed once, in this great wilderness here?" She says that what he had never nurtured in her had never nurtured in himself. If he had only neglected her, she would have been a much better and much happier creature. On hearing this, after all his care, Mr. Gradgrind bows his head upon his hand and groans aloud. Louisa says that had she been allowed to exercise fancy of the heart, she should have been "a million times wiser, happier, more loving, more contented, more innocent and human in all good respects" than her present state of being. She has almost repulsed and crushed her better angel into a demon: "What I have learned has left me doubting, misbelieving, despising, regretting, what I have not learned; and my dismal resource has been to think that life would soon go by, and that nothing in it could be worth the pain and trouble of a contest."

In fact, Gradgrind's guidance and instructions have ultimately connected Louisa with death and led her to deviation from the path of moral uprightness. So, she is desperate, direct and trenchant in her criticism of the Gradgrindery system of education. This is evident in her speech in which she bluntly and directly accuses her father: "All that I know is your philosophy and your teaching will not save me." She suggests very poignantly that her growth has been a constant straying away from her essential nature. Not only that she has not been provided with the mental pabulum, even the basic human element of 'wonder' has been stifled in her. Her utilitarian and irrevocable marriage to Mr. Bounderby has proved fatal. She complains that her father proposed her husband to her, and she married him. She never made a pretence to Bounderby or her father that she loved Bounderby. She was not wholly indifferent, for she had a hope of being pleasant and useful to Tom. Tom had been the subject of all the little tenderness of her life; perhaps he became so because she knew so well how to pity him. Louisa resumes that when she was irrevocably married, there rose up into rebellion against the tie, the old strife, made fiercer by all those causes of disparity which arose out of the two individual natures, and which no general laws would ever rule or state for her. At last Louisa comes to confess that this has encouraged the young man Harthouse to exploit the situation in his favour. She has escaped with her honour but the vexation of her temporary slip is so agonising that it seems unbearable. No word from her father has the power to console her as she faints up on the ground before his ashy eyes. The "metallurgical Louisa" realizes herself and gets obfuscated to find no meaning in her present identity. This feeling of frustration is fraught with some tragic potentiality because Louisa pours forth her accusations from the pressure of self-realization, from a sense of wasted life. In this scene Mr. Gradgrind also learns his lesson, obviously at a tremendous cost. If in the beginning he asserted the efficacy of education based on facts, the same teaching has boomeranged upon himself in the end when he realizes that the summation of his facts is going to crush his own daughter. The claim of the scene to be the most moving one is also justified in that the Gradgrind thread is central in the thematic structure of the novel.

But Dickens is famous as much for creating pathetic scenes as for depicting humorous and extremely amusing situations. Although it is difficult to trace any true, typically Dickensian scene of humour in *Hard Times* which was concerned with fighting the contemporary menus of Benthamite Utilitarianism and with preaching a grave moral lesson, there are in this novel a few funny situations and amusing scenes of which the one described in the chapter, called 'Philosophical', is most enjoyable in many senses. Although it is said that the Dickens of *Hard Times* is much inferior to and different from the Dickens of other novels, like *David Copperfield* or *Oliver Twist* or *Pickwick Papers*, G.B. Shaw in his article "Hard Times" writes, "...you need not fear to find Dickens losing his good humor and sense of fun and becoming serious in Mr. Gradgrind's way. On the contrary, Dickens in this book casts off, and casts off for ever, all restraint on his wild sense of humor." One can also remember Chesterton here: "Humour was his medium; his only way of approaching emotion. Wherever you do not get humour, you get unconscious humour" (Ford 185). Dickens takes special delight in throwing the real villain and the enemy of humanitarianism into the tight corner in the chapter, "Philosophical".

In the process of the development of the plot, Gradgrind undergoes much remorse as a consequence of the apparently unpredictable results of his fact-based education. We can feel something of his remorse when he is made to realise that it is he who alone is responsible for ruining his daughter and also for his son's being a robber. Tom himself has confessed his role in the robbery. The agonised father is eager to save his son by any means. The only way left open is to send him to a foreign country like America. When everything is settled with the help of Sleary, Bitzer stands in the way. He takes possession of Tom and is bent on delivering him over to Mr. Bounderby for by doing so he will be able to further his self-interest which will be fulfilled through his promotion to the post of Tom. Mr. Gradgrind resorts to 'compassionate influence' but fails to soften Bitzer. Gradgrind becomes so desperate as to offer bribe to Bitzer for releasing Tom, but without any results. As a last resort he implores as Bitzer's teacher to the latter's good sense of gratitude and the most amusing situation is when the alumnus answers Gradgrind back by saying, "My schooling was paid for, it was a bargain, and when I came away, the bargain ended." Thus, quite bluntly he confesses that as he learnt in the school of Gradgrind on cash payments, he feels no urge for gratitude. Besides, as a student he learnt from Gradgrind to pursue his own interest and nothing else. So his action is justifiable from the point of view of Gradgrind himself. When he refuses to budge even an inch from his position, Sleary comes to intervene into it. He poses to side with Bitzer and promises to help him carry Tom upto the stations. The cart begins to move, but very soon at the signal of the driver, the horse begins to dance, so much so that Bitzer is forced to come down. The dog fixes its eyes upon Bitzer so that he cannot stir a step. Thus Tom is provided with the opportunity to escape and Bitzer is not allowed to move until Tom reaches the point of safety.

So far as plotting of the novel is concerned the situation shows Dickens's resourcefulness. Moreover, the skilful management of the whole process by Sleary and his associates stupefies Bitzer. Credit goes more to Sleary but not less to his trained horse and dog. Poetic justice is maintained in two senses. First, Mr. Gradgrind's own philosophy is made to recoil upon himself in a bitterly plaguing manner and secondly, he is also offered the highest tribute for protecting Sissy in her days of distress. Admittedly, therefore, imaginatively and morally viewed, this is the most amusing situation in the novel.

(X) FLAWED CLASSIC

Hard Times was written somewhat hurriedly to fill a blank in the schedule of *Household Words*; and it was constructed in the weekly and constricted installments with which Dickens had last contended in *The Old Curiosity Shop* and *Barnaby Rudge*. Despite the fact that the thesis of *Hard Times* is an integral part of his narrative intentions, he found less room for developing his contrasting plot sequences. He also had difficulty in focusing all his narrative technical resources on his subject, so that the novel does not call upon many of his best devices. The sequences which interlocked the large monthly parts of *Bleak House* had no similar opportunity in the smaller pieces which were required by the magazine's weekly issues. The novel sometimes gives the effect of choppy episodes, of undeveloped contrasts, of unfinished business, and this kind of effect is exactly un-Dickensian. *Hard Times* is an underrated novel. Its thesis is challenging, it contributes materially to Dickens's total study of the social microcosm, but it is something less than a great novel for several reasons. Since it has been enthusiastically praised by George Bernard Shaw, and since F.R. Leavis called it "a completely serious work of art" (*The Great Tradition* 275)—one needs to look closely at the reasons for finding it less effective than *Bleak House* or *Little Dorrit*.

F.R. Leavis observes in *Dickens: The Novelist* that "In the books and essays on Dickens...it [*Hard Times*] is passed over as a very minor thing; too slight and insignificant to distract us for more than a sentence or two from the works worth critical attention.... Of all Dickens's works it is the one that, having the distinctive strength that makes him a major artist, has it in so compact a way, and with a concentrated significance so immediately clear and penetrating, as, one would have thought, to preclude the reader's failing to recognize that he had before him a completely serious, and, in its originality, a triumphantly successful, work of art" (251). Leavis argued that though *Hard Times* is not without certain defects, it is a classic of sustained seriousness.

Dickens's art of characterization in *Hard Times* has been seriously faulted. It has been alleged that Dickens's characters are either virtuous or vicious to a fault. They are either too white or too black, never bichromatic as in life, and the language in which they are embodied fixes them in their "given" condition. They can only die like Stephen or be broken like Mr. Gradgrind. Dickens falters in the handling of the character of Tom precisely because he uses a device for fixing character (whelp) to express a process of change. Rachael reveals none of her faults, for Dickens believes her to have none. The caricature technique fights a losing battle in *Hard*

Times; the speech devices are less effective than usual. The shadowy ghost of caricature shows itself in the early description of Gradgrind and of M'Choakumchild. Mrs. Sparsit has a Coriolanian nose and dense black eyebrows. Her great-aunt, Lady Scadgers, is an immensely gross woman who loves meat and possesses a leg which has refused to get out of bed for fourteen years. Probably the best characters are the circus people. Mr. Sleary, the proprietor, is a fat man with one fixed and one loose eye, a voice like a broken bellows, a head which is never either completely sober or sufficiently drunk, and a manner of speaking which is affected by his asthma and comes out in a lisp which makes his speeches difficult to read. Master Kidderminster is a dwarf who assists Childers, being carried on the palm of Childers' hand, feet upward, while the daring vaulting act goes on.

The presentation of the very poor and the very unhappy paralyzes Dickens and deprive him of his comic power. He will not have the reader laugh at them. The novelist's purpose was to have them admiration, but the modern reader tends to find them unspeakably tedious. About Stephen and Rachael, the novelist had harboured the singular illusion. Dickens wrote to Forster, "I have done what I hope is a good thing with Stephen, taking his story as a whole." In this connection S. Monod observes: "Perhaps he had done a good thing in the sense of a well meant and virtuous attempt, but not in the sense of a successful artistic creation."

It is said that Dickens did not succeed in putting forward a clear, coherent, persuasive thesis. In 1854, Charles Knight sent Dickens a copy of his *Knowledge is Power*, a kind of elementary guide to contemporary process of commerce and more particularly manufacture; and said that he was afraid that Dickens, then busy writing *Hard Times*, would set him down as "a cold-hearted political economist'. And Dickens replied: 'My satire is against those who see *figures and averages, and nothing else*—the representatives of the wickedest and most enormous vice of this time.... Bah! What have you to do with these?" [Charles Knight, *Passages of a Working Life* (1873 ed.), Vol. III, 187-88]

John Holloway in "*Hard Times*: A History and a Criticism" says, "Dickens stood much too near to what he criticized in the novel, for his criticism to reach a fundamental level. This is not a matter of his having a balanced view of the whole situation as between manufacture, labour, and capital; but of his sharing the somewhat naïve enthusiasms, and with them to some extent the brusque middle-class hostilities and presumptions, of those whom he thought he was criticizing" (Gross 166). Almost the very moment when he was beginning *Hard Times*, Dickens could write:

> Mighty, indeed, are the dealings of these cotton monarchs. Complicated are their transactions; numberless the interests they affect; and far away and strange the lands they give vitality to, the mouths they feed, the forms they clothe. (Lancashire Witchcraft, *Household Words*, 4 Feb. 1654)

A year before, writing then too of the Lancashire mills, he wrote:

> ...the factory itself is certainly not a "thing of beauty" in its externals. But it is a grand machine in its organization —the men, the fingers, and the iron and steel, all work together for one common end. (*Household Words*, 5 Feb. 1653)

The article concludes with a eulogy of the 'captain of industry' (Mr. Titus Salt) who was building new model factories at Saltaire. 'Captain of industry' is of course a phrase of Carlyle's. Dickens dedicated *Hard Times* to that fiery and apocalyptic bourgeois, and assured him that there was nothing in the book with which he would disagree. It is plain that Dickens's whole love-hate relation to Victorian industry was deeply influenced by the writings of Carlyle. Again, Dickens stands against the world of 'addition, subtraction, multiplication, and division'. John Holloway in "*Hard Times*: A History and a Criticism" says that Dickens's "alternative is neither the determined individuality and, in a certain degree, genuine cultivation of the best masters (as Charlotte Bronte saw this when she depicted Hunsden in *The Professor*, or as Mrs. Gaskell did with John Thornton in *North and South* or indeed, to some extent, Dickens himself with Mr. Rouncewell in *Bleak House*); nor the desperate need, communal feeling, and strengthening responsibility which he saw for himself among the 'hands'. His alternative was something which lay altogether outside the major realities of the social situation with which he dealt: the circus world of Mr. Sleary" (Gross 167-68).

In the conversation between Louisa and her father when Bounderby has proposed, it is apparent at once that neither character is a true embodiment of the standpoint—or predicament—which is their allotted role; they are creatures of stick, arguing a case or obligingly but unconvincingly tongue-tied.

In *Hard Times*, in fact, Utilitarianism largely means 'Manchester School' political economy: 'Utilitarian economists, skeletons of schoolmasters, Commissioners of fact' (II, VI)—there is an implicit reference back to the 'unlucky infants' who are told to 'take everything on political economy'. The gradual degeneration of Tom, until the superb moment when, in his ridiculous and degrading disguise, 'he came down, bench by bench (like a monkey) until he stood in the sawdust' (III, VIII), is barely related to Dickens's major problems in the book. Dickens's satire was directed against the contemporary forces of enlightenment and is written from the standpoint of the mid-Victorian middle-class Philistine. This, broadly speaking, is the Dickens who wrote with a low-brow vulgarity about Millais's 'Christ in the Carpenter's Shop' in the Pre-Raphaelite exhibition. His attitude can be defined as a kind of sentimental socialism. He was conscious of the existence of a problem, but it was one that acted on his emotions rather than on his intelligence, and thus the solutions he contemplated were all of the benevolent, patronizing kind.

Predictability, as pointed out by Earl Davis, is another technical flaw of the work. From the very beginning events turn up accordingly to our expectation and there is hardly any suspense in the entire work. The Harthouse episode does not seem to have been meticulously planned. First of all, it has been grossly thrust upon the wreck of Louisa. Besides it is beyond understanding how a weak, unassertive girl like Sissy prevails upon the cunning philanderer and forces him to leave Coketown. The description of Slackbridge in the novel is vague, and the metaphorical inventiveness that characterizes Dickens's creations is missing in the case. Dickens's understanding of worker's solidarity in *Hard Times* 'betrays a marked limitation'. G.B. Shaw writes in his article "Hard Times", "...even at their worst trade union organizers are not a bit like Slackbridge. All this is pure middle-class ignorance. It is much as if a tramp were to write a description of millionaires smoking large cigars in church, with their wives in low necked dresses and diamonds. We cannot say that Dickens did not know the working classes, because he knew humanity too well to be ignorant of any class. But this sort of knowledge is as compatible with ignorance of class manners and customs as with ignorance of foreign languages. Dickens knew certain classes of working folk very well: domestic servants, village artisans, and employees of petty tradesmen, for example. But of the segregated factory populations of our purely industrial towns he knew no more than an observant professional man can pick up on a flying visit to Manchester" (Ford 133).

Excessive sentimentality is counted as another weakness of *Hard Times*. The suffering of Stephen and Rachael has obviously been exploited for maudlin purposes. Stephen's faulty grammar is a form of sentimental blackmailing, for the reader cannot refuse to be moved by such ignorance or to see in it the incontrovertible evidence of Stephen's purity of mind. The parallel between Bounderby's and Stephen's matrimonial troubles is unconvincing; and one feels that probability, psychology and everything else had been sacrificed to symmetry. A.O.J. Cochshut comments in "Hard Times—Dickens's Masterpiece?": "The last chapter summarizes in a few hundred words events which might fill a whole novel. Here Dickens's sense of the superiority of life to fact, which is the guiding star of the novel,...seems ironically to have deserted him."

Notwithstanding these flaws, *Hard Times* impresses us as an immortal work of art. Prof. Leavis has defended its 'foregone conclusions' on the ground of its being a 'moral fable'. *Hard Times* retains force because of its purpose. Dickens planned three separate plot sequences for *Hard Times*, each of them presenting opportunities for development and contrast. His main action was to center around Thomas Gradgrind, a retired wholesale hardware merchant who had become a member of Parliament. The second division of action centers about Mr. Bounderby, who is an even more vicious portrait of the hard-hearted capitalist than was Scrooge. The third division of action concerns the power-loom weaver, Stephen Blackpool. These three plot sequences illustrate Dickens's general plan for revolving his action around attack on utilitarian economy, since it also encompasses criticism of the educational system, the caste system, and divorce laws. The sincerity of Dickens's social feeling is not to be called in doubt. Few men have been so vividly struck as he was by the sufferings of the poor, by the unfairness of fate, and by the frequent cruelty of privileged people. A careful reading of the novel shows that he succeeded in giving them a unified purpose.

As to characterization, it may be noted that the character of Mr. Gradgrind is not without pity and sympathy. And we see that he goes through a metamorphic transformation. He learns his lesson, obviously at a tremendous cost. If in the beginning he asserted the efficacy of education based on facts, the same teaching has boomeranged upon himself in the end when he realizes that the summation of his facts is going to crush his own daughter.

Though Dickens earned fame for his humour, *Hard Times* shows the triumph of his ironic art. F.R. Leavis writes in *Dickens: The Novelist*: "The final stress may fall on Dickens's command of word, phrase, rhythm and image: in ease and range there is surely no greater master of English except Shakespeare. This comes back to saying that Dickens is a great poet: his endless resource in felicitously varied expression is an extraordinary responsiveness to life. His senses are charged with emotional energy, and his intelligence plays and flashes in the quickest and sharpest perception. That is, his mastery of 'style' is of the only kind that matters—which is not to say that he hasn't a conscious interest in what can be done with words; many of his felicities could plainly not have come if there had not been, in the background, a habit of such interest" (274-75). Fielding writes:

> The novel has...a broad purpose even though it included references to some of Dickens's living contemporaries which most of them were unable to recognize, and satire of specific abuses which was too pointed to be understood by the general reader; and it is only by understanding this broader purpose (which is not so obvious that it can be taken for granted) that one can see how it unifies Dickens's remarks on Stephen Blackpool's marriage, the aesthetic theories of the 'third gentleman' in the second chapter, the problems of Trade Unionism, Louisa's marriage to Bounderby, and her brother's theft from the bank. Dickens once wrote that the ideas took him 'by the throat' and forced him to write...that he succeeded in giving them a unified purpose, and that *Hard Times* has coherence and power which deserve great respect even though it is not as entertaining as most of the other novels. (133)

6

Characters in *Hard Times*

MR. THOMAS GRADGRIND

In *Hard Times*, Dickens is possessed by a comprehensive vision, one in which the inhumanities of Victorian civilization are seen as fostered and sanctioned by a hard philosophy, the aggressive formulation of an inhumane spirit. The philosophy is represented by Thomas Gradgrind, Esquire, Member of Parliament for Coketown, who has brought up his children on the lines of the experience recorded by John Stuart Mill as carried out on himself. What Gradgrind stands for is, though repellent, nevertheless respectable; his Utilitarianism is a theory sincerely held and there is an intellectual disinterestedness in its application. Dickens here makes a just observation about the affinities and practical tendency of Utilitarianism, as, in his presentment of the Gradgrind home and the Gradgrind elementary school, he does about the Utilitarian spirit in Victorian education. One of the reasons why, in the fifties, Dickens's novels begin to show a greater complication of plot than before, is, according to Humphry House in the article "Hard Times" that "he was intending to use them as a vehicle of more concentrated sociological argument. All his journalism shows too that he was thinking much more about social problems, whereas earlier he had been content to feel mainly, and to record a thought, when it occurred, in emotional dress. The objection to such a character as Gradgrind is not just that he is a burlesque and an exaggeration—so are Squeers and Pecksniff—but rather that in him the satire is directed against a kind of thought..." (Dyson 215).

Gradgrind is Mr. Utilitarian: "A man of realities. A man of facts and calculations. A man who proceeds upon the principle that two and two are four, and nothing over...." With no allowances for the tender or susceptible emotions, Mr. Gradgrind conducts all the business of life practically, because this is the way one gets ahead, makes money, and becomes financially and socially successful according to Victorian standards. Mr. Gradgrind bows to Carlyle's God of Cash-Payment, and he intends to conduct his life and bring up his children according to his philosophy. Gradgrind is the only major Dickens character who is meant to be an 'intellectual': "His character was not unkind, all things considered; it might have been a very kind one indeed if he had only made some round mistake in the arithmetic that balanced it, years ago." Dickens was caught with the idea of a man like Gradgrind living by a certain philosophy. Humphry House wrote in "Hard Times" that Dickens obviously "felt during the fifties, when Public Health and Administrative Reform were keeping him so closely to social-political problems, that there must be some essential flaw in the reasoning of such a man as Bright. The character of Gradgrind is an attempt to track it down" (Dyson 215).

Gradgrind is a man of good instincts victimized by his own system. Mr. Gradgrind is shown as a man with a heart underneath his philosophy, for he aids Sissy. He betrays his initial kindness, ungenial enough, but properly rebuked by Bounderby, to Sissy. But Gradgrind's system is a dangerous nonsense. Although we are never led into a dramatic engagement with the conflict within Gradgrind's mind, he has an ego-investment in the Utilitarian calculus. In itself it is pure error, pure folly. Dickens's imaginative mode and symbolic methods do not function as devices for the critical exploration of a way of thinking or for the dramatization of a complex conflict of human interest. They function as the theatrical virtuoso's mode of execution of his powerfully simple refutation of the Utilitarian algebra. The confutation of

Utilitarianism by life is conducted with great subtlety. The inadequacy of his calculus in life is starkly exposed when he brings it to bear on the problem of marriage on the consummate scene with his eldest daughter:

> He waited, as if he would have been glad that she said something. But she said never a word.
>
> Louisa, my dear, you are the subject of a proposal of marriage that has been made to me.

Again he waited, and again she answered not one word. This so far surprised him as to induce him gently to repeat, "a proposal of marriage, my dear". To which she returned, without any visible emotion whatsoever:

> I hear you, father. I am attending, I assure you.

His embarrassment is caused by the perfect rationality with which she receives his overture. He is still more disconcerted when, with a completely dispassionate matter-of-factness that does credit to his *regime,* she gives him the opportunity to state in plain terms precisely what marriage should mean for the young Houyhnhnm. The instinct-free rationality of the emotionless Houyhnhnm is a void. Louisa proceeds to try and make him understand that she is a living creature, but it escapes Mr. Gradgrind. He marries Louisa to Josiah Bounderby, 'banker, merchant, manufacturer', about whom there is no disinterestedness whatever, and nothing to be respected.

Gradgrind sees the error of his ways after his children experience unhappiness or ruin because of his utilitarian philosophy. Louisa's relation with Harthouse is the first complication in the Gradgrind plot; Dickens handles it as he had occasionally done in the past, by showing his heroine on the verge of succumbing to temptation, but successfully resisting it at the last moment. Certainly Louisa's upbringing and her father's philosophy are of no help to her. Louisa pours forth her accusations from the pressure of self-realization, from a sense of wasted life: "All that I know is, your philosophy and your teaching will not save me.... Save me by some other means!" Gradgrind saw the pride of his heart and the triumph of his system, lying an insensible heap, at his feet. If in the beginning Mr. Gradgrind asserted the efficacy of education based on facts, the same teaching has boomeranged upon himself in the end when he realizes that the summation of his facts is going to crush his own daughter. Tom's bank robbery is the outcome of Gradgrind's aggressive formulation of an inhumane spirit. Gradgrind questions Tom as to the how and why of the bank robbery. Tom replies that a certain number of people holding positions of trust are bound to prove dishonest and that he is one of them: "The father buried his face in his hands, and the son stood in his disgraceful grotesqueness, biting straw..." (III, VII). His philosophy again boomeranged upon himself when Bitzer declined his request to free Tom and he questioned Bitzer's feelings:

> Bitzer, still holding the paralysed culprit by the collar, stood in the Ring, blinking at his old patron through the darkness of the twilight.
>
> "Bitzer", said Mr. Gradgrind, broken down and miserably submissive to him, "have you a heart?"
>
> "The circulation, Sir", returned Bitzer, smiling at the oddity of the question, "couldn't be carried on without one. No man, sir, acquainted with the facts established by Harvey relating to the circulation of the blood, can doubt that I have a heart." (III, VIII)

Bitzer's selfish interest regarding Tom's arrest explained itself the philosophy of Gradgrind:

> It was a fundamental principle of the Gradgrind philosophy, that everything was to be paid for. Nobody was ever on any account to give anybody anything, or render anybody help without purchase. Gratitude was to be abolished, and the virtues springing from it were not to be. Every inch of the existence of mankind, from birth to death, was to be a bargain across a counter. And if we didn't get to Heaven that way, it was not a politico-economical place, and we had no business there. (III, VIII)

Gradgrind is a class-name for the hard Victorian employer. Gradgrind is a Utilitarian seen by Dickens as one of the *feeloosofers* against whom Cobbett thundered, or as one of the *steam-engine intellects* described by Carlyle. Dickens has Mill's *Political Economy* (1849) very much in mind in his general indictment of the ideas which built and maintained Coketown. In condemning Thomas Gradgrind, the representative figure, we condemn the kind of thinking and the methods of enquiry and legislation which in fact promoted a large measure of social and industrial reform. One wonders, for example, what a typical Fabian feels when he is invited to condemn Gradgrind, not as an individual but as a type. Public commissions, Blue Books, Parliamentary legislation—all these, in the world of *Hard Times*—are Gradgrindery. Although Humphry House says in "Hard Times" that "...the satire of Mr. Gradgrind is comparatively ineffective, for Dickens is not even intending to attack the whole philosophy which he thought was represented in the Manchester men; he is only attacking the excessive emphasis on statistics..." (Dyson 217), F.R. Leavis observes: "Gradgrind, in the nature of the fable, has to *experience* the confutation of his philosophy, and to be capable of the change involved in admitting that life has proved him wrong" (262).

MR. BOUNDERBY

Ruskin calls Bounderby "a dramatic monster, instead of a characteristic example of a worldly master". Josiah Bounderby is the embodiment of the aggressive money-making and power-seeking ideal which was a driving force of the Industrial revolution. He is also a braggart, a liar and in general personally repellent. The conjunction of these personal defects with the aggressive ideal is not a necessary conjunction. A large part of the Victorian reader's feelings against Bounderby rests on the older and rather different feeling that trade, as such, is gross. The very name—and Dickens uses his names with conscious and obvious effect—incorporating *bounder*, incorporates this typical feeling. The social criticism represented by *bounder* is, after all, a rather different matter from the question of aggressive economic individualism. Bounderby, in his odd, inverted way, illustrates the principle of inner life and growth. Bounderby's story of character and industry triumphant is a sham; and his mock humility is a form of snobbery and pride. His relations with Mrs. Sparsit perfectly illustrate the real source of his feelings and his lies. The important point is that the low "down-to-earth" materialistic attitude takes its origin in an idealistic illusion.

The arch-hypocrite Bounderby in *Hard Times* wishes it to be believed, despite his perfectly secure childhood, that he fought his way up from the gutter. He employs Mrs. Sparsit, a fellow hypocrite posing as a great lady in reduced circumstances, so that he can feel superior to her fallen grandeur. Bounderby invents elaborate degradations for his own early years, and compares these with the imagined glories of the Sparsit past. In this way both hypocrites can draw satisfaction from completely fictitious accounts of themselves. "At a time when", says Bounderby, "to have been a tumbler in the mud of the streets, would have been a godsend to me, a prize in the lottery to me, you were at the Italian Opera. You were coming out of the Italian Opera, ma'am, in white satin and jewels, a blaze of splendour, when I hadn't a penny to buy a link to light you." "I certainly, sir", returned Mrs. Sparsit, with a dignity serenely mournful, "was familiar with the Italian Opera at a very early age". Adroitly Mrs. Sparsit embraces the grandeur and rejects the implication of relative seniority. Dickens's hypocrites are the prime beneficiaries of his inventive genius.

Mr. Gradgrind marries his eldest daughter to Bounderby, 'banker, merchant, manufacturer', about whom there is no disinterestedness whatever, and nothing to be respected. Bounderby is Victorian 'rugged individualism' in its grossest and most intransigent form. Concerned with nothing but self-assertion and power and material success, he has no interest in ideals or ideas—except the idea of being the completely self-made man.

> Utilitarian economists, skeletons of schoolmasters, commissioners of Fact, genteel and used-up infidels,

> gabblers of many little dog's-eared creeds, the poor you will have always with you. Cultivate in them, while there is yet time, the utmost graces of the fancies and affections to adorn their lives so much in need of ornament; or, in the day of your triumph when romance is utterly driven out of their souls, and they and a bare existence stand face to face, Reality will take a wolfish turn and make an end of you.

'A wolfish turn...' for Reality, as for Fancy, since the two may, after all, be inseparably linked. The most astonishing, though not of course the most painful, manifestation of this theme in *Hard Times* concerns Bounderby and Mrs. Sparsit in their domestic life. Bounderby, whose war to the death with Fancy is the ruination of the woman he chooses to marry, turns out to be a creature of Fancy himself. His one flight of Fancy turns out to be the lie about his upbringing, and the curious game of inverted snobbery which he plays out with Mrs. Sparsit's ironic help. Both live out a fantasy, mutually satisfying to their snobbery, and satisfying also—to Mrs. Sparsit, anyway—to some darkly sardonic streak below. In fact, both of them come from almost precisely the same kind of background—middle to lower middle class—and their respective roles represent nothing so much as an exquisitely balanced marriage of untrue minds. The Powler who is a 'born lady' is a fitting trophy for the Bounderby who has risen from nowhere precisely because both are a sordid sham. It is this game, however, which justifies Bounderby's treatment of all his hands, including Stephen, and which underlies his one habitual flight of verbal imagery: "I know 'em all pretty well. I always tell that man, whoever he is, that I know what he means. He means turtle soup and venison, with a gold spoon, and that he wants to be set up with a coach and six." The robber Fancy returns for revenge in his minimal and irreducible form of a brutal lie. Even by brutal standards, moreover, Bounderby exemplifies egotism in its most coarsely paradoxical garb: "No, by George! I don't forget that I am Josiah Bounderby of Coketown. For years upon years, the only pictures in my possession, or that I could have got into my possession by any means unless I stole 'em, were the engravings of a man shaving himself in a boot, on the blacking bottles that I was overjoyed to use in cleaning boots with, and that I sold when they were empty for a farthing apiece, and glad to get it!"

Bounderby is an even more vicious portrait of the hardhearted capitalist than was Scrooge. Mr. Bounderby is part of the Louisa-Harthouse triangle, but he also has a separate course of action, based upon his relationship to his housekeeper, Mrs. Sparsit. In a non-theatrical novel we might not be so easily satisfied that Bounderby is the bosom-friend of Gradgrind, who comes to us defined as a man of goodwill. In *Hard Times*, Gradgrind's relationship to Bounderby means that he is the victim of his own system, which hides his own instincts from himself. Although Gradgrind's heart sometimes softens, Bounderby's is a relentless case. Bounderby's ever-contemptuous attitude towards Sissy is a contrast to that of Sleary who really feels a paternal interest in her. When Bounderby sharply says to Sissy that her father has absconded and deserted her, some of the members of the circus troupe mutter words like 'shame', 'brute' as a protest against Bounderby's way of talking to an unhappy girl. After the Harthouse episode, when Louisa was staying at Stone Lodge, Gradgrind asked Bounderby to allow Louisa a period of repose and reflection at Stone Lodge, for a gradual alteration for the better in many respects. Bounderby took the suggestion as an insult to him. He blustered that if Louisa would not return to his house by twelve o'clock at noon the next day, he would send her clothes and so forth over at Stone Lodge and Gradgrind would have to take charge of her permanently for the future. Accordingly, the next day, he directed Mrs. Bounderby's property to be carefully packed up and sent to Stone Lodge. He advertised his country house for sale by private contract. He then resumed, what might be called, a bachelor life. Bounderby also has a mother he is ashamed of, and there is a small intrigue which shows her visiting Coketown on occasion just to look at her son from a distance. Bounderby thus illustrates false pride as well as a lack of filial affection. He is exposed at the end as having fabricated much of the story he tells about his youth and the lack of opportunities afforded him in his climb to fortune and power. In the final chapter we come to know that Bounderby died in a fit in the Coketown street.

The overthrow of Bounderby is a simple enough business. Dickens's methods here are the traditional ones which we are familiar with from, for instance, Fielding's account of the overthrow of Thwackum and Square in *Tom Jones*. But it took no miracle of flexibility on Dickens's part to 'reconcile' this kind of characterization with central fable of his novel, for the completely successful rendering of Gradgrind's self-discovery is not notably more complex and more inward than the rendering of Bounderby.

SISSY JUPE

Sissy Jupe, the tumbler's child in *Hard Times*, belongs to a long line of Dickens's heroines whose influence is universally benevolent. From the time Sissy appears in the novel she is identified with heavenly light, described as 'irradiated Sissy'. She is shown in different relationships and through various trials in this novel. Dickens's first presentation of Sissy Jupe is worth quoting:

> The square finger, moving here and there, lighted suddenly on Bitzer, perhaps because he chanced to sit in the same ray of sunlight which, darting in at one of the bare windows of the intensely whitewashed room, irradiated Sissy. For, the boys and girls sat on the face of the inclined plane in two compact bodies, divided up the centre by a narrow interval; and Sissy, being at the corner of a row on the sunny side, came in for the beginning of a sunbeam, of which Bitzer, being at the corner of a row on the other side, a few rows in advance, caught the end. But, whereas the girl was so dark-eyed and dark-haired, that she seemed to receive a deeper and more lustrous colour from the sun, when it shone upon her, the boy was so light-eyed and light-haired that the self-same rays appeared to draw out of him what little colour he ever possessed. (I, II)

There is no need to insist on the force—representative of Dickens's art in general in *Hard Times*—with which the moral and spiritual differences are rendered here in terms of sensation, so that the symbolic intention emerges out of metaphor and the vivid evocation of the concrete. What may, perhaps, be emphasized is that Sissy stands for vitality as well as goodness—they are seen, in fact, as one; she is generous, impulsive life, finding self-fulfilment in self-forgetfulness—all that is the antithesis of calculating self-interest. Dickens forgot about Sissy Jupe's lustrous dark eyes and dark hair for a good reason—good in terms of the Dickens theatre. What he had in mind as Sissy's further career could not be conveniently adjusted to the earlier, vivid registration of her 'vital impulse'. Sissy can't define a horse, though she belongs to Sleary's horse-riders, whereas Bitzer knows it's a graminivorous quadruped with forty teeth. Sissy's quiet potency makes a significant—and of course effective—contrast with the aggressiveness and bluster of Gradgrind and Bounderby, the tension of Louisa, the sullenness of the whelp, Tom. Nor do Sissy's actions—consisting as they do mostly of nursing, receiving confidences, understanding, and being patient—strike us as inept or trivial or sentimental manifestations of what is lacking in the Utilitarian home.

Louisa and Sissy become friends and their relation grows deeper when the latter comes to stay at Stone Lodge. She introduces herself as Sissy Jupe. Gradgrind takes offence at this version of her given name and insists that she is properly called Cecelia. Sissy tells story of her life to Louisa, her love of her father, she even speaks despairingly regarding her scanty progress at school and her stories move the heart of Louisa to pity and sympathy:

> Father, soon after they came home from performing, told Merrylegs to jump up on the backs of the two chairs and stand across them—which is one of his tricks. He looked at father and didn't do it at once. Everything of father's had gone wrong that night, and he hadn't pleased the public at all. He cried out that the very dog knew he was failing, and had no compassion on him.

> Then he beat the dog, and I was frightened, and said, 'Father, father! Pray don't hurt the creature who is so fond of you! O Heaven forgive you, father, stop!' And he stopped, and the dog was bloody, and father lay down crying on the floor with the dog in his arms, and the dog licked his face.
>
> Louisa saw that she was sobbing; and going to her, kissed her, took her hand, and sat down beside her. (*HT*. I, IX)

Louisa's friendliness however turns into utter coldness when Sissy disapproves of Louisa's marriage with a much older man than herself. She "had turned her head and looked, in wonder, in pity, in sorrow, in doubt, in multitudes of emotions towards Louisa". From then onwards Sissy is kept by Louisa at a distance. However, Sissy never wavers in her affection towards Louisa but remains loyal to her.

Dickens exposes the fallacy of the Utilitarian system of education through the character of Sissy. Her answers to the questions, though not factual, have a core of truth in them. When she is asked if the Nation is prosperous, her answer is that she cannot know whether it is a prosperous nation or not unless she knows who has got the money and whether any of it belongs to her. Gradgrind, though dissatisfied with her answers, has some kind of affection for her chiefly because she has become very useful to his household and an incalculable help for tending his ailing wife. As a matter of fact, it is Sissy, who with her instinctive goodness, vitality and a fund of goodwill and benevolence for all, brings sunshine to the gloomy atmosphere of the Gradgrind family. Indeed, Sissy is most vividly portrayed and as F.R. Leavis said: "She is the most crucial character in the novel because she not only offers a commentary on the Utilitarian philosophy but also a corrective to it." When the married Louisa comes on a short visit to see her ailing mother she finds her younger sister Jane grown up differently from her due to the guiding influence of Sissy. After her marriage has been wrecked Louisa returns to 'Stone Lodge' in a miserable condition. Sissy begs her permission to attend upon her and she nurses her back to the normal rhythm of life. Louisa, deeply affected by the sisterly kindness of Sissy, senses her unspoken, anxious sympathy and reproach when their eyes meet and her pride makes her eyes withdraw. Thus, Louisa is able at last to be receptive to Sissy.

There are two persons in *Hard Times*, Louisa Gradgrind and Sissy Jupe, who are serious throughout. But Sissy is nothing if not natural; and though Sissy is as true to nature in her character as Mrs. Sparsit, she "speaks like a book" in the most intolerable sense of the words. In her interview with Mr. Harthouse, her unconscious courage and simplicity, and his hopeless defeat by them, are quite natural and right; and the contrast between the humble girl of the people and the smart sarcastic man of the world whom she so completely vanquishes is excellently dramatic; "but Dickens has allowed himself," as G.B. Shaw writes in his article "Hard Times", "to be carried away by the scene into a ridiculous substitution of his own most literary and least colloquial style for any language that could conceivably be credited to Sissy."

Sissy Jupe, who might be taken for a merely conventional *persona,* has already, as a matter of fact, been established in a potently symbolic role: she is part of the poetically creative operation of Dickens's genius in *Hard Times*. Sissy's symbolic significance is bound up with that of Sleary's Horse-riding where human kindness is very insistently associated with vitality. Sissy is serene, and survives the Gradgrind onslaught upon her vitality. Sissy points the irony, of course, of Gradgrind's system, particularly when her answers on political economy, drawn straight from the Sermon of the Mount, cover her with schoolroom disgrace. Sissy is not consciously quoting from scripture—the effect would be destroyed if one supposed this—and Dickens shows that uncorrupted nature and the New Testament speak with one voice. She does shame Mr. Harthouse into leaving the neighbourhood just as Louisa seems on the verge of joining him, and she helps Tom escape when he is about to be arrested for stealing, sending him to the circus where Mr. Sleary, the owner, conceals him and gets him safely abroad. The role of one who soothes and cures is to be a major one for Sissy. Sissy, like a character in a morality play, illustrates all the ideas opposite from the utilitarian philosophy taught at school. Dr. Leavis regards the whole characterization of Sissy as an unqualified success:

> A general description of her part in the fable might suggest the worst, but actually she has nothing in common with Little Nell: she shares in the strength of the Horse-riding. She is wholly convincing in the function Dickens assigns to her.... (*The Great Tradition* 235)

STEPHEN BLACKPOOL

Dickens was a champion of social realism and was gifted with a humanitarian zeal and a reforming spirit. The bitter curse of poverty which he had experienced in his early youth had made him acutely sensitive to the miseries of the poor and the working masses. In many of his novels, his heart is seen to bleed in sympathy for the downtrodden and the exploited class of people. *David Copperfield*, *Nicholas Nickleby*, *Great Expectations*, *A Tale of Two Cities*—all these novels owe much of their appeal to the deeply moving picture they contain of the utterly miserable condition of the lives of the poor and working people. *Hard Times,* the very title of which implies that it is steeped in the spirit of social realism, also brings out Dickens's sympathy for the poor and the downtrodden mainly through his depiction of Coketown and his portrayal of the life of Stephen Blackpool. In the works of early fifties of the 19th century, the idea of muddle was spreading over wider and wider social fields. *Hard Times* came out between April and August 1854, and Stephen Blackpool's reiterated comment, "Tis a muddle" is superficially the least hopeful moral to be got from any novel Dickens wrote. If Macaulay condemned *Hard Times* as 'sullen socialism' and Mr. Edwin Pugh called it 'dry', hard, Dickens said of it himself that he had not meant to write a new story for a year, when the idea laid hold of him by the throat in a very violent manner. Dickens was a good deal influenced by Mary Barton in writing *Hard Times* and it is one of Dickens's most thought-about books.

The novelty in *Hard Times* is not in the sufferings of the victims or the wickedness of their tormentors, but in the arid waste of their hearts and lives. Like Louisa, Stephen is defeated in his attempt to do good (as indeed is Rachael) and he enjoys no inward peace arising from pure intentions and duty done. Emptiness is embodied in Stephen's laboured and stately rhetoric—which, whether or not it is true to dialect, is true to the man. Stephen says life is 'aw a muddle'. He has an unhappy married life with his drunkard wife and loves Rachael, but he finds the expenses of the divorce laws proceedings too high to let him divorce his wife and marry Rachael. Bounderby, his master, does not help him in this matter; instead, he frightens him by saying that divorce is only for rich men. The novel comes close at one point to being a tract for divorce reform, but this possibility is not, in the end, pursued. Stephen refuses to join Union as he has given his word to Rachael that he will not do so. Treated as an outcast by his mates, he is approached by Bounderby who, assuming that he is on the side of the employers, questions him about 'the set of rascals and rebels' who have joined the Tribunal. Stephen defends them by saying that they believe they are doing their duty by each other in banding themselves together for protection. Stephen delivers a speech which has little profundity, but is inspired by sincere emotion:

> Deed we are in a muddle, Sir. Look around town—so rich as 'tis—and see the numbers o' people as has been broughten into bein heer, fur to weave, an to card, an to piece out a living, aw the same one way, somehows, twixt their cradles and their graves. Look how we live, an wheer we live, an in what numbers, an by what chances, and wi' what sameness; and look how the mills is awlus a goin, and how they never works us no nigher to any dis'ant object-ceptin awlus, Death. ...Who can look on 't, sir, and fairly tell a man 'tis not a muddle? (II, V)

Like Louisa, Stephen loses his reputation when he is cast off by his fellow workers and then by his employer for disloyalty. Advertised for as a suspected accomplice in the Bounderby bank robbery (really carried out by young Gradgrind), he disappears and is found at the bottom of a disused mine-shaft by Rachael. He recognizes her, requests her to clear his name and then dies. Since it is Stephen who is used by Tom Gradgrind in his scheme to shift responsibility for the theft from the bank, Stephen is connected with the Gradgrind sequence of the plot.

Stephen is shown almost falling into evil, as if to fulfil some curse upon his life. The night when Stephen is racked by his terrible dream of weddings and gallows, and wakes or half-wakes as his drunken wife reaches towards the poison bottle, is the most nightmarish stretch of the book. His wife is saved only by Rachael, to whom Stephen confesses the murder in his heart. It seems, then, that Stephen comes close to joining the ranks of murderers in Dickens's works, who are depicted as either totally mad, or wicked, or at the very least as driven distracted by lust or pride. But Stephen avoids the path of Edith Dombey, Miss Wade, Miss Havisham and so many other Dickens people, who nourish bitterness in their hearts and embark on darkly destructive and self-destructive paths of revenge. Stephen keeps alive some pure love for Rachael. When he is cast out, he takes to the road, with nothing but Rachael's blessing to lighten his way. He is able to preserve some citadel of good in the inner self, even with circumstances wholly against him and no sustaining ease of conscience in his life. Dickens examines the problem of suffering and of God's nature in a specifically Christian context. Stephen Blackpool, who represents the case of man crucified by the contemporary world, puts the tragic irony of the situation:

> How 'tis...that what is best in us folk, seems to turn us most to trouble an' misfort'n an' mistake, I dunno. But 'tis so. I know 'tis, as I know the heavens is over me ahint the smoke. We're patient too, an' wants in general to do right. An' I canna think the fawt is aw wi' us.

In his notes, Dickens plans a Christian answer: "STEPHEN AND RACHAEL Bear and forbear The star that leads the way" (Chap. XXXIV). Stephen is able to attain a Christian view of forbearance returned for suffering, which transcends his earlier concept of providence, through the star of diving guidance with its strong New Testament associations:

> "It ha' shined upon me", he said reverently, "in my pain and trouble down below. It ha' shined into my mind. I ha' look'n at it an thowt o' thee, Rachael, till the muddle in my mind have cleared awa, above a bit, I hope." (III, VI)

The muddle turns out to have been only in Stephen's mind, a paranoid delusion of a persecuting fate. It is dispelled by a compassionate Christian love which is also enlightenment. As Sucksmith writes in *The Narrative Art of Charles Dickens*: "The irony was a double one. Stephen was deceived in thinking that providence was cruelly ironic. Unfortunately, the solution, which is expressed with the conventional, sometimes the sentimental, Christian feeling of Dickens's time, fails to convince us. It is much less impressive than that other vision of malevolent energy at work in the universe which is usually fresh and compelling in Dickens's fiction and points to a deeper conviction" (356).

Stephen Blackpool is victimized by the fall-outs of *Laissez Faire* and utilitarian system as propounded by J.S. Mill and Jeremy Bentham respectively. The kind of self-respecting steadiness and conscientious restraint that he represents in Stephen did certainly exist on a large scale among the working-classes, and this is an important historical fact. In Stephen Dickens tried to rescue the idea of personality in an individual industrial worker. Stephen's successive defeats by the Law, by the Trade Union, and by his employer might have become the material of genuine tragedy, if Dickens had been prepared to accept his death from the beginning as inevitable and unanswerable; but he was hankering all the time after a way to avoid the proper tragic solution, and the result is nothing but a slow record of inglorious misery and defeat. Humphry House says in "Hard Times":

> Dickens did not want to admit that Stephen's bargaining power—whether against Bounderby, his marriage, or life itself—was negligible, but wrote as if there might be an unexpected solution at every turn. There is no difficulty about Stephen's relation of the Law or about his relation to Bounderby; the true crux is in the part

> of the plot that deals with the Trade Union, and in making it so Dickens was apparently trying to work out, in the actual writing of the book, the implications of his old ideal of man to man benevolence in the relations between employers and labour in large-scale industry. (Dyson 216)

The sincerity of Dickens's social feeling is not to be called in doubt. Few men have been so vividly struck as he was by the sufferings of the poor, by the unfairness of fate, and by the frequent cruelty of privileged people. Dickens in *Hard Times* questions the social and judicial systems, and attacks the industrial organization in which the worker has nothing to do but mind a machine with no variety of work or psychological outlet in the form of, say, in the running of the concern, in which productivity is pursued at the expense of human satisfaction he is supposed to serve. We have sentimentality in Stephen whose perfect patience under infliction is supremely edifying and irresistibly touching as the agonies are piled on for his martyrdom. Stephen does justice to his name through his holy character as Dickens took the name from the Bible in which Stephen is the name of a holy saint.

LOUISA

Dickens in *Hard Times* planned three separate plot sequences for *Hard Times*, each of them presenting opportunities for development and contrast. His main action was to centre around Thomas Gradgrind, a retired wholesale hardware merchant who had become a member of Parliament. In the line of action Louisa, Tom, and Sissy carry the main action. Louisa is something of a breakthrough for Dickens, escaping the two categories of pure maid and frump. The Victorian effort to restrict the role of women to such stereotypes, both in fiction and in real life, suggests a lurking awareness of woman's threat to male supremacy. The woman must be constrained to certain kinds of servitude—domestic pet, angel, mother, clown—to meet the male's need for entertainment or spiritual uplift. But behind the man-made categories women were waiting to get out—women with talents and intellects which the nineteenth century stifled. It is worthwhile to quote John Carey:

> The phenomenon of woman expecting to be treated, in political or intellectual matters, as if she were a normal human being, provoked Dickens, in real life, to sportive derision: "she has found out that she ought to go and vote at elections; ought to be competent to sit in Parliament; ought to be able to enter the learned professions—the army and navy, too, I believe". For a woman to 'go out speechifying', besides being preposterous in itself, was to forfeit the 'hold' upon her husband which shrinking femininity could naturally reckon on. His own wife's bids to broaden her mind, he treated with little respect. 'Kate wants to know whether you have "any books to send her"', he wrote to Forster. 'If you have any literary rubbish on hand, please to shoot it here.' (162)

Louisa Gradgrind in *Hard Times* is an exceptional Dickensian heroine because she has some inkling of the more passionate side of marriage and is even prepared to talk about it. That seems to be what she is referring to in an interview with her father where they discuss her forthcoming marriage to Bounderby, though the phrasing is veiled enough for the modest reader to miss the point if he wishes. Louisa, having failed repeatedly to get her father to acknowledge the need for love in marriage, stares out of the window at the factory chimneys of Coketown so fixedly that he asks her why she's looking at them.

> "There seems to be nothing there but languid and monotonous smoke. Yet when the night comes, Fire bursts out, father!" she answered, turning quickly.
>
> "Of course I know that, Louisa. I do not see the application of the remark."

This is a new kind of frankness, even if it escapes Mr. Gradgrind and a new kind of woman. Having no outlet for her emotional life except in her love for her brother, she lives for him, and marries Bounderby—under pressure from

Tom—for Tom's sake ('What does it matter?'). Thus, by the constrictions and starvations of the Gradgrind *regime,* are natural affection and capacity for disinterested devotion turned to ill. The vacuum in Louisa's life comes to be filled by Harthouse who, produced by a background wholly unlike Coketown, has nonetheless arrived at a philosophy of life congruent with hers. Harthouse's careless hedonism, nurtured on leisure, boredom and cynicism, is in one wholly surprising way the mirror-image of Gradgrind's world. In her extreme temptation, Louisa summons up the will to flee to her father and seek protection.

The temptation of Louisa is the first complication in the Gradgrind plot. It is natural that Louisa, having sacrificed herself for this unrepaying object of affection, should be found not altogether unresponsive when Harthouse, having sized up the situation, pursues his opportunity with well-bred and calculating tact. Dickens handles it as he had occasionally done in some other novels, by showing his heroine on the verge of succumbing to temptation, but successfully resisting it at the last moment. This is a sensitive spot in the Victorian novel, since writers had to treat adultery as a sin more abominable than they probably really thought it, and no fictional adulteress could expect forgiveness, or even survival, after the act. In this book, Dickens proclaims that marriages are not made in heaven, and that those which are not confirmed there, should be dissolved. When, fleeing from temptation, she arrives back at her father's house, she tells him her plight. She looks colourless, despairing and defined. Without any introduction she accuses her father of imparting wrong education to her. Louisa curses the hour in which she was born. She says that her father's education through which she had been brought up has taken away the graces of her soul, the sentiments of her heart and the bliss of life: "What have you done, O father, what have you done, with the garden that should have bloomed once, in this great wilderness here?" She says that what he had never nurtured in her had never nurtured in himself. If he had only neglected her, she would have been a much better and much happier creature. On hearing this, after all his care, Mr. Gradgrind bows his head upon his hand and groans aloud. Louisa says that had she been allowed to exercise fancy of the heart, she should have been "a million times wiser, happier, more loving, more contented, more innocent and human in all good respects" than her present state of being. She has almost repulsed and crushed her better angel into a demon: "What I have learned has left me doubting, misbelieving, despising, regretting, what I have not learned; and my dismal resource has been to think that life would soon go by, and that nothing in it could be worth the pain and trouble of a contest."

In fact, Gradgrind's guidance and instructions have ultimately connected Louisa with death and led her to deviation from the path of moral uprightness. So, she is desperate, direct and trenchant in her criticism of the Gradgrindery system of education. This is evident in her speech in which she bluntly and directly accuses her father: "All that I know is, your philosophy and your teaching will not save me." She suggests very poignantly that her growth has been a constant straying away from her essential nature. Not only that she has not been provided with the mental pabulum, even the basic human element of 'wonder' has been stifled in her. Her utilitarian and irrevocable marriage to Mr. Bounderby has proved fatal. She complains that her father proposed her husband to her, and she married him. She never made a pretence to Bounderby or her father that she loved Bounderby. She was not wholly indifferent, for she had a hope of being pleasant and useful to Tom. Tom had been the subject of all the little tenderness of her life; perhaps he became so because she knew so well how to pity him. Louisa resumes that when she was irrevocably married, there rose up into rebellion against the tie, the old strife, made fiercer by all those causes of disparity which arose out of the two individual natures, and which no general laws would ever rule or state for her. At last Louisa comes to confess that this has encouraged the young man Harthouse to exploit the situation in his favour. She has escaped with her honour but the vexation of her temporary slip is so agonising that it seems unbearable. No word from her father has the power to console her as she faints up on the ground before his ashy eyes. The "metallurgical Louisa" realizes herself and gets obfuscated to find no meaning in her present identity. This feeling of frustration is fraught with some tragic potentiality because Louisa pours forth her accusations from the pressure of self-realization, from a sense of wasted life.

It becomes apparent that Louisa's spirit, as it matures in Coketown under its educative influences, finds its dismal reflection almost equally in Harthouse and in Stephen Blackpool: in Harthouse, whose libertinism is the fruit of a similar emptiness and boredom, and in Blackpool, whose crushed decency she can admire but not reach over or connect with barriers of class. All Louisa's relationships or attempted relationships develop a horrifying logic, bred in the desolation of her heart. Between herself and her father there is an insuperable barrier, which extends naturally enough to her relationship with Bounderby when she is delivered over to him as wife. She tries to help Blackpool, and succeeds in ruining him—through the treachery of a worthless brother who is the recipient, nonetheless, of her only real love. Harthouse almost ruins her as part of a normal libertine's strategy, yet she experiences with him her only illusion of requited love. There is the further desolating fact that she is unfitted for the one relationship of ordinary friendship which could have helped her. Sissy's tenderness is repulsed because of a moment's pity and amazement, which Louisa, understandably, cannot accept. The novelty in *Hard Times* is not in the sufferings of the victims or the wickedness of their tormentors, but in the arid waste of their hearts and lives. Louisa and Stephen are defeated in their attempt to do good (as indeed is Rachael) and enjoy no inward peace arising from pure intentions and duty done. Emptiness is embodied in Louisa's speech habits, formal even when she is with her brother or her lover.

In the final chapter of the novel, Louisa is "watching the fire as in the days of yore, though with a gentler and a humbler face". The question "How much of the future might arise before her vision?" is answered in a long series of noun fragments and participles in an overall present tense of anticipated futurity, which foresees in the fire, among other things, Louisa "grown learned in childish lore" and dedicating herself, on behalf of Sissy's children, to "those imaginative graces and delights, without which the heart of infancy will wither up". Louisa is a figure of poetic tragedy, and the reader is likely to sympathize with her difficulties.

TOM

With no allowances for the tender or susceptible emotions, Mr. Gradgrind conducts all the business of life practically, because this is the way one gets ahead, makes money, and becomes financially and socially successful according to Victorian standards. Mr. Gradgrind bows to Carlyle's God of Cash-Payment, and he intends to conduct his life and bring up his children according to his philosophy. As for Tom, the *regime* has made of him a bored and sullen whelp, and "he was becoming that not unprecedented triumph of calculation which is usually at work on number one"—the Utilitarian philosophy has done that for him. According to the overall pattern of *Hard Times*, Tom and Louisa are to act as indices of the failure of Mr. Gradgrind's philosophy of education, and should thus never be allowed to stray aside the area of our pity, since they are both victims rather than free agents. But Tom's actions take him beyond the readers' pity, and diminish the interest of his character.

Tom is presented as selfish, ill-natured, sensual, and completely mercenary. Tom said that Louisa was the only pleasure he had. Tom's disgust against Fact and Figures is evident as he says, "I wish I could collect all the Facts we hear so much about...and all the Figures, and all the people who found them out: and I wish I could put a thousand barrels of gunpowder under them, and blow them all up together!" He expressed his hope that when he would go to live with Bounderby, he would have his revenge. He would enjoy a little, and go about and see something, and hear something. Louisa said that Mr. Bounderby thought as their father thought, and was a great deal rougher, and not half so kind. Tom said that he knew very well how to manage and smooth Bounderby.

Louisa was his tram-card: "It's you. You are his little pet, you are his favourite; he'll do anything for you. When he says to me what I don't like, I shall say to him, 'My sister Loo will be hurt and disappointed', Mr. Bounderby." He declares that when he goes to live with Bounderby as having a post in the bank, 'he'll have his revenge'.—"I mean I'll enjoy myself a little, and go about and see something and hear something. I'll recompense myself for the way in which I've been brought up." He is employed as a clerk in the bank owned by his sister's husband, Mr. Bounderby, and eventually steals money from the bank in order to cover his debts contracted in dissipation and idleness. His descent into debt and bank-robbery is natural. He contrives a scheme to throw the blame on Stephen, a workman in Mr. Bounderby's factory, and the resulting action which establishes Stephen's innocence and fixes the blame properly on Tom brings the novel to its conclusion.

More in the tradition of Cracker's parrot is the scene where Tom Gradgrind sits on the terrace with Harthouse, picking roses and tearing them to pieces with his teeth. The sorry state of Tom's soul, implied by such behaviour, is fully explained in the later interview between Louisa Gradgrind and her father, when she strikes herself on the bosom and asks "what have you done O father, what have you done, with the garden that should have bloomed once, in this great wilderness here!".

"Whelp" is a cliché, and the word was first used by Harthouse, and then adopted by the novelist in his authorial capacity. David Lodge says that when a novelist does this, it is usually with ironical intent, suggesting some inadequacy in the speaker's habits of thought. Dickens plays on Gradgrind's "facts" to this effect. But in the case of Harthouse's "whelp" he has taken a moral cliché from Tom who is morally unreliable, and invested it with his own authority as narrator. This gives away the fact that Tom is being forced into a new role halfway through the novel. For Tom's degeneration should be related to the major problems with which Dickens is concerned in the novel.

Tom, is the centre, is sardonic comedy, imagined with great intensity and done with the sure touch of genius. There is the pregnant scene in which Mr. Gradgrind, in the deserted ring of a third-rate travelling circus, has to recognize his son in a comic negro servant; and has to recognize that his son owes his escape from justice to a peculiarly disinterested gratitude—to the opportunity given him to assume such a disguise by the non-Utilitarian Mr. Sleary, grateful for Sissy's sake: "In a preposterous coat, like a beadle's, with cuffs and flaps exaggerated to an unspeakable extent; in an immense waistcoat, knee breeches, buckled shoes, and a mad cocked-hat; with nothing fitting him and everything of coarse material, moth-eaten and full of holes; with seams in his black face, where fear and heat had started through the greasy composition daubed all over it; anything so grimly, detestably, ridiculously shameful as the whelp in his comic livery, Mr. Gradgrind never could by any other means have believed in, weighable and measurable fact though it was. And one of his model children had come to this!" (III, VII). Gradgrind questions Tom as to the how and why of the bank robbery. Tom replies that a certain number of people holding positions of trust are bound to prove dishonest and that he is one of them:

> The father buried his face in his hands, and the son stood in his disgraceful grotesqueness, biting straw: his hands, with the black partly worm away inside, looking like the hands of a monkey. The evening was fast closing in; and from time to time, he turned the whites of his eyes restlessly and impatiently towards his father. They were the only parts of his face that showed any life or expression, the pigment upon it was so thick. (III, VII)

Tom says that he had had the key that was found, made long before. He did not take the money all at once and he had been stealing money in small sums from time to time. This revenging attitude in the case of Tom Gradgrind is even prepared for earlier in the novel, when Tom explains that he has been treated for so long as a mule or donkey that "I should like to kick like one" (I, VIII).

Tom was feeling happy that he would be sent abroad because he was feeling miserable in the circus. The note of ironic satiric discomfiture of the Utilitarian philosopher by the rebound of his formulae upon himself is developed in the ensuing scene with Bitzer, the truly successful pupil, the real triumph of the system. He arrives to intercept Tom's flight. Sleary forged a stratagem, involving an intelligent dog, which succeeded in getting Tom off to Liverpool. He pretended to be on Bitzer's side and said that he would have Tom and Bitzer conveyed to the railway station. While they were in Sleary's carriage, the trained horse started dancing at a signal from the carriage-driver, without moving an inch further, and it oblized Bitzer to get down. One of the trained circus-dogs then took charge of Bitzer and would not let him move a step in any direction. Tom's escape is contrived, successfully in every sense, by means belonging to Dickensian high-fantastic comedy. And there follows the solemn moral of the whole fable, put with the rightness of genius into Mr. Sleary's asthmatic mouth.

MR. SLEARY

Dickens was a life-long champion of amusement. Many of the issues on which his voice is clearest, his opposition to teetotalism and Sabbath laws, became clear to him precisely because of his Sleary philosophy of life. When Dickens sees, as he sees so readily, the common manifestations of human kindness, and the essential virtues, asserting themselves in the midst of ugliness, squalor and banality, his warmly sympathetic response has no disgust to overcome. There is no suggestion, for instance, of recoil—or of distance-keeping—from the game-eyed, brandy-soaked, flabby-surfaced Mr. Sleary, who is successfully made to figure for us a humane, anti-Utilitarian positive. Dickens opens *Hard Times* with Sleary's Circus in which the natural goodness and generosity of members of the troupe are displayed; he closes the novel with an act of kindness shown by Sleary to the very magnates who regard his troupe as vagabonds and their entertainment as a time-and-money-wasting opportunity for their operatives.

Mr. Sleary, the circus proprietor, is undoubtedly an able organizer and a kind-hearted man.

Mr. Sleary is a stout man, with one fixed eye, and one loose eye, a voice "like the efforts of a broken old pair of bellows, a flabby surface, and a muddled head which was never sober and never drunk" (I, VI). He is troubled with asthma, and his breath comes "far too thick and heavy for the letters". The kindness of the horse-riding is embodied chiefly in the figure of Sleary, and we are accordingly conscious mostly of the meanings enforced by his character. The circus party is marked by fellow-feeling and there is an untiring readiness to help and pity one another. Mr. Sleary really feels a paternal interest in Sissy and this attitude is contrasted with Bounderby's contemptuous attitude. Sissy's father who finds himself unable any longer to amuse the audience, runs away, leaving his daughter to an uncertain fate. The vitality of the circus people has nicely been conveyed through their association with animals like dog and horse. Mr. Sleary has a simple philosophy of life. He says that people must be amused, they are not machines to do work all the time. In his lisping manner what he says is that circus-shows make life worthwhile by creating fun and entertainment. In addition to learning and working, common people need some diversion also. The concluding words of Mr. Sleary, with their emphasis on amusement are as follows:

> ...Don't be croth with uth poor vagabondth. People mutht be amuthed. They can't alwayth be a learning, nor yet they can't be alwayth a working, they an't made for it. You *mutht* have uth, Thquire. Do the withe thing and the kind thing too, and make the betht of uth; not the wurtht! (III, VIII)

The scenes in which Sleary helps Gradgrind get Tom out of the country derive their meaning from the eminently theatrical contrast between practical hard-headed Gradgrind, now menaced by his prize-pupil Bitzer and sloppy, lisping Sleary. He has his natural resourcefulness to tackle a critical situation. Dickens's point is the surprising *practicality* of the incompetent-seeming Sleary, and the surprising *usefulness* of the horse that can dance the polka. This does not in any important way *feel* inconsistent with Dickens's earlier view of the Horse-riding which emphasizes, as Dr. Leavis points out, the fact that the skills of the Horse-riding contain their end within themselves and are therefore 'wasteful' in terms of Gradgrind's algebra. The broad-hearted Sleary offers a contrast to the money-minded brutes like Bounderby. When Gradgrind offers Sleary some money he declines the offer. He accepts only a five-pound note for Mr. Childers who is a family man and asks him to buy a collar for the dog and a belt for the horse. The final scenes focus emphatically on Sissy's richness and luster and the Horse-riding's triumphant activity. Dickens keeps his symbolic intentions continuously in hand throughout the moral fable.

Sleary and his circus troupe express vital human impulse, and they minister to vital human needs. The horse-riding, frowned upon as frivolous and wasteful by Gradgrind and malignantly scorned by Bounderby, brings the machine-hands of Coketown what they are starved of. It brings to them, not merely amusement, but art, and the spectacle of triumphant activity that, seeming to contain its end within itself, is, in its easy mastery, joyously self-justified. Through the character of Sleary, which represents the fundamental qualities of the circus troupe, Dickens expresses a profounder reaction to industrialism than might have been expected of him.

MR. JAMES HARTHOUSE

Dickens's understanding of Victorian civilization and his moral perception work in alliance with a clear insight into the English social structure. The character of Mr. James Harthouse is necessary not only for the plot of *Hard Times* but also for his representative function. Harthouse has adopted the dogmas of political economy out of boredom, out of that weary assumption of originality, which is always a mark of dullness of mind. Also Harthouse knows in advance that the devotees of political economy will be secretly impressed with his upper-class connections. Therefore, he will carry more weight in their councils than he would in circles more accustomed to enjoying aristocratic support. His pose is one of cynicism. He has no real interest in the cynical principles of the political economists; his cynicism is only an attractive line. A.O.J. Cochshut comments in "*Hard Times*—Dickens's Masterpiece?" that Harthouse is "the ancestor of a long line of 'brutally frank and courageously outspoken' publicists of the twentieth century; and it can be fairly claimed that Dickens may well have been the first person to understand and analyse the type."

The vacuum in Louisa's life comes to be filled by Harthouse who, produced by a background wholly unlike Coketown, has nonetheless arrived at a philosophy of life congruent with hers. Harthouse's careless hedonism, nurtured on leisure, boredom and cynicism, is in one wholly surprising way the mirror-image of Gradgrind's world. "The Gradgrind party", we are told, "wanted assistance in cutting the throat of the Graces. They went about recruiting, and where could they enlist recruits more hopefully than among the fine gentlemen who, having found out everything to be worth nothing, were equally ready for anything?" Nothing could be more direct than this perception that because want of fancy and want of humanity are such near neighbours, Gradgrind has prepared for himself the curious tragedy of his daughter's near-seduction by a libertine, Harthouse. Gradgrind's own goodness of heart proves inadequate to foresee or forestall the situation, since it has been disciplined into total insensitivity by his rigid beliefs.

Harthouse is one of the most purely realistic characters in *Hard Times*, possibly because he exists only in relation to Louisa's fate. Dickens is not concerned with Harthouse's personal destiny, as he is with that of certain similar characters—Steerforth in *David Copperfield* for instance and Eugene Wrayburn in *Our Mutual Friend*. But it is also true that Dickens was particularly fascinated by the blend of cynicism and irresponsibility present in Harthouse, which may explain why the depiction is directly realistic, and without grotesqueries or mythic overtones of any kind. The line of good-looking, or at the very least darkly compelling, lechers in his novels stretches from Sir John Chester and Carker through Steerforth, Harthouse and Sydney Carton to Eugene Wrayburn. There are continual variants in his depictions, since

Dickens never repeated the same character, or the same particular moral dilemma. Of all these characters Harthouse is the most assured and in his own way perfect, since his sole *raison d'etre* is to seem to us as to Louisa, what he chooses to seem. His torments if he has any are not relevant, and perhaps he really is as free from such weaknesses as he leads us to think. He comes into the novel to tempt Louisa, and it is enough that the temptation should be plausible and strong. Later, Dickens has merely to remove him from Coketown, and this again is easy; it is enough to allow the minimal good in his nature—helped along by the stirring of humour, and the natural desire to be well rid of complications—to respond to Sissy's appeal. This is a great help to his credibility, and to the novel's progress at this tricky moment since Sissy's rhetoric, however sincere, is hardly sophisticated, and Harthouse might have found it easy enough to resist at some other time. Dickens lets him move off to other scenes—he is lucky enough not to be imprisoned like the primary characters in Coketown—and we are merely told that his one virtuous action of leaving Louisa unmolested is, by a law among such men, the action he feels most ashamed of in after life. It becomes apparent that Louisa's spirit, as it matures in Coketown under its educative influences, finds its dismal reflection almost equally in Harthouse and in Stephen Blackpool: in Harthouse, whose libertinism is the fruit of a similar emptiness and boredom, and in Blackpool, whose crushed decency she can admire but not reach or connect with over barriers of class. The main point, however, is that Harthouse comes as close as he does to seducing Louisa, whose father has created in her an answering abyss. Harthouse almost ruins her as part of a normal libertine's strategy, yet she experiences with him her only illusion of requited love. A near marriage of untrue minds is arranged by the robber Fancy, intent the vacuum, on his revenge.

SLACKBRIDGE

Slackbridge, the trade union organizer, is a mere figment of the middle-class imagination. No such man would be listened to by a meeting of English factory hands. Not that such meetings are less susceptible to humbug than meetings of any other class. Not that trade union organizers, worn out by the terribly wearisome and trying work of going from place to place repeating the same commonplaces and trying to "stoke up" meetings to enthusiasm with them are less apt than other politicians to end as windbags, and sometimes to depend on stimulants to pull them through their work. Not, in short, that the trade union platform is any less humbug ridden than the platforms of the more highly placed political parties. G.B. Shaw writes in his article "Hard Times", "...even at their worst trade union organizers are not a bit like Slackbridge. All this is pure middle-class ignorance. It is much as if a tramp were to write a description of millionaires smoking large cigars in church, with their wives in low necked dresses and diamonds. We cannot say that Dickens did not know the working classes, because he knew humanity too well to be ignorant of any class. But this sort of knowledge is as compatible with ignorance of class manners and customs as with ignorance of foreign languages. Dickens knew certain classes of working folk very well: domestic servants, village artisans, and employees of petty tradesmen, for example. But of the segregated factory populations of our purely industrial towns he knew no more than an observant professional man can pick up on a flying visit to Manchester" (Ford 133). It is especially important to notice that Dickens expressly says in *Hard Times* that the workers were wrong to organize themselves in trade unions. In *Our Mutual Friend,* he appeals again and again to the governing classes. Nowhere does he appeal to the working class to take their fate into their own hands and try the democratic plan.

Three points may be worthwhile to observe in Dickens's treatment of the Union—Stephen's inexplicable obstinacy in refusing to join it; Dickens's hatred of Slackbridge; and the difference of mood and attitude of the other workers towards Stephen as men and as Union members under Slackbridge's influence. In his article "On Strike" in *Household Words* (11 Feb. 1854), Dickens describes the two Union meetings of the cotton strikers that he attended, and they are obviously the foundation for the Union meeting in *Hard Times*. The article stresses their order and courtesy of the strikers, the efficiency of the business and the competence of the men's local leaders; it decries the influence of an outside orator who is a prototype of Slackbridge; it makes clear that the men fully believed in the justice of their case, but that, at the same time, they had no hatred or resentment for most of the employers. The moral approval seems to be all on the side of the strikers. But the political conclusion is not that the strike is right:

> In any aspect in which it can be viewed, this strike and lock-out is a deplorable calamity. In its waste of time, in its waste of a great people's energy, in its waste of wages, in its waste of wealth that seeks to be employed, in its encroachment on the means of many thousands who are laboring from day to day, in the gulf of separation it hourly deepens between those whose interests must be understood to be identical or must be destroyed, it is a great national affliction. But, at this pass, anger is of no use, starving out is of no use—for what will that do, five years hence, but overshadow all the mills in England with the growth of a bitter remembrance?—political economy is a mere skeleton unless it has a little human covering and filling out, a little human bloom upon it, and a little human warmth in it.

Dickens accepts the fundamental ethical and political proposition of the political economy he generally so much deplores. The interests of employers and the employed must be assumed to be identical or must be destroyed. What Humphry House said in "Hard Times" is worth quoting: "On the whole the 'Combinations' of the thirties and forties, whether organized locally, by trades, or nationally, had avowed revolutionary aims. The extent to which their members advocated the use of physical force was less important than the fact that they were widely believed to do so; but, physical force aside, they were revolutionary in the sense that they did not accept the doctrine of the natural identity of interests between Capital and Labour, and were in their political activities more or less conscious of a class-struggle; and this consciousness was shared by their opponents. The Chartist failure of '48 meant widespread disillusionment in the possibilities of working-class political action, and the reviving unions of the fifties concentrated more on the immediate problem of collective bargaining within particular trades than on the formation of huge amalgamations with political aims. Dickens seems to have realized that this change was happening, but he shared two common popular misconceptions about it; the first was that the leaders of such unions were bound to be demagogic frauds like Gruffshaw and Slackbridge; and the second was that the unions were likely to violate liberty by being exclusive and tyrannical towards workers who refused to join them: both points were heavily underlined in *Hard Times*" (Dyson 218).

Persuasion is a very special anathema of the time when advertising, propaganda, and indoctrination have been pushed to the point of brain washing and mass lunacy. Though Dickens's creation, Slackbridge, the stump orator, addressing an assembly of the United Aggregate Tribunal in the crowded, stuffy, little Hall of Coketown may be a pale preview of certain giant demagogues of the 19th century with their monstrous rallies in vast sports stadiums, still a suggestion of the frightening possibilities is there in *Hard Times*. Dickens, in fact, was so aware of a false and immoral rhetoric that in his attempt to show its hollowness he has seriously weakened the impact that Slackbridge makes on the reader.

But, in *Hard Times,* Dickens regarded local opinion as dynamically inferior to Slackbridge's bluster; he meant to imply that Stephen was socially boycotted in spite of a predominating feeling in his favour, and the other workers bamboozled out of their better selves; and he made the distortion seem more serious by giving Stephen no better reason for not joining them than his promise to Rachael. Dickens realized that when Stephen had been both boycotted by his fellow-workers and sacked by Bounderby he had no scope of securing another job; but he did not draw the inference that an individual worker cannot be the equal of an employer in bargaining power, and that the ideal bargaining for labour-price talked of by the economists only had any meaning when the bargaining was done by a unanimous combinations. In fact, Dickens did not give up all hope of locating some means other than the unions by which such men as Stephen might be politically and socially articulate; he was still grouping after it later in the year in the address "To Working Men" and his other articles on Public Health.

RACHAEL

Rachael is the name of a woman in the Bible who had undergone much suffering. It has been alleged that Dickens's characters are either virtuous or vicious to a fault. They are either too white or too black, never bichromatic as in life. The language in which they are embodied fixes them in their "given" condition. They can only die like Stephen or be broken like Mr. Gradgrind. Rachael reveals none of her faults, for Dickens believes her to have none. Despite the cynically critical consternation, it is seen that Rachael is a crucial character in the novel and through her activities Dickens expresses the soft, positive values of life.

Stephen was standing in the street, with the old sensation upon him which the stoppage of the machinery always produced—the sensation of its having worked and stopped in his own head. He was waiting to see Rachael. It was a wet night, and many groups of young women passed him, with their shawls drawn over their bare heads and held close under their chins to keep the rain out. He knew Rachael well, for a glance at any one of these groups was sufficient to show him that she was not there. At last, there were no more to come; and then he turned away in disappointment, thinking that he had missed her. But he had not gone the length of three streets, when he saw another of the shawled figures in advance of him. Making his pace at once much quicker and much softer, he darted on until he was very near this figure, then fell into his former walk, and called "Rachael"! Rachael turned, being then in the brightness of a lamp; and raising her hood a little, showed a quiet oval face, dark and rather delicate, irradiated by a pair of very gentle eyes, and further set off by the perfect order of her shining black hair. It was not a face in its first bloom of youth. She was a woman of thirty-five years of age. He looked at her with some disappointment in his face, but with a respectful and patient conviction that must be right in whatever she did. Stephen praised her beauty that she looked as young as ever she had been. Stephen laments that his life is a muddle, always a muddle and he can never get beyond it.

Rachael, Stephen's "angel", was attending his sick wife in his lodging. From the outside of his home Stephen gloomily passed to the inside, with suspended breath and with a slow footstep. He went up to his door, opened it, and entered the room. Quiet and peace were there; Rachael was there, sitting by the bed. She turned her head. Her face lightened Stephen's mind. She sat by the bed, watching and tending his wife. Everything was in its place and order as he had always kept it. The little fire was newly trimmed. The hearth was freshly swept. It appeared to him that he saw all this in Rachael's face, and looked at nothing besides. While looking at her face, it was shut out from his view by the softened tears that filled his eyes. He had seen how earnestly she looked at him, and how her own eyes were filled too, with tears. Rachael turned towards the bed, and all was quiet there.

There were wounds about the neck of the 'self-made outcast', Stephen's wife. Rachael was dressing them. She steeped a piece of linen in a basin, into which she poured some liquid from a bottle, and laid it with a gentle hand upon the sore. The three-legged table had been drawn close to the bedside, and on it there were two bottles. Rachael said she had the hope that when his wife would get better she would leave him to himself again, and do him no more hurt. Then Rachael kept silence, for she wanted Stephen to sleep. He closed his eyes, more to please her than to rest his weary head. His imperfect consciousness faded away at last, and he dreamed a long, troubled dream. Rachael also fell asleep in the chair to the bed. He waked to see his wife, craving for drink, took up the bottle of poison with which Rachael had been dressing her wounds. He sat spell-bound, making no move to stop her.

However, at that critical moment, Rachael started up and averted the danger. As it was early morning, she had to leave. Stephen hoped that one day, even in death perhaps, he and Rachael might be together.

To keep his promise to Rachael Stephen did not join the union and consequently suffered. Stephen informed Rachael that Bounderby's work and he were parted, that he had lost his job. Stephen left Coketown in search of a job while the suspicion of the bank robbery fell gravely on him. Rachael told Sissy that she held a firm confidence in Stephen. She said that she has had the mistrust that some one had put Stephen out of way, as by his coming back of his own accord, and showing himself innocent before them all, some one would be confounded. That is why he might be stopped, and it would not be unlikely to think that he might be murdered. The confidence Rachael holds in her heart against all discouragement is not likely to be wrong. Rachael caps this careful phrasing with a claim still more positive: "God knows my heart, I have never once left trusting Stephen Blackpool!" Stephen had fallen into the pit while coming to Coketown in response to Rachael's letter to clear himself of the charges related to the bank robbery. When he was rescued from the pit, Stephen said to Rachael, "Ah, Rachael, aw' a muddle! From first to last, a muddle!"

So, Rachael, kindly, patient, tolerant, plays a useful part throughout the novel, *Hard Times*, as a centre of affection and guidance. The sweet-tempered and serene working-woman is a character whose 'heart' is in the right place and who suffers from the Coketown world of fact.

BITZER

Bitzer is integrally threaded into the fabric of the story of *Hard Times* in a compact plot. As per the criteria and code of the Gradgrind-Bounderby philosophy, Bitzer represents a model of perfectibility. He remains unchanged throughout the movement of the story.

Mr. Gradgrind told the pupils, 'the little pitchers', that as Sissy was unable to define a horse she possessed of no facts, in reference to one of the commonest of animals. The square finger of Mr. Gradgrind, moving here and there, lighted suddenly on Bitzer, perhaps because he chanced to sit in the same ray of sunlight which irradiated Sissy. The boys and girls sat on the face of the inclined plane in two compact bodies, divided up the centre by a narrow interval. Sissy, being at the corner of a row on the sunny side, came in for the beginning of a sunbeam, of which Bitzer who was at the corner of a row on the other side, a few rows in advance, caught the end. But Sissy was so dark-eyed and dark-haired, that she seemed to receive a deeper and more lustrous colour from the sun, when it shone upon her. Bitzer was so light-eyed and light-haired that the self-same rays appeared to draw out of him what little colour he ever possessed. His "cold eyes would hardly have been eyes, but for the short ends of lashes which, by bringing them into immediate contrast with something paler than themselves, expressed their form." His short-cropped hair might have been a mere continuation of the sandy freckles on his forehead and face. His skin was so unwholesomely deficient in the natural tinge, that he looked as though if he were cut he would bleed white. Thomas Gradgrind asked Bitzer to give the definition of a horse. Bitzer defined it: "Quadruped. Graminivorous. Forty teeth, namely twenty-four grinders, four eye-teeth, and twelve incisive. Sheds coat in the spring; in marshy countries, sheds hoofs, too. Hoofs hard, but requiring to be shod with iron. Age known by marks in mouth." The schoolroom contrast of Sissy Jupe and Bitzer is a contrast between the education, practical but often inarticulate which is gained by living and doing, and the education, highly articulated, which is gained by systemization and abstraction. The instinctive, un-intellectual, unorganized life is the ground of genuine feeing and of all good relationships.

Bitzer serves as the light porter at Bounderby's bank: "He was a very light porter indeed; as light as in the days when he blinkingly defined a horse, for girl number twenty." Bitzer is a career of tales, humourless, without passion, even without filial affection, looking down upon the workpeople of Coketown with disdain and condescension. When Mrs. Sparsit asked him whether the clerks were trustworthy, punctual and industrious, Bitzer answered in the affirmative, adding the words, "the usual exception". Bitzer held the respectable office of general spy and informer in the establishment, for which volunteer service he received a present at Christmas, over and above his weekly wage. He had grown into an extremely clear-headed, cautious, prudent young man, who was safer to rise in the world. His mind was exactly regulated. He had no affections or passions. All his proceedings were the result of the nicest and coldest calculation. Bitzer told Mrs. Sparsit that he doubted Tom very much and he did not like his ways at all. He opined that Tom was a dissipated, extravagant idler. Bitzer needed no recreations in life and to him it was stuff and nonsense to want recreations. He said that he does not want recreations, he never did, and he never would. As to people's combining together, by watching and informing upon one another, he said that one could earn a trifle now and then, whether in money or goodwill, and improve their livelihood. To improve the livelihood would be the first consideration of a rational creature. It would become quite nauseous, concerning their wives and families. Bitzer said, "I don't want a wife and family."

Bitzer is nonplussed by the robbery. He is the real success of the system, and its strongest condemnation. Gradgrind's philosophy again boomeranged upon himself when Bitzer declined his request to free Tom and he questioned Bitzer's feelings:

> Bitzer, still holding the paralysed culprit by the collar, stood in the Ring, blinking at his old patron through the darkness of the twilight.
>
> "Bitzer", said Mr. Gradgrind, broken down and miserably submissive to him, "have you a heart"?
>
> "The circulation, sir", returned Bitzer, smiling at the oddity of the question, "couldn't be carried on without one. No man, sir, acquainted with the facts established by Harvey relating to the circulation of the blood, can doubt that I have a heart." (III, VIII)

Bitzer held 'the paralyzed culprit', Tom, by the collar, and stood in the Ring, blinking at his old patron, Mr. Gradgrind, through the darkness of the twilight. Interrupting Mr. Gradgrind's words about Bitzer's self-interest, Bitzer retorted that he was sure Mr. Gradgrind knew that "the whole social system is a question of self-interest." He said that he was brought up in that catechism when he was very young. It was a fundamental principle of the Gradgrind philosophy that everything was to be paid for. Nobody was ever on any account to give anybody anything, or render anybody help without purchase. Gratitude was to be abolished, and the virtues springing from it were not to be. Every inch of the existence of mankind, from birth to death, was to be a bargain across a counter. Bitzer's bloodless arguments menace the broken Gradgrind. Sleary pretended to be on Bitzer's side and said that he would have Tom and Bitzer conveyed to the railway station. While they were in Sleary's carriage, the trained horse started dancing at a signal from the carriage-driver, without moving an inch further, and it oblized Bitzer to get down. One of the trained circus-dogs then took charge of Bitzer and would not let him move a step in any direction.

Although Bitzer was deprived of his conquest, we know of his future, maintained by his master in the Bounderby model. So, the real success of the Utilitarian doctrine is its strongest shame and sham.

MRS. SPARSIT

An elderly lady, Mrs. Sparsit, presided over Mr. Bounderby's establishment, in consideration of a certain annual stipend. Mrs. Sparsit was a highly-connected lady. She had a great aunt living in those very times called Lady Scadgers. Mr. Sparsit, deceased, of whom she was the relict, had been by the mother's side what Mrs. Sparsit called "a Powler". The late Mr. Sparsit, being by the mother's side a Powler, married the lady, being by the father's side a scadgers. Lady Scadgers contrived the marriage. Mr. Sparsit inherited a fair fortune from his uncle, but owed it all before he came into it, and spent it twice over immediately afterwards. When he died, at twenty-four, he did not leave Mrs. Sparsit in affluent circumstances. And they had been separated soon after the honeymoon. "That bereaved lady, fifteen years older than he, fell presently at deadly feud with her only relative, Lady Scadgers; and, partly to spite her ladyship, and partly to maintain herself, went out at a salary. And here she was now, in her elderly days, with the Coriolanian style of nose and dense black eyebrows which had captivated Sparsit,...."

Mrs. Sparsit's "sir", in addressing Mr. Bounderby, was a word of ceremony, rather exacting consideration for herself in the use, than honouring him. Bounderby invents elaborate degradations for his own early years, and compares these with the imagined glories of the Sparsit past. Mrs. Sparsit thus embraces the grandeur and rejects the implication of relative seniority. Mr. Bounderby gave her the news that he was going to marry 'Tom Gradgrind's daughter'. Bounderby resumed that under the circumstances, he thought it would be better for her to go to his Bank where there were apartments, where 'a born-and-bred lady' would be rather a catch than otherwise if the same annual compliment would be acceptable there. Bounderby said that she would have her private apartments, coals and candles, and all the rest of it; and she would have her maid to attend upon her, and her light porter to protect her. Mrs. Sparsit accepted his offer gratefully with many acknowledgments for past favours.

A subtle hint of Mrs. Sparsit's cat-like nature is found in the following words: "A lady so decorous in herself, and so highly connected, was not to be suspected of dropping over the banisters or sliding down them, yet her extraordinary facility of locomotion suggested the wild idea. Another noticeable circumstance in Mrs. Sparsit was, that she was never hurried. She would shoot with consummate velocity from the roof to the hall, yet would be in full possession of her breath and dignity on the moment of her arrival there. Neither was she ever seen by human vision to go at a great pace." After the bank robbery, Mrs. Sparsit made a stay of some weeks in duration at Mr. Bounderby's retreat. Mrs. Sparsit's greatest point, first and last, was her determination to pity Mr. Bounderby. And she had a curious propensity to call

Mrs. Bounderby "Miss Gradgrind". Her repetition of this mistake covered her (Mrs. Sparsit) with modest confusion, but indeed, she said, it seemed so natural to say Miss. Gradgrind. When ultimately she left the house, she was invited by Bounderby to visit the house every weekend. During the whole term of stay at Bounderby's house, Mrs. Sparsit was a pattern of consistency, continuing to take care and pity on Mr. Bounderby to his face; and to call his portrait, with the greatest acrimony and contempt, a Noodle, in private. Mrs. Sparsit was not a poetical woman. But she took an idea in the nature of an allegorical fancy, into her head. She erected in her mind a mighty Staircase, with a dark pit of shame and ruin at the bottom; and down those stairs, from day to day and hour to hour, she saw Louisa descending. It became the task of Mrs. Sparsit's life, to look up at her staircase, and to watch Louisa coming down and down, but never turning back.

Perhaps the most vividly memorable part of the whole novel is that of Mrs. Sparsit spying on Louisa and Harthouse, and following the fleeing Louisa, through the thunderstorm, to the railway station and to Coketown. It is the culmination of one of the great imaginative strokes of the book, Dickens's likening of her temptation to the descent of a great staircase, into chaos at its foot. He extracts the image, with great skill and economy, from Louisa's own 'what does it matter?' and then imposes it on Mrs. Sparsit, and modulates it, with a truly poetic movement, into the 'deep water' and universal deluge of the railway scene.

Mrs. Sparsit reached London where Bounderby happened to be at that time, and told him that his wife had eloped with Harthouse. Utterly heedless of the wear and tear of her clothes and constitution, and adamant to her pathetic sneezes, Mr. Bounderby immediately crammed her into a coach, and bore her off to Stone Lodge. Mr. Bounderby informed Mr. Gradgrind that Mrs. Sparsit, by accident, in a situation overheard a conversation out of doors between her daughter and his precious gentleman-friend, Mr. James Harthouse. Gradgrind told Bounderby that he had known what passed in the conversation, and he informed that the moment

Louisa could detach herself from that interview, she hurried by the train to town and ran from town to his house through a raging storm, and presented herself before him in a state of distraction; and from then, Louisa was in his house. Mr. Bounderby silently gazed about him for some moments, in every direction except Mrs. Sparsit's direction. Bounderby demanded apology from Mrs. Sparsit who took refuge in tears, seeing no way to defend herself. Bounderby ordered Mrs. Sparsit to go to her apartment at the bank without delay. Bounderby extended his right hand to the weeping lady, and escorted her to the conveyance.

Mr. Bounderby felt inappeasably indignant with her for her triumphant discovery of Mrs. Pegler. He felt that Mrs. Sparsit had audaciously anticipated him and presumed to be wiser than he. At last he made the discovery as to how to discharge Mrs. Sparsit. He decided to punish Mrs. Sparsit according to her deserts. Since the Pegler affair, Mrs. Sparsit had covered her pity for Mr. Bounderby with a veil of quiet melancholy and contrition. It had become her habit to assume a woeful look. Mr. Bounderby rebuked Mrs. Sparsit that she might be highly connected, but she could not be permitted to bother and badger a man in his position, and he was not going to put up with it. He said that a different sort of establishment altogether would bring out a lady of her powers. In unambiguous terms she expressed her contempt against him and even mentioned that she had often stood before his portrait and called him a 'noodle'.

Dickens hated privilege and systems of patronage: he despised snobbishness and self-righteousness and bigotry. In his portrait of the life and eventual distress of Mrs. Sparsit he sums up much of these feelings with telling caricature and burlesque and it makes the truth so sharp and painful.

MRS. GRADGRIND

Like Mrs. Matthew Pocket in Dickens's *Great Expectations,* Mrs. Gradgrind was an ineffectual mother. The 'little, thin, white, pink-eyed bundle of shawls, of surprising feebleness', Mrs. Gradgrind was dominated by her husband

and his utilitarian doctrination. Mrs. Gradgrind was not a scientific character. She usually dismissed her children to their studies with the general injunction to go and be 'somethingological'. Mrs. Gradgrind's stock of facts in general was woefully defective, but "Mr. Gradgrind in raising her to her high matrimonial position had been influenced by two reasons. Firstly, she was most satisfactory as a question of figures; and secondly, she had 'no nonsense' about her. By nonsense he meant fancy; and truly it is probable she was as free from any alloy of that nature, as any human being not arrived at the perfection of an absolute idiot, ever was." Mrs. Gradgrind scolded Louisa in no uncertain terms for wondering while she had expressly been warned by her father never to wonder. She rebuked Thomas that it was really shameful that a boy brought up as he had been should be found encouraging his sister to wonder. When Louisa denied Tom's participation in the offence their mother said that unless she had been encouraged, it was morally and physically impossible that she could have done it. She said that if such stuff was to reach their father's ears she would not hear the last of it. It was poor Mrs. Gradgrind's perpetual fear of fancy as a dreaded intruder. Whenever and however it manifests itself, she fears she will never hear the last.

Bitzer brought a note to say that Mrs. Gradgrind was very ill at Stone Lodge. Louisa returned hastily to her old home. Sissy was tending her mother. When Louisa wanted to hear of her mother, she said that it was something new when somebody wanted to hear of her. Mrs. Gradgrind was incoherent in her talk. When Louisa asked her whether she was feeling pain, she said that there was a pain somewhere in the room, but she couldn't positively say that she had got it. Left alone with her mother, Louisa saw her lying with an awful lull upon her face, "like one who was floating away upon some great water, all resistance over, content to be carried down the stream". Mrs. Gradgrind said that whenever she said anything on any subject, she had never heard the last of it: and consequently, that she had long left off saying anything. She said that Louisa and her brother learnt 'Ologies' a great deal, of all kinds from morning to night and if there was any 'Ology' left, of any description, she would not be able to hear its name. She resumed that there was something, not an 'Ology' at all, that their father had missed, or forgotten: "I don't know what it is. I have often sat with Sissy near me, and thought about it. I shall never get its name now. But your father may. It makes me restless. I want to write to him, to find out for God's sake, what it is. Give me a pen, give me a pen." The power of restlessness was gone. She fancied, however, that her request had been complied with. Mrs. Gradgrind died.

Mrs. Gradgrind's "somethingological" concern or obsession with "Ology" hints at Dickens's fundamental satirical intent on utilitarian statistics.

MRS. PEGLER

The 'maligned old lady', Mrs. Pegler, provides some of the most comic yet most ironical scenes in *Hard Times*. In Book III, Chapter V, of the novel we get almost every information about Mrs. Pegler and her words reveal the hypocrisy and filial disodedience of Mr. Bounderby.

As Sissy and Rachael were passing Mr. Bounderby's house on foot, and somehow they looked round involuntarily, the bright gaslight over Mr. Bounderby's steps showed them Mrs. Sparsit in a coach, in an ecstasy of excitement, struggling to open the door. Mrs. Sparsit seeing them at the same moment, called to them to stop. They saw that Mrs. Pegler came out of the coach. Mrs. Sparsit incontinently collared her. Mr. Bounderby appeared, accompanied by Mr. Gradgrind and Tom, with whom he had been holding conference upstairs. Mr. Bounderby looked more astonished than hospitable, at the sight of the uninvited party in his dining-room. Mr. Bounderby's visage exhibited an extraordinary combination of all possible colours and expressions of discomfiture as old Mrs. Pegler was disclosed to his view.

Mr. Bounderby roared against Mrs. Sparsit, asking explanation as to why she had interfered into his family affairs. Mrs. Pegler asked not to blame her (Mrs. Pegler) as it was not her fault. She told her darling son, Josiah, that she suggested Mrs. Sparsit over and over again that what she was doing would not be agreeable to him. But she threatened her that if she (Mrs. Pegler) resisted her, she should be brought by constables. Mrs. Pegler reminded him that she had never broken the condition laid down: that she had never said that she was his mother, and that she had always admired him at a distance. Even when she had visited the town sometimes to take 'a proud peep' at him, she had done it unbeknown, and gone away. Mr. Gradgrind observed with severity that he was surprised to see that in her old age she was not ashamed to claim Mr. Bounderby for her son, after her unnatural and inhuman treatment of him. She said that she herself had brought up Josiah (Bounderby) as best as she could, handicapped as she was by her stark poverty. And it came to light that Bounderby's grandmother had died before he was born. It was disclosed from the words of Mrs. Pegler that Bounderby had pensioned his mother off on thirty pounds a year, and he laid the condition that she was to remain in the countryside and never introduce herself for his mother. The spectators greedily took in every syllable of Mrs. Pegler's appeal, and at each succeeding syllable became more and more astonished. It was plain to all present there that Bounderby's story about his mother and grandmother was a pack of damned lies. Although Bounderby did not deny the account given by Mrs. Pegler, he said that he was not bound to explain his family affairs to anyone. Thus he dismissed the crowd from his house. However, Mrs. Pegler was offered a bed at her son's (Bounderby's) house.

7

Some Critical Responses

G.K. CHESTERTON

The early 19th century spirit produced great men, because it believed that men were great. It made strong men by encouraging weak men. Its education, its public habits, its rhetoric, were all addressed towards encouraging the greatness in everybody. And by encouraging the greatness in everybody, it obviously encouraged superlative greatness in some. Superiority emerged from the great ecstasy of equality and in this ambience of passionate unconsciousness and bewildering community of thought men do become more than themselves. Almost without exception all the great men have come out of this atmosphere of equality. Great men may make despotisms; but democracies make great men. The other main factory of heroes besides a revolution is a religion. And a religion again, is a thing which, by its nature, does not think of men as more or less valuable, but of men as all intensely and painfully valuable, a democracy of eternal danger. For religion all men are equal, as all pennies are equal, because the only value in any of them is that they bear the image of the King. This fact has been quite insufficiently observed in the study of religious heroes. Piety produces intellectual greatness precisely because piety in itself is quite indifferent to intellectual greatness. The strength of Cromwell was that he cared for religion. But the strength of religion was that it did not care for Cromwell; did not care for him, that is, any more than for anybody else. He and his footman were equally welcomed to warm places in the hospitality of hell. It has often been said, very truly, that religion is the thing that makes the ordinary man feel extraordinary; it is an equally important truth that religion is the thing that makes the extraordinary man feel ordinary. The typical child of the French Revolution, Carlyle, began with the wildest hopes from the Reform Bill and he had been made and moulded by those hopes. He was disappointed with Equality; but Equality was not disappointed with him. In the post-Carlylean period, every man examines himself, every man examines his neighbours, to see whether they or he quite come up to the exact line of greatness. But the whole atmosphere was replete with a faith in the infinity of human souls, which is in itself not only Christian but orthodox. If Christianity said that any man could be a saint if he chose, democracy said that any man could be a citizen if he chose. It was a world that expected everything of everybody. It was a world that encouraged anybody to be anything. And in England and literature its living expression was Charles Dickens. Dickens was the humane voice in England of this encouraging of anybody to be anything. His best books are a carnival of liberty, and there is more of the real spirit of the French Revolution in *Nicholas Nickleby* than in *The Tale of Two Cities*. His work has the great glory of the Revolution, the call for every man to be himself.

As a fact, there is no shred of evidence to show that those who have had sad experiences tend to have a sad philosophy. There are numberless points upon which Dickens is spiritually at one with the poor, that is, with the great mass of mankind. But there is no point in which he is more perfectly at one with them than in showing that there is no kind of connection between a man being unhappy and a man being pessimistic. Sorrow and pessimism are indeed, in a sense, opposite things, since sorrow is founded on the value of something, and pessimism upon the value of nothing. And in practice we find that those poets or political leaders who come from the people, and whose experiences have really been searching and cruel, are the most sanguine people in the world. These men out of the old agony are always optimists; they are sometimes offensive optimists. A man like Robert Burns, whose father (like Dickens's father) goes bankrupt, whose whole life is a struggle against miserable external powers and internal weaknesses yet more miserable—a man whose life begins grey and ends black—Burns does not merely sing about the goodness of life, he positively rants and cants about it. Rousseau, whom all his friends and acquaintances treated almost as badly as he treated them—Rousseau, does not grow merely eloquent, he grows gushing and sentimental, about the inherent goodness of human nature. Charles Dickens, who was most miserable at the receptive age when most people are most happy, is afterwards happy when all men weep. Circumstances break men's bones; it has never been shown that they break men's optimism. These great popular leaders do all kinds of desperate things under the immediate scourge of tragedy. They become drunkards; they become demagogues; they become morphomaniacs. They never become pessimists. Most unquestionably there are ragged and unhappy men whom we could easily understand being pessimists. But as a matter of fact they are not pessimists. Most unquestionably there are whole dim hordes of humanity whom we should promptly pardon if they cursed God. But they don't. The pessimists are aristocrats like Byron; the men who curse God are aristocrats like Swinburne. But when those who starve and suffer speak for a moment, they do not profess merely an optimism, they profess a cheap optimism; they are too poor to afford a dear one. They cannot indulge in any detailed or merely logical defence of life; that would be to delay the enjoyment of it. These higher optimists, of whom Dickens was one, do not approve of the universe; they do not even admire the universe; they fall in love with it. They embrace life too close to criticize or even to see it. Existence to such men has the wild beauty of a woman, and those love her with most intensity who love her with least cause.

The hardest thing to remember about our own time, of course, is simply that it is a time; we all instinctively think of it as the Day of Judgement. But all the things in it which belong to it merely as this time will probably be rapidly turned upside down; all the things that can pass will pass. It is not merely true that all old things are already dead; it is also true that all new things are already dead; for the only undying things are the things that are neither new nor old. The more you are up with this year's fashion, the more (in a sense) you are already behind next year's. Consequently, in attempting to decide whether an author will, as it is cantly expressed, live, it is necessary to have very firm convictions about what part, if any part, of man is unchangeable. And it is very hard to have this if you have not a religion or, at least, a dogmatic philosophy.

The equality of men needs preaching quite as much as regards the ages as regards the classes of men. To feel infinitely superior to a man in the twelfth century is just precisely as snobbish as to feel infinitely superior to a man in the Old Kent Road. There are differences between the man and us, there may be superiorities in us over the man; but our sin in both cases consists in thinking of the small things wherein we differ when we ought to be confounded and intoxicated by the terrible and joyful matters in which we are at one. But here again the difficulty always is that the things near us seem larger than they are, and so seem to be a permanent part of mankind, when they may really be only one of its parting modes of expression. Few people, for instance, realize that a time may easily come when we shall see the great outburst of Science in the nineteenth century as something quite as splendid, brief, unique, and ultimately abandoned, as the outburst of Art at the Renascence. Few people realize that the general habit of fiction, of telling tales in prose, may fade, like the general habit of the ballad, of telling tales in verse, has for the time faded. Few people realize that reading and writing are only arbitrary, and perhaps temporary sciences, like heraldry.

The immortal mind will remain, and by that writers like Dickens will be securely judged. That Dickens will have a high place in permanent literature there is, I imagine no prig surviving to deny. But though all prediction is in the dark, I would devote this chapter to suggesting that his place in nineteenth-century England will not only be high, but altogether the highest. At a certain period of his contemporary fame, an average Englishman would have said that there were at that moment in England about five or six able and equal novelists. He could have made a list, Dickens, Bulwer Lytton, Thackeray, Charlotte Bronte, George Eliot, perhaps more. Forty years or more have past and some of them have slipped to a lower place. Some would now say that the highest platform is left to Thackeray, and Dickens; some to Dickens, Thackeray, and George Eliot; some to Dickens, Thackeray, and Charlotte Bronte. I venture to offer the proposition that when more years have passed and more weeding has been effected, Dickens will dominate the whole England of the nineteenth century; he will be left on that platform alone.

I know that this is an almost impertinent thing to assert, and that its tendency is to bring in those disparaging discussions of other writers in which Mr. Swinburne brilliantly embroiled himself in his suggestive study of Dickens. But my disparagement of the other English Novelists is wholly relative and not in the least positive. It is certain that men will always return to such a writer as Thackeray, with his rich emotional autumn, his feeling that life is a sad but sacred retrospect in which at least we should forget nothing. It is not likely that wise men will forget him. So, for instance, wise and scholarly men do from time to time return to the lyrists of French Renascence, to the delicate poignancy of Du Bellay: so they will go back to Thackeray. But I mean that Dickens will bestride and dominate our time as the vast figure of Rabelais dominates Du Bellay, dominates the Renascence and the world.

Let me put a negative reason first. The particular things for which Dickens is condemned (and justly condemned) by his critics, are precisely those things which have never prevented a man from being immortal. The chief of them is the unquestionable fact that he wrote an enormous amount of bad work. This does lead to a man being put below his place in his own time: it does not effect his permanent place, to all appearance, at all. Shakespeare, for instance, and Wordsworth wrote not only an enormous amount of bad work, but an enormous amount of enormously bad work. Humanity edits such writers' works for them. Virgil was mistaken in cutting out his inferior lines; we would have undertaken the job.

Moreover in the particular case of Dickens there are special reasons for regarding his bad work, as I have previously suggested, under a kind of general ambition that had nothing to do with his special genius; an ambition to be a pubic provider of everything, a warehouse of all human emotions.

He held a kind of literary day of judgement. He distributed bad characters as punishments and good characters as rewards. My meaning can be best conveyed by one instance out of many. The character of the kind old Jew in "Our Mutual Friend" (a needless and unconvincing character) was actually introduced because some Jewish correspondent complains that the bad old Jew in "Oliver Twist" conveyed the suggestion that all Jews were bad. The principle is so lightheadedly absurd that it is hard to imagine any literary man submitting to it for an instant. If ever he invented a bad auctioneer he must immediately balance him with a good auctioneer; if he should have conceived an unkind philanthropist, he must on the spot, with whatever natural agony and toil, imagine a kind philanthropist. The complaint is frantic; yet Dickens, who tore people in pieces for much fairer complaints, liked this complaint of his Jewish correspondent. It pleased him to be mistaken for a public arbiter: it pleased him to be asked (in a double sense) to judge Israel. All this is so much another thing, a non-literary vanity, that there is much less difficulty than usual in separating it from his serious genius: and by his serious genius, I need hardly say, I mean his comic genius. Such irrelevant ambitions as this are easily passed over, like the sonnets of great statesmen. We feel that such things can be set aside, as the ignorant experiments of men otherwise great, like the politics of Professor Tyndall or the philosophy of Professor Haeckel. Hence, I think, posterity will not care that Dickens has done bad work, but will know that he has done good.

Again, the other chief accusation against Dickens was that his characters and their actions were exaggerated and impossible. But this only meant that they were exaggerated and impossible as compared with the modern world and with certain writers (like Thackeray or Trollope) who were making a very exact copy of the manners of the modern world. Some people, oddly enough, have suggested that Dickens has suffered or will suffer from the change of manners. Surely, this is irrational. It is not the creators of the impossible who will suffer from the process of time: Mr. Bunsby can never be any more impossible than he was when Dickens made him. The writers who will obviously suffer from time will be the careful and realistic writers, the writers who have observed every detail of the fashion of this world which passeth away. It is surely obvious that there is nothing so fragile as a fact, that a fact flies away quicker than a fancy. A fancy will endure for two thousand years. For instance, we all have fancy for an entirely fearless man, a hero; and the Achilles of Homer still remains. But exactly the thing we do not know about Achilles is how far he was possible. The realistic narrators of the time are all forgotten (thank God) so we cannot tell whether Homer slightly exaggerated or wildly exaggerated or did not exaggerate at all, the personal activity of a Mycenaean captain in battle; for the fancy has survived the facts. So the fancy of Podsnap may survive the facts of English commerce: and no one will know whether Podsnap was possible, but only know that he is desirable, like Achilles.

The positive argument for the permanence of Dickens comes back to the thing that can only be stated and cannot be discussed: creation. He made things which nobody else could possibly make. He made Dick Swiveller in a very different sense from that in which Thackeray made Colonel Newcome. Thackeray's creation was observation: Dickens's was poetry, and is therefore permanent. But there is one other test that can be added. The immortal writer, I conceive, is commonly he who does something universal in a special manner. I mean that he does something interesting to all men in a way in which only one man or one land can do. Other men in that land, who do only what other men in other lands are doing as well, tend to have a great reputation in their day and to sink slowly into a second or a third or a fourth place. A parallel from war will make the point clearer. I cannot think that any one will doubt that, although Wellington and Nelson were always bracketed, Nelson will steadily become more important and Wellington less. For the fame of Wellington rests upon the fact that he was a good soldier in the service of England, exactly as twenty similar men were good soldiers in the service of Austria or Prussia or France. But Nelson is the symbol of a special mode of attack, which is at once universal and yet especially English, the sea. Now Dickens is at once as universal as the sea and as English as Nelson. Thackeray and George Eliot and the other great figures of that great England, were comparable to Wellington in this, that the kind of thing they were doing,—realism, the acute study of intellectual things, numerous men in France, Germany and Italy were doing as well or better than they. But Dickens was really doing something universal, yet something that no one but an Englishman could do. This is attested by the fact that he and Byron are the men who, like pinnacles, strike the eye of the continent. The points would take long to study: yet they may take only a moment to indicate. No one but an Englishman could have filled his books at once with a furious caricature and with a positively furious kindness. In more central countries, full of cruel memories of political change, caricature is always inhumane. No one but an Englishman could have described the democracy as consisting of free men, but yet of funny men. In other countries where the democratic issue has been more bitterly fought, it is felt that unless you describe a man as dignified you are describing him as a slave. This is the only final greatness of a man; that he does for all the world what all the world cannot do for itself. Dickens, I believe, did it.

The hour of absinthe is over. We shall not be much further troubled with the little artists who found Dickens too sane for their sorrows and too clean for their delights. But we have a long way to travel before we get back to what Dickens meant: and the passage is along rambling English road, a twisting road such as Mr. Pickwick travelled. But this at least is part of what he meant; that comradeship and serious joy are not interludes in our travel; but that rather our travels are interludes in comradeship and joy, which through God shall endure for ever. The inn does not point to the road; the road points to the inn. And all roads point at last to an ultimate inn, where we shall meet Dickens and all his characters: and when we drink again it shall be from the great flagons in the tavern at the end of the world.

(*Charles Dickens*)

HUMPHRY HOUSE

On the whole the 'Combinations' of the [eighteen] thirties and forties, whether organized locally, by trades, or nationally, had avowed revolutionary aims. The extent to which their members advocated the use of physical force was less important than the fact that they were widely believed to do so; but, physical force aside, they were revolutionary in the sense that they did not accept the doctrine of the natural identity of interests between Capital and Labour, and were in their political activities more or less conscious of a class-struggle; and this consciousness was shared by their opponents. The Chartist failure of '48 meant widespread disillusionment in the possibilities of working-class political action, and the reviving unions of the fifties concentrated more on the immediate problem of collective bargaining within particular trades than on the formation of huge amalgamations with political aims. Dickens seems to have realized that this change was happening, but he shared two common popular misconceptions about it; the first was that the leaders of such unions were bound to be demagogic frauds like Gruffshaw and Slackbridge; and the second was that the unions were likely to violate liberty by being exclusive and tyrannical towards workers who refused to join them: both points were heavily underlined in *Hard Times*.

***

...a careful study of actual affairs at the time, of what Dickens wrote in *Hard Times*, what he said in his letters, and what he wrote in *Household Words*, show that the conditions described in *Hard Times* are much closer to the engineering strike of 1852 than to the dispute at Preston. For, at this time, there was no trade unionism there among the spinners and weavers; their leaders were not permanent organizers but local workmen; and the story of Stephen Blackpool, the weaver who is sent to Coventry because he refuses to join the union, is false in fact as well as in characterization. The novel is weakest, therefore, just where certain recent writers on Dickens would like to see it come out strongest as a study of industrial capitalism.

Too much, however, ought not to be made of the industrial scenes in the novel in comparison with the domestic life of the Gradgrinds and Mr. Sleary's circus. Unfortunately, Dickens himself was responsible for calling attention to them when he began to write. He chose as part of his subject a dispute in the cotton industry just when the Preston strike was in everyone's mind. He was publicly said to have visited the north to verify his impressions. He published the article on Preston in *Household Words* a few weeks before the first instalment of the novel, and made it clear to attentive traders that the agitator, Slackbridge, was drawn from one of the local leaders at Preston; on top of everything else, even before *Hard Times* had finished its run in *Household Words*, he advertised as its successor a novel by Mrs. Gaskell called *North and South*, which also turned out to be based on the Preston dispute. His subsequent denial that there was any necessary connection between Coketown and Preston made no difference therefore. The *Westminster Review* declared that: when it was announced...that Mr. Dickens was about to write a tale called *Hard Times*, the general attention was instantly arrested. It was imagined the main topic of the story would be drawn from the fearful struggle being enacted in the north. In fact, it went on, his readers had been disappointed. The purpose of the book seemed to be to show that if a child were brought up in a circus it would be a prodigy of virtue, while if it were sent to a model school it might grow up to rob a bank or make a prostituted marriage. Such misunderstandings were a natural consequence of reading the story with nothing but topical events in mind; and although this was not the fault of the novel, the author himself was partly responsible.

Wrong as the reviewers were, present day critics such as Edgar Johnson who try to see it as an expression of 'Dickens's violent hostility to industrial capitalism and its entire scheme of life', are even more misleading. Dickens wanted to help the workers but he did not condemn capitalism. The story should be interpreted as a moral fable, in the everyday sense. It may even be called a morality drama, which is Johnson's term. But, like the Christmas books and the other novels serialized in *Household Words* and *All the Year Round*, it is based on a Christian morality.

("*Hard Times*" in *Dickens: Modern Judgements*)

G.B. SHAW

There is nothing more in the book that needs any glossary, except, perhaps, the strange figure of the Victorian "swell", Mr. James Harthouse. His pose has gone out of fashion. Here and there you may still see a man—even a youth—with a single eyeglass, an elaborately bored and weary air, and a little stock of cynicisms and indifferentisms contrasting oddly with a mortal anxiety about his clothes. All he needs is a pair of Dundreary whiskers, like the officers in Desanges' military pictures, to be a fair imitation of Mr. James Harthouse. But he is not in the fashion: he is an eccentric, as Whistler was an eccentric, as Max Beerbohm and the neo-dandies of the *fin de siecle* were eccentrics. It is now the fashion to be strenuous, to be energetic, to hustle as American millionaires are supposed (rather erroneously) to hustle. But the soul of the swell is still unchanged. He has changed his name again and again, become a Masher, a Toff, a Johnny and what not; but fundamentally he remains what he always was, an Idler, and therefore a man bound to find some trick of thought and speech that reduces the world to a thing as empty and purposeless and hopeless as himself. Mr. Harthouse reappears, more seriously and kindly taken, as Eugene Wraburn and Mortimer Lightwood in *Our Mutual Friend*. He reappears as a club in The Finches of the Grove of *Great Expectations*. He will reappear in all his essentials in fact and in fiction until he is at last shamed or coerced into honest industry and becomes not only unintelligible but inconceivable.

("*Hard Times*" in *The Dickens Critics*)

Bibliography

Ackroyd, Peter. *Dickens*. New York: Harper Collins, 1990.

———. *Dickens: Public Life and Private Passions*. Irvington, NY: Hydra, 2002.

———. *Introduction to Dickens*. London: Sinclair-Stevenson, 1991.

Adderley, James, et al. *Christian Social Reformers of the Nineteenth Century*. 1927; Freeport, NY: Books for Libraries, 1970.

Adrian, Arthur A. *Dickens and the Parent-Child Relationship*. Athens, OH: Ohio UP, 1984.

———. *Georgina Hogarth and the Dickens Circle*. Oxford: Oxford UP, 1957.

Alexander, Doris. *Creating Characters with Charles Dickens*. University Park: Pennsylvania State UP, 1991.

Allan, Janice M. *Charles Dickens's Bleak House: A Sourcebook*. London: Routledge, 2004.

Allbut, Robert. *London Rambles with Charles Dickens*. London: Drewett, 1886.

Allen, Michael. *Charles Dickens' Childhood*. London: Macmillan, 1988.

Allen, Walter. *Six Great Novelists: Defoe, Fielding, Scott, Dickens, Stevenson, Conrad*. London: Hamilton, 1955.

Amalric, Jean-Claude, ed. *Studies in the Later Dickens*. Montpellier: Universite Paul Valery, 1973.

Andrew, Malcom. *Dickens on England and the English*. Hassocks, Sussex: Harvester, 1979.

Andrews, Malcolm. *Charles Dickens and his Performing Selves: Dickens and the Public Readings*. Oxford: Oxford UP, 2006.

Arac, Jonathan. *Commissioned Spirits: The Shaping of Social Motion in Dickens, Carlyle, Melville, and Hawthorne*. New Brunswick, NJ: Rutgers UP, 1979.

Armstrong, Frances. *Dickens and the Concept of Home*. London: UMI Research, 1990.

Arnds, Peter O. *Wilhelm Raabe's Der Hungerpastor and Charles Dickens's David Copperfield: Intertextuality of Two Bildungsromane*. New York: Peter Lang, 1997.

Axton, William F. *Circle of Fire: Dickens' Vision and Style and the Popular Victorian Theater*. Lexington, KY: U of Kentucky P, 1966.

Axton, William. *Charles Dickens and Shorthand*. Manchester: Manchester UP, 1892.

Aylmer, Felix. *Dickens Incognito*. London: Rupert Hart-Davis, 1959.

———. *The Drood Case*. London: Rupert Hart-Davis, 1964.

Ayres, Brenda. *Dissenting Women in Dickens' Novels: The Subversion of Domestic Ideology*. Wesport, CT: Greenwood, 1998.

Baker, Ernest A. *The Age of Dickens and Thackeray*. London: H.F. and G. Witherby, 1936.

Baker, George P., ed. *Charles Dickens and Maria Beadnell: Private Correspondence*. Boston: Bibliophile Society, 1908.

Baker, Richard M. *The Drood Murder Case*. Berkeley, CA: U of California P, 1951.

Barickman, Richard, Susan MacDonald, and Myra Stark. *Corrupt Relations: Dickens, Thackeray, Trollope, Collins, and the Victorian Sexual System*. New York: Columbia UP, 1982.

Barlow, Eleanor P. *The Master's Cat: The Story of Charles Dickens as Told by His Cat*. Exeter, NH: J.N. Townsend, 1999.

Barlow, G. *The Genius of Dickens*. 1909; New York: Haskell House, 1975.

Barnard, Fred, et al. *Scenes and Characters from the Works of Charles Dickens: Being Eight Hundred and Sixty-Six Drawings*. London: Chapman and Hall, 1908.

Barnard, Robert. *Imagery and Theme in the Novels of Dickens*. New York: Humanities, 1974.

Barnes, A.W. *A Dickens Guide*. London, 1929.

Barnes, John. *A Critical Commentary on Dickens's 'Great Expectations'*. Critical Commentaries. London: Macmillan, 1966.

Baugh, Albert C. *Literary History of England: The Nineteenth Century and After*. London: Routledge, 2006.

Becker, May L. *Introducing Charles Dickens*. New York: Dodd, Mead, 1940.

Beckwith, Charles E., ed. *Twentieth Century Interpretations of A Tale of Two Cities: A Collection of Critical Essays*. Englewood Cliffs, NJ: Prentice-Hall, 1972.

Beer, John. *Post-Romantic Consciousness: Dickens to Plath*. Basingstoke, UK: Palgrave Macmillan, 2003.

Bell, Aldon D. *London in the Age of Dickens*. Norman, OK: U of Oklahoma P, 1967.

Bentley, Nicolas, Michael Slater and Nina Burgis. *The Dickens Index*. Oxford: Oxford UP, 1988.

Berard, Jane Helen. *Dickens and Landscape Discourse*. New York: Peter Lang, 2006.

Bevis, Matthew. *The Art of Eloquence: Byron, Dickens, Tennyson, Joyce*. Oxford: Oxford UP, 2007.

BL. *Charles Dickens: The J.F. Dexter Collection: Accessions to the General Catalogue of Printed Books, Manuscripts, Prints and Drawings*. London: British Museum, 1974.

Bloom, Harold, ed. *Charles Dickens*. Philadelphia: Chelsea House, 1987.

———. *Charles Dickens's A Tale of Two Cities*. New York: Chelsea House, 1987.

———. *Charles Dickens's Bleak House*. Modern Critical Interpretations. New York: Chelsea House, 1987.

———. *Charles Dickens's David Copperfield*. Modern Critical Interpretations. New York: Chelsea House, 1987.

———. *Charles Dickens's Great Expectations*. Broomall, PA: Chelsea House, 1996.

———. *Charles Dickens's Hard Times*. Modern Critical Interpretations. New York: Chelsea House, 1987.

———. *Charles Dickens*. New York: Chelsea House, 2006.

Blount, Trevor. *Charles Dickens: The Early Novels*. London: Longman, 1968.

Boarman, J.C. and J.L. Harte. *Boz: An Intimate Biography of Charles Dickens*. Boston, 1935.

Bodenheimer, Rosemarie. *Knowing Dickens*. Ithaca: Cornell UP, 2007.

Bolm, Adolf and R. Vaughan Williams. *On Christmas Night: A Masque with Dancing, Singing, and Miming: Freely Adapted from Dickens's "A Christmas Carol"*. London: Oxford UP, 1957.

Bolton, H. Philip. *Dickens Dramatized*. Novels on Stage. Vol. 1. London: Mansell, 1987.

Born, Daniel. *The Birth of Liberal Guilt in the English Novel: Charles Dickens to H.G. Wells*. Chapel Hill, NC: U of North Carolina P, 1995.

Bowen, John. *Other Dickens: Pickwick to Chuzzlewit*. New York: Oxford UP, 1999.

———. *Palgrave Advances in Charles Dickens Studies*. Basingstoke: Palgrave Macmillan, 2006.

Bowen, W.H. *Charles Dickens and His Family: A Sympathetic Study*. Cambridge: W. Heffer, 1956.

Brannan, Robert L., ed. *Under the Management of Mr. Charles Dickens: His Production of "The Frozen Deep"*. Ithaca, NY: Cornell UP, 1966.

Brattin, Joel J. and Bert G. Hornback. *Our Mutual Friend: An Annotated Bibliography*. The Garland Dickens Bibliographies. Vol. 1. New York: Garland, 1984.

Braybrooke, Patrick, ed. *A Child's Charles Dickens*. London: Cecil Palmer, 1930.

Bredsdorff, Elias. *Hans Andersen and Charles Dickens: A Friendship and Its Dissolution*. Cambridge: W. Heffer, 1956.

Brewer, Lether A. *Leigh Hunt and Charles Dickens: The Skimpole Caricature*. 1930; New York: Haskell House, 1971.

Bridgham, Elizabeth A. *Spaces of the Sacred and Profane: Dickens, Trollope, and the Victorian Cathedral Town*. New York: Routledge, 2008.

Brook, G.L. *The Language of Dickens*. London: Andre Deutch, 1970.

Brooks, Peter N., ed. *Reformation Principle and Practice: Essays in Honour of Arthur Geoffrey Dickens*. London: Scolar, 1971.

Brooks-Davies, Douglas. *Chesterton on Dickens*. London: J.M. Dent, 1992.

———. *Charles Dickens, Great Expectations*. Penguin Critical Studies. London: Penguin, 1989.

———. *Fielding, Dickens, Gosse, Iris Murdoch and Oedipal Hamlet*. Basingstoke: Macmillan, 1989.

Brown, Arthur W. *Sexual Analysis of Dickens's Props*. New York, 1971.

Brown, Ivor, comp. *Charles Dickens, 1812-1870*. London: Jackdaw, 1970.

———. *Dickens and His World*. London: Lutterworth, 1970.

———. *Dickens in His Time*. London: Thomas Nelson, 1963.

Brown, James M. *Dickens: Novelist in the Market-Place*. London: Macmillan, 1982.

Browne, Hablot K. *Phiz and Dickens as They Appeared to Edgar Browne*. London: James Nisbet, 1913.

Bruce, Sylvia. *Dickens Portrayal of Women and Other Essays.* San Bernardino: Borgo, 1990.

Buchanan-Brown, John. *Phiz! Illustrator of Dickens' World.* New York: Charles Scribner, 1978.

Buckley, Jerome H. *Season of Youth: The Bildungsroman from Dickens to Golding.* Bridgewater, NJ: Replica, 1974.

Burton, H.M. *Dickens and His Works.* London: Methuen Educational, 1968.

Burton, Richard. *Charles Dickens.* Indianapolis: Bobbs-Merrill, 1919.

Busch, Frederick. *The Mutual Friends.* Hassocks, Sussex: Harvester, 1978.

Butt, John and Kathleen Tillotson. *Dickens at Work.* London: Methuen, 1957.

Butt, John. *Pope, Dickens and Others.* Edinburgh: Edinburgh UP, 1969.

Cain, Lynn. *Dickens, Family, Authorship (Nineteenth Century).* Farnham, UK: Ashgate, 2008.

Callow, Simon. *Dickens' Christmas: A Victorian Celebration.* New York: Harry N. Abrams, 2003.

Campbell, Elizabeth A. *Fortune's Wheel: Dickens and the Iconography of Women's Time.* Athens, OH: Ohio UP, 2003.

Camus, Marianne. *Gender and Madness in the Novels of Charles Dickens.* Lewiston, NY: Edwin Mellen, 2004.

Canning, A.S.G. *Philosophy of Charles Dickens.* London: Smith, Elder, 1880.

———. *Dickens and Thackeray: Studies in Three Novels.* Port Washington, NY: Kennikat, 1911.

Canning, John, ed. *The Illustrated Mayhew's London: The Classic Account of London Street Life and Characters in the Time of Charles Dickens and Queen Victoria.* London: Weidenfeld and Nicolson, 1986.

Caravantes, Peggy. *Best of Times: The Story of Charles Dickens.* Greensboro, NC: Morgan Reynolds Pub., 2005.

Carey, John. *The Violent Effigy: A Study of Dickens' Imagination*. London: Faber, 1973.

Carlisle, Janice. *The Sense of an Audience: Dickens, Thackeray, at George Eliot and Mid-Century*. Brighton: Harvester, 1982.

Carlton, William J. *Charles Dickens, Shorthand Writer: The Prentice Days of A Master Craftsman*. London, 1947.

Caserio, Robert L. *Plot, Story, and the Novel: From Dickens and Poe to the Modern Period*. Princeton, NJ: Princeton UP, 1979.

Cash, Catherine. *Commodity Culture in Dickens's Household Words: The Social Life of Goods*. Aldershot, Hants., England; Burlington, VT: Ashgate, 2008.

Cazamian, Louis. *The Social Novel in England 1830-1850: Dickens, Disraeli, Mrs. Gaskell, Kingsley*. Trans. Martin Fido. London: Routledge and Kegan Paul, 1973.

Champion, Neil. *Charles Dickens*. Melbourne: Heinemann Library, 2001.

Chancellor, E. Beresford. *The London of Charles Dickens: Being an Account of the Haunts of His Characters and the Topographical Setting of His Novels*. London: Richards, 1924.

———. *Dickens and His Times*. London: Richards, 1932.

Charles, Edwin. *Some Dickens Women*. London: Laurie, 1926.

Chase, Karen. *Eros and Psyche: The Representation of Personality in Charlotte Bronte, Charles Dickens, and George Eliot*. New York: Methuen, 1984.

Chatterjee, Sisir K. "Materials on *Hard Times*" (unpublished).

Chesterton, G.K. *Charles Dickens*. London: Methuen, 1906.

Chittick, Kathryn. *Dickens and the 1830s*. Cambridge: Cambridge UP, 1990.

———. *The Critical Reception of Charles Dickens, 1833-1841*. New York: Garland, 1989.

Christianson, Frank. *Philanthropy in British and American Fiction: Dickens, Hawthorne, Eliot, and Howells.* Edinburgh: Edinburgh UP, 2007.

Christie, John. *The Ancestry of Catherine Thomas Hogarth.* Edinburgh, 1912.

Christie, O.F. *Dickens and His Reader.* New York: Gordian, 1974.

———. *Dickens and His Age: An Essay.* London: H. Cranton, 1939.

Churchill, R.C., ed. *A Bibliography of Dickensian Criticism, 1838-1975.* London, 1975.

Clair, Colin. *Charles Dickens: Life and Character.* London, 1963.

Clark, Cumberland. *Charles Dickens and the Yorkshire Schools: With His Letter to Mrs. Hall.* London: Chiswick, 1918.

———. *Dickens and Democracy and Other Studies.* London: Palmer, 1930.

———. *Dickens and Talfourd.* London, 1919.

———. *Shakespeare and Dickens: A Lecture as Delivered to the Dickens Fellowship, Shakespeare Reading Society, Etc., London, and the Shakespeare Club, Stratford-on-Avon.* 1918; New York: Haskell House, 1973.

———. *The Dogs in Dickens.* London: Chiswick, 1926.

———. *The Story of a Great Friendship: Charles Dickens and Clarkson Stanfield.* London: Chiswick, 1918.

Clark, William R., ed. *Discussions of Charles Dickens.* Boston: D.C. Heath, 1961.

Clayton, Jay. *Charles Dickens in Cyberspace: The Afterlife of the Nineteenth Century in Postmodern Culture.* New York: Oxford UP, 2003.

Cockshut, A.O.J. *The Imagination of Charles Dickens.* London: Collins, 1961.

Cody, Sherwin. *Scott, Dickens, Thackeray.* Chicago: A.C. McClurg, 1917.

Cohen, Jane R. *Charles Dickens and His Original Illustrators*. Columbus, OH: Ohio State UP, 1980.

Cohn, Alan M. and K.K. Collins. *The Cumulated Dickens Checklist, 1970-1979*. Troy, NY: Whitston, 1982.

Colin, Gibson. *Art and Society in the Victorian Literature: Essays on Dickens and His Contemporaries*. Basingstoke: Macmillan, 1989.

Collins, P.A.W. *Dickens and Adult Education*. Rev. ed. Leicester: U of Leicester, 1962.

Collins, Philip, ed. *Charles Dickens: The Public Readings*. Oxford: Clarendon, 1975.

———. ed. *Dickens: The Critical Heritage*. London: Routledge and Kegan Paul, 1971.

———. *A Critical Commentary on Dickens's 'Bleak House'*. Critical Commentaries. London: Macmillan, 1971.

———. *Charles Dickens: David Copperfield*. Studies in English Literature. London: Edward Arnold, 1977.

———. *Dickens and Crime*. London: Macmillan, 1962.

———. *Dickens and Education*. London: Macmillan, 1963.

———. *Dickens, Interviews and Recollections*. London: Macmillan, 1981.

———. *Dickens: Interviews and Recollections*, 2 vols. New York: Barnes and Noble, 1981.

Collins, Philip, et al. *Charles Dickens, Our Mutual Friend: Essays from Britain and Japan*. Tokyo: Nan'un-do, 1983.

Conner, Stephen. *Charles Dickens*. Oxford: Basil Blackwell, 1985.

Connolly, Thomas E. *Essays on Fiction: Dickens, Melville, Hawthorne, and Faulkner*. Lewiston, NY: Edwin Mellen, 1999.

Connor, Steven, ed. *Charles Dickens*. London: Longman, 1996.

———. *Charles Dickens*. Rereading Literature, ed. Terry Eagleton. Oxford: B. Blackwell, 1985.

Coolidge, A.C., Jr. *Charles Dickens as Serial Novelist*. Ames, IA: Iowa State UP, 1967.

Cooper, Lettice. *A Hand Upon the Time: A Life of Charles Dickens*. London: V. Gollancz, 1971.

Cooper, T.P. *With Dickens in Yorkshire*. London, 1923.

Cotsell, Michael A. *Critical Essays on Charles Dickens's A Tale of Two Cities*. New York: G.K. Hall, 1998.

Cotsell, Michael, ed. *Critical Essays on Charles Dickens's Great Expectations*. Boston, MA: G.K. Hall, 1990.

Cotsell, Michael. *The Companion to Our Mutual Friend*. London: Unwin Hyman, 1986.

Coustillas, Pierre. *Gissing's Writings on Dickens: A Bio-Bibliographical Survey*. London: Enitharmon, 1969.

Cox, Don R. *Charles Dickens's The Mystery of Edwin Drood: An Annotated Bibliography*. New York: AMS, 1998.

Cox, Helen. *Mr and Mrs Charles Dickens Entertain at Home*. Oxford: Pergamon, 1970.

Crotch, W. Walter. *The Pageant of Dickens*. London: Chapman, 1917.

———. *The Secret of Dickens*. London: Chapman and Hall, 1919.

———. *The Soul of Dickens*. London: Chapman and Hall, 1916.

———. *The Touchstone of Dickens*. London: Chapman and Hall, 1920.

———. *Charles Dickens: The Social Reformer*. London: Chapman and Hall, 1913.

Crothers, Samuel M. and Jessie W. Smith. *The Children of Dickens*. New York: Scribner, 1925.

Crothers, Samuel M., et al. *The Children of Dickens*. Chicago, IL: Academy Chicago, 2000.

Cruikshank, R.J. *Charles Dickens and Early Victorian England*. London: Pitman, 1949.

Curry, George. *Charles Dickens and Annie Fields*. San Marino, CA: Henry E. Huntington Lib., 1988.

Cusumano, Joseph D. *Transforming Scrooge: Dicken's Blueprint for a Spiritual Awakening*, St. Paul, MN: Llewellyn, 1996.

Dabney, Ross H. *Love and Property in the Novels of Dickens*. London: Chatto and Windus, 1967.

Daldry, Graham. *Charles Dickens and the Form of the Novel*. London: Croom Helm, 1987.

Dale, Alzina S., introd. *Chesterton on Dickens*. San Francisco: Ignatius, 1989.

Daleski, H.M. *Dickens and the Art of Analogy*. London: Faber, 1970.

Dark, Sidney. *Charles Dickens*. London: T.C. and E.C. Jack, 1919.

Darton, Harvey. *Dickens, Positively the First Appearance: A Centenary Review with a Bibliography of "Sketches by Boz"*. London: Argonaut, 1933.

Darwin, Bernard. *Dickens*. London: Duckworth, 1933.

———. *The Dickens Advertiser: A Collection of the Advertisements in the Original Parts of Novels by Charles Dickens*. 1930; Whitefish, MT: Kessinger, 2004.

Davies, James A. *The Textual Life of Dickens's Characters*. London: Macmillan, 1989.

———. *The Textual Life of Dickens' Characters*. London: Macmillan, 1990.

Davis, Earle R. *The Flint and the Flame: The Artistry of Charles Dickens*. Columbia, MO: U of Missouri P, 1963.

Davis, Paul B. *Critical Companion to Charles Dickens: A Literary Reference to His Life and Work*. New York: Facts on File, 2007.

Davis, Paul. *The Penguin Dickens Companion: The Essential Reference to His Life and Work*. Harmondsworth: Penguin, 1999.

De Fontaine, F.G., comp. *A Cyclopedia of the Best Thoughts of Charles Dickens*. New York: E.J. Hale, 1873.

Den Hartog, Dirk. *Dickens and Romantic Psychology: The Self in Time in Nineteenth-Century Literature*. London: Macmillan, 1987.

Dent, H.C. *The Life and Character of Charles Dickens*. London, 1933.

Dever, Carolyn. *Death and the Mother from Dickens to Freud: Victorian Fiction and the Anxiety of Origins*. Cambridge: Cambridge UP, 1998 and 2006.

DeVries, Duane. *Bibliographies, Catalogues, Collections, and Bibliographical and Textual Studies of Dickens's Works*. New York: AMS, 2004.

———. *Dickens's Apprentice Years: The Making of a Novelist*. Hassocks, West Sussex: Harvester, 1976.

———. *General Studies of Charles Dickens and His Writings and Collected Editions of His Works*. New York: AMS, 2000.

Dexter, Walter and J.W.T. Ley. *The Origin of Pickwick: New Facts Now First Published in the Year of the Centenary*. London: Chapman and Hall, 1936.

Dexter, Walter, ed. *Dickens to His Oldest Friend: The Letters of a Lifetime from Charles Dickens to Thomas Beard*. London: Putnam, 1932.

———. ed. *The London of Dickens*. London: Cecil Palmer, 1930.

———. ed. *The Unpublished Letters of Charles Dickens to Mark Lemon*. London: H. and T. Smith, 1927.

———. ed. *Mr. and Mrs. Charles Dickens: His Letters to Her*. London: Constable, 1935.

———. *Some Rogues and Vagabonds of Dickens*. London: C. Palmer, 1927.

———. *The England of Dickens*. London: Cecil Palmer, 1925.

———. *The Kent of Dickens*. London: C. Palmer, 1924.

———. *The Love Romance of Charles Dickens: Told in His Letters to Maria Beadnell (Mrs. Winter)*. London: Argonaut, 1936.

Dickens, Cedric C. and Alan S. Watts, ed. *Sayings of Charles Dickens by Charles Dickens*. London: Duckworth, 1995.

Dickens, Cedric C. *Dining with Dickens*. Goring-on-Thames, Oxfordshire: Elvendon, 1984.

———. *Drinking with Dickens*. London: Mears Caldwell Hacker, 1980.

Dickens, Charles. *Hard Times*. New Delhi: Oxford, 2004.

Dickens, Henry F. *Memories of My Father*. London: Victor Gollancz, 1928.

———. *The Recollections of Sir Henry Dickens*. London: William Heinemann, 1934.

Dickens, Kate (Mrs. Perugini). *The Comedy of Charles Dickens: A Book of Chapters and Extracts Taken from the Writer's Novels*. London: Chapman and Hall, 1906.

Dickens, Mamie and Georgina Hogarth, eds. *The Letters of Charles Dickens, 1833-1870*. 3 vols. London: Macmillan, 1893.

Dickens, Mamie. *Charles Dickens*. 1885; London: Cassell, 1894.

———. *My Father as I Recall Him*. New York: E.P. Dutton, 1897.

Dickens, Monica. *The London of Charles Dickens: Dickens Centenary 1970*. London: London Transport Executive, 1970.

Dolby, George. *Charles Dickens as I Knew Him: The Story of the Reading Tours in Great Britain and America (1866-1870)*. London: T. Fisher Unwin, 1885.

Donovan, Frank. *The Children of Charles Dickens*. London: Leslie Frewin, 1969.

Donovan, Robert A. *The Shaping Vision: Imagination in the English Novel from Defoe to Dickens*. Ithaca, NY: Cornell UP, 1966.

Drake, Jane, ed. *Charles Dickens*. London: Pitkin Pictorials, 1993.

Drew, John M.L. *Dickens the Journalist*. Basingstoke: Palgrave Macmillan, 2003.

Du Cann, C.G.L. *The Love-Lives of Charles Dickens*. London: Frederick Muller, 1961.

Dubberke, Ray. *Dickens, Drood, and the Detectives*. New York: Vantage, 1992.

Duncan, Ian. *Modern Romance and Transformations of the Novel: The Gothic, Scott, Dickens*. Cambridge, UK: Cambridge University Press, 2005.

Dunn, Richard J. *A Routledge Literary Sourcebook on Charles Dickens's David Copperfield*. New York: Routledge, 2004.

Dunn, Richard J. and Ann M. Tandy. *David Copperfield: An Annotated Bibliography-Supplement I, 1981-1998*. New York: AMS, 2000.

Dunn, Richard J. *David Copperfield: An Annotated Bibliography*. The Garland Dickens Bibliographies. Vol. 8. New York: Garland, 1981.

Dupee, F.W., ed. *The Selected Letters of Charles Dickens*. New York: Farrar, Straus and Cudahy, 1960.

Dyson, A.E. *The Inimitable Dickens: A Reading of the Novels*. London: Macmillan, 1970.

———. ed. *Dickens: Bleak House: A Casebook*. Casebook Series. London: Macmillan, 1969.

———. ed. *Dickens: Modern Judgements*. London: Macmillan, 1968.

Eck, John C. *The First Editions of the Writings of Charles Dickens: Their Points and Values: A Bibliography*. London: Maggs, 1932.

Eckel, John C. *The First Editions of the Writings of Charles Dickens and Their Values: A Bibliography*. London: Chapman, 1913.

Edmondson, John. *Dickens on France*. Northampton, MA: Interlink, 2007.

———. *Dickens on France*. Oxford: Signal, 2006.

Edmondson, Reg, Ron Cook, and Peter Park. *Eating Out With Charles Dickens*. Basildon, Essex: Jingle, 2003.

Edwards, P.D. *Dickens's 'Young Men': George Augustus Sala, Edmund Yates and the World of Victorian Journalism*. Aldershot, Hampshire: Ashgate, 1997.

Eigner, Edwin M. *The Dickens Pantomime*. Berkeley, CA: U of California P, 1989.

———. *The Metaphysical Novel in England and America: Dickens, Bulwer, Melville, and Hawthorne*. U of California P, 1978.

Elliott, Ralph W.V. *A Critical Commentary on Dickens's 'A Tale of Two Cities'*. Critical Commentaries. London: Macmillan, 1966.

Ellis, Stephen. *Charles Dickens*. Northamptonshire: First and Best in Education, 1996.

Ellison, Owen. *Charles Dickens*. London, 1908.

Elsna, Hebe. *Unwanted Wife: A Defence of Mrs. Charles Dickens*. London: Jarrolds, 1963.

Elton, Oliver. *Dickens and Thackeray*. London: Arnold, 1924.

Engel, Monroe. *The Maturity of Dickens*. Cambridge, MA: Harvard UP, 1959.

Epstein, Norrie. *The Friendly Dickens: Being a Good-Natured Guide to the Art and Adventures of the Man Who Invented Scrooge*. New York: Viking, 1998.

Eysell, Joanne. *A Medical Companion to Dickens's Fiction*. New York: Peter Lang, 2005.

Fanger, Donald. *Dostoevsky and Romantic Realism: A Study of Dostoevsky in Relation to Balzac, Dickens, and Gogol*. Cambridge: Harvard UP, 1965.

Farr, Chester N., Jr. *Random Thoughts on Dickens*. Philadelphia: C. Sessler, Philadelphia, 1931.

Faulkenburg, Marilyn T. *Church, City, and Labyrinth in Bronte, Dickens, Hardy, and Butor*. New York: Peter Lang, 1993.

Fawcett, F. Dubrez. *Dickens the Dramatist: On Stage, Screen and Radio*. London: W.H. Allen, 1952.

Fawkner, H.W. *Animation and Reification in Dickens's Vision of the Life Denying Society*. Uppsala, 1977.

Fenstermaker, John J. *Charles Dickens 1940-1975: An Analytical Subject Index to Periodical Criticism of the Novels and Christmas Books (Reference Publication in Literature)*. Boston: G.K. Hall, 1979.

Fido, Martin. *Charles Dickens*. London: Routledge and Kegan Paul, 1968.

———. *Charles Dickens: An Authentic Account of His Life and Times*. New York: Hamlyn, 1970.

Field, Kate. *Pen Photographs of Charles Dickens's Readings: Taken from Life*. Troy, NY: Whitston, 1998.

Fielding, K.J. *Studying Charles Dickens*. Harlow, Essex: Longman, 1986.

———. ed. *The Speeches of Charles Dickens*. Oxford: Clarendon, 1960.

———. *Charles Dickens*. London: Longman, 1953.

———. *Charles Dickens: A Critical Introduction*. London: Longmans, 1958.

Fields, James T. *In and Out of Doors with Charles Dickens*. Boston: J.R. Osgood, 1876.

Fisher, Leona W. *Lemon, Dickens, and Mr. Nightingale's Diary: A Victorian Farce*. Victoria, BC: U of Victoria P, 1988.

Fitzgerald, Percy H. *The Life of Charles Dickens as Revealed in His Writings*. 2 vols. London: Chatto and Windus, 1905.

Fitzgerald, Percy. *Bozland: Dickens' Places and People*. London: Downey, 1895.

———. *Memories of Charles Dickens*. Bristol: J.W. Arrowsmith, 1913.

Fitz-Gerald, S.J. Adair. *Dickens and the Drama*. London: Chapman and Hall, 1910.

Fitzsimons, Raymund. *Garish Lights: The Public Reading Tours of Charles Dickens*. New York: J.B. Lippincott, 1970.

———. *The Charles Dickens Show: An Account of His Public Readings 1858-1870*. London: Geoffrey Bles, 1970.

Fleissner, Robert F. *Dickens and Shakespeare*. New York: Haskell House, 1965.

Fletcher, Geoffrey. *The London Dickens Knew*. London: Hutchinson, 1970.

Flint, Kate. *Dickens*. London: Harvester Wheatsheaf, 1985.

Foltinek, Herbert. *Imagination all Compact: How did Charles Dickens Compose His Novels?*. Wien: Verlag der Osterreichischen Akademie der Wissenschaften, 2005.

Ford, Boris, ed. *From Dickens to Hardy*. The New Pelican Guide to English Literature. Vol. 6. 1969; Harmondsworth: Penguin, 1991.

Ford, G.H. and Lauriat Lane Jr. *The Dickens Critics*. Ithaca, NY: Cornell UP, 1961.

Ford, George H. *Dickens and His Age*. New York: Phaeton, 1974.

———. *Dickens and His Readers: Aspects of Novel-Criticism Since 1836*. Princeton, NJ: Princeton UP, 1955.

Ford, George H., et al. *Dickens Criticism: Past, Present, and Future Directions: A Symposium*. Cambridge, MA: CDRC, 1962.

Foreman, Peter. *Tales of the Supernatural*. Genoa: Black Cat, 2006.

Forster, John. *The Life of Charles Dickens*. 3 vols. London: Chapman and Hall, 1872-74.

Forsyte, Charles. *The Decoding of Edwin Drood*. New York: Scribner, 1980.

Fossard, Adelaide R. *Wit and Wisdom from Dickens: A Treasury of Choice Passages*. London: Blackie, 1912.

Frank, Lawrence. *Charles Dickens and the Romantic Self*. Lincoln, NE: U of Nebraska P, 1984.

———. *Victorian Detective Fiction and the Nature of Evidence: The Scientific Investigations of Poe, Dickens and Doyle.* Basingstoke, UK: Palgrave Macmillan, 2003.

Frederick, Rideal C. *Charles Dickens' Heroines and Womenfolk: Some Thoughts Concerning Them.* Haskell House, 1974.

Friedman, Stanley. *Dickens's Fiction: Tapestries of Conscience.* New York: AMS, 2003.

Frost, Thomas. *In Kent with Charles Dickens.* London: Tinsley, 1880.

Fyfe, Thomas A. *Who's Who in Dickens.* 1912; Ann Arbor, MI: Gryphon, 1971.

Gadd, W. Laurence. *The Great Expectations Country.* London: Cecil Palmer, 1929.

Gager, Valerie L. *Shakespeare and Dickens: The Dynamics of Influence.* Cambridge: Cambridge UP, 2006.

Ganz, Margaret. *Humor, Irony, and the Realm of Madness: Psychological Studies in Dickens, Butler, and Others.* New York: AMS, 1990.

Gardner, Joseph. *Dickens in America: Twain, Howells, James, and Norris.* New York: Garland, 1988.

Garis, Howard R. *Dickens Theatre a Reassessment of the Novels.* New York: Oxford UP, 2000.

Garis, Robert. *The Dickens Theatre: A Reassessment of His Novels.* Oxford: Clarendon, 1965.

Gaskell, E. *Dickens and Medicine.* London: Wellcome Institute, 1970.

Gattegno, Jean. *Dickens.* Paris: Seuil, 1975.

Gearing, Nigel. *Dickens in America.* New York: Theatre Communications Group, 1999.

Gerson, Stanley. *Sound and Symbol in the Dialogue of the Works of Charles Dickens.* Stockholm: Almqvist and Wiksell, 1967.

Giddings, Robert, ed. *The Changing World of Charles Dickens.* London: Vision, 1983.

Giddings, Robert. *Student Guide to Charles Dickens*. Billericay, Essex: Greenwich Exchange, 2002.

Gilbert, Elliot L., ed. *Critical Essays on Charles Dickens's Bleak House*. Boston: G.K. Hall, 1989.

Gilfillan, Ross. *The Snake-Oil Dickens Man*. London: Fourth Estate, 1998.

Gissing, George, abr. *Forster's Life of Dickens*. London: Chapman and Hall, 1903.

Gissing, George. *Charles Dickens: A Critical Study*. London: Blackie, 1898.

———. *Critical Studies of the Works of Charles Dickens*. New York: Greenberg, 1924.

———. *The Immortal Dickens*. London: Cecil Palmer, 1925.

Glancy, Ruth F. *A Tale of Two Cities: An Annotated Bibliography*. The Garland Dickens Bibliographies. Vol. 12. New York: Garland, 1993.

Glancy, Ruth F. *Dickens's Christmas Books, Christmas Stories, and Other Short Fiction: An Annotated Bibliography*. The Garland Dickens Bibliographies. Vol. 4. New York: Garland, 1985.

Glancy, Ruth. *A Tale of Two Cities: Dickens's Revolutionary Novel*. Boston, MA: G.K. Hall, 1991.

———. *Student Companion to Charles Dickens*. Wesport, CT: Greenwood, 1999.

Glavin, John, ed. *Dickens on Screen*. Cambridge: Cambridge UP, 2003.

Glavin, John. *After Dickens: Reading, Adaptation and Performance*. Cambridg: Cambridge UP, 1999.

Gold, Joseph, comp. *The Stature of Dickens: A Centenary Bibliography*. Toronto: U of Toronto P, 1971.

Gold, Joseph. *Charles Dickens: Radical Moralist*. London, 1972.

Goldberg, Michael. *Carlyle and Dickens*. Athens, GA: U of Georgia P, 1972.

Golden, Morris. *Dickens Imagining Himself: Six Novel Encounters with a Changing World*. Lanham, MD: UP of America, 1992.

Golding, Robert. *Idiolects in Dickens: The Major Techniques and Chronological Development*. London: Macmillan, 1985.

Gomme, A.H. *Dickens*. London: Evans, 1971.

Gordon, Elizabeth H. *The Naming of Characters in the Work of Charles Dickens*. Lincoln, NE: U of Nebraska P, 1917.

Graham, Eleanor. *The Story of Charles Dickens*. London: Methuen, 1952.

Graham, Paul. *The Dickens Connection*. London: Local History, 1995.

Grant, Allan. *A Preface to Dickens*. London: Longman, 1984.

Greaves, John. *Dickens at Doughty Street*. London: Elm Tree, 1975.

———. *Who's Who in Dickens*. London: Elm Tree, 1972.

Green, Frank. *As Dickens Saw Them*. London, 1933.

———. *London Homes of Dickens*. 1928; Folcroft, PA: Folcroft Library, 1970.

Grego, Joseph. *Pictorial Pickwickiana: Charles Dickens and His Illustrators with 350 Drawings and Engravings* by Robert Seymour, et al. 2 vols. London: Chapman and Hall, 1899.

Grigsby, Ann M. *The Victorian Craze: The Appeal of Madness in Charles Reade, Wilkie Collins, and Charles Dickens*. Ann Arbor, MI: UMI Dess. Services, 1998.

Grillo, Virgil. *Charles Dickens' "Sketches by Boz": End in the Beginning*. Boulder: Colorado Associated UP, 1974.

Gross, John and Gabriel Pearson, eds. *Dickens and the Twentieth Century*. London: Routledge, 1962.

Guerard, Albert J. *The Triumph of the Novel: Dickens, Dostoevsky, Faulkner*. New York: Oxford UP, 1976.

———. *The Triumph of the Novel: Dickens, Dostoevsky, Faulkner*. Oxford: Oxford UP, 1977.

Guida, Fred. *A Christmas Carol and Its Adaptations*. Jefferson, NC: McFarland, 1999.

———. *A Christmas Carol and Its Adaptations: A Critical Examination of Dickens's Story and Its Productions on Screen and Television*. Jefferson, NC: McFarland, 2000.

Guiliano, Edward and Philip Collins, eds. *The Annotated Dickens*. 2 vols. London: Orbis, 1986.

Gummer, Ellis N. *Dickens's Work in Germany*. Oxford, 1946.

Haines, Charles. *Charles Dickens*. Studies in Language and Literature. Immortals of Literature. New York: F. Watts, 1969.

Hammerton, J.A. *The Dickens Companion: A Book of Anecdote and Reference*. Charles Dickens Library. London: Educational Book, 1910.

———. *The Dickens Picture-Book: A Record of the Dickens Illustrators*. London: Educational Book, 1910.

Hammond, R.A. *The Life and Writings of Charles Dickens: A Memorial Volume*. 1870; New York: Haskell House, 1972.

Hanaford, Phebe A. *The Life and Writings of Charles Dickens: A Woman's Memorial Volume*. Boston: B.B. Russell, 1871.

Hanna, Robert C. *Dickens's Nonfictional, Theatrical, and Poetical Writings: An Annotated Bibliography, 1820-2000*. New York: AMS, 2007.

———. *The Dickens Christian Reader: A Collection of New Testament Readings and Biblical References from the Works of Charles Dickens*. New York: AMS, 2000.

———. *The Dickens Family Gospel*. San Diego, CA: Legacy, 1998.

Harbage, Alfred H. *A Kind of Power: The Shakespeare-Dickens Analogy*. 1925; Philadelphia: American Philosophical Soc., 1975.

Hardwick, Michael and Mollie, comp. *The Charles Dickens Quiz Book*. London: Luscombe, 1974.

Hardwick, Michael and Mollie. *Dickens's England*. London: J.M. Dent, 1970.

———. *The Charles Dickens Companion*. New York: E.P. Dutton, 1968.

———. *The Charles Dickens Encyclopedia*. Reading: Osprey Publishing Ltd., 1973.

Hardy, Barbara Nathan. *Dickens and Creativity*. London: Continuum, 2008.

———. *Charles Dickens: The Writer and His Work*. Windsor, Berkshire: Profile Books, 1983.

———. *Dickens: The Later Novels*. London: Longman, 1968.

———. *The Moral Art of Dickens: Essays*. London: Athlone, 1970.

Harris, Edwin. *Gad's Hill Place and Charles Dickens*. Rochester: Edwin Harris, 1910.

Harrison, Michael. *Charles Dickens: A Sentimental Journey in Search of an Unvarnished Portrait*. London: Cassell, 1953.

Hatton, Thomas and Arthur H. Cleaver. *A Bibliography of the Periodical Works of Charles Dickens: Bibliographical Analytical and Statistical*. London: Chapman and Hall, 1933.

Hawes, Donald. *Charles Dickens*. London: Continuum, 2007.

———. *Who's Who in Dickens*. London: Routledge and Kegan Paul, 1997.

———. *Who's Who in Dickens*. New York: Routledge, 2002.

Hawksley, Lucinda. *Katey: The Life and Loves of Dickens's Artist Daughter*. London: Doubleday, 2006.

Hayward, Arthur L. *The Days of Dickens: A Glance at Some Aspects of Early Victorian Life in London*. London: George Routledge, 1924.

———. *The Dickens Encyclopaedia*. 1924; London: Folio Soc., 1989.

Heineman, Helen K. *Three Victorians in the New World: Interpretations of the New World* in the works of Frances Trollope, Charles Dickens and Anthony Trollope.

Herst, Beth F. *The Dickens Hero: Selfhood and Alienation in the Dickens World*. London: Weidenfeld and Nicolson, 1990.

Hewett, Edward and W.F. Axton. *Convivial Dickens: The Drinks of Dickens and His Times*. Athens, OH: Ohio UP, 1983.

Hibbert, Christopher. *The Making of Charles Dickens*. London: Longmans, 1967.

Higbie, Robert. *Dickens and Imagination*. Gainesville, FL: UP of Florida, 1998.

Hill, Nancy K. *A Reformer's Art: Dickens' Picturesque and Grotesque Imagery*. Athens, OH: Ohio UP, 1981.

Hobsbaum, Philip. *A Reader's Guide to Charles Dickens*. London: Thames and Hudson, 1972.

Hochman, Baruch and Ilja Wachs. *Dickens: The Orphan Condition*. Madison, NJ: Fairleigh Dickinson UP, 1999.

Holbrook, David. *Charles Dickens and the Image of Women*. New York: New York UP, 1993.

———. *Charles Dickens and Woman*. London: Vision, 1991.

Holdsworth, William S. *Charles Dickens as a Legal Historian*. New Haven: Yale UP, 1928.

Hollingsworth, Keith. *The Newgate Novel, 1830-1847: Bulwer, Ainsworth, Dickens, and Thackeray*. Detroit: Wayne State UP, 1963.

Hollington, Michael, ed. *Charles Dickens: Critical Assessments*. 4 vols. Mountfield, East Sussex, Helm Information, 1995.

Hollington, Michael. *Dickens and the Grotesque*. London: Croom Helm, 1984.

Homer, Bryan. *Charles Dickens and Leamington Spa: Fact, Fiction and Fancy*. Coventry, UK: Jones-Sands, 1992.

Hori, Masahiro. *Investigating Dickens' Style: A Collocational Analysis*. Basingstoke, UK: Palgrave Macmillan, 2004.

Hornback, Bert G. *Noah's Arkitecture: A Study of Dickens's Mythology*. Athens, OH: Ohio UP, 1972.

———. *The Hero of My Life: Essays on Dickens*. Athens, OH: Ohio UP, 1981.

Horsman, E.A. *Dickens and the Structure of the Novel.* Folcroft, PA: Folcroft Library, 1970.

Horton, Susan R. *Interpreting, Interpreting: Interpreting Dickens's Dombey*. Baltimore, MD: Johns Hopkins, 1979.

———. *The Reader in the Dickens World: Style and Response.* London: Macmillan, 1981.

Hotten, J.C. *Charles Dickens, the Story of His Life: With Illustrations and Facsimiles*. New York: Harper, 1870.

House, Humphry. *The Dickens World.* Oxford: Oxford UP, 1941.

Houston, Gail Turley. *From Dickens to Dracula: Gothic, Economics, and Victorian Fiction.* Cambridge: Cambridge UP, 2005.

Hughes, James L. *Dickens as an Educator*. New York: D. Appleton, 1900.

Hughes, William R. *A Week's Tramp in Dickensland: Together with Personal Reminiscences of the 'Inimitable Boz' Therein Collected*. Illust. F.G. Kitton and other artists. London: Chapman and Hall, 1891.

Humphreys, Arthur. *Charles Dickens and His First Schoolmaster*. Manchester, 1926.

Huntington, Trumbull, ed. *The Dickens Reader*. New York: Howell Soskin, 1948.

Hutchings, Richard J. *Dickens on an Island*. Bath: Brodie, 1970.

Hutton, Laurence, ed. *Letters of Charles Dickens to Wilkie Collins, 1851-1870*. London: J.R. Osgood, 1892.

Hyatt, Alfred H. *The Pocket Dickens: Being Favourite Passages Chosen from the Works of Charles Dickens*. London: Chatto and Windus, 1906.

Imahayashi, Osamu. *Charles Dickens and Literary Dialect.* Hiroshima: Keisuisha, 2006.

Ingham, Patricia. *Dickens, Women and Language.* London: Harvester Wheatsheaf, 1992.

Jackson, T.A. *Charles Dickens: The Progress of a Radical.* 1937; New York: Haskell House, 1971.

Jacobson, Wendy S., ed. *Dickens and the Children of Empire.* Basingstoke, UK: Palgrave Macmillan, 2001.

Jacobson, Wendy. *The Companion to The Mystery of Edwin Drood.* London: Unwin Hyman, 1986.

Jaffe, Audrey. *Vanishing Points: Dickens, Narrative, and the Subject of Omniscence.* Berkeley: U of California P, 1991.

James, Elizabeth. *Charles Dickens.* London: BL, 2004.

Jaques, E.T. *Charles Dickens in Chancery: Being an Account of His Proceedings in Respect of the 'Christmas Carol' With Some Gossip in Relation to the Old Law Court.* Union, NJ: Lawbook Exchange, 2000.

Jarmuth, Sylvia L. *Dickens's Use of Women in His Novels.* New York: Excelsior, 1967.

Jarvie, Paul A. *Ready to Trample on All Human Law: Financial Capitalism in the Fiction of Charles Dickens.* New York: Routledge, 2005.

Johannsen, Albert. *Phiz Illustrations from the Novels of Charles Dickens.* Chicago: U of Chicago P, 1956.

John, Juliet. *Dickens's Villains: Melodrama, Character, Popular Culture.* New York: Oxford UP, 2001.

Johnson, Derek. *Pastoral in the Work of Charles Dickens.* New York: Peter Lang, 1992.

Johnson, E.D.H. *Charles Dickens: An Introduction to His Novels.* New York: Random, 1969.

Johnson, Edgar and Eleanor. *The Dickens Theatrical Reader.* London: Victor Gollancz, 1964.

Johnson, Edgar, introd. *Letters from Charles Dickens to Angela Burdett-Coutts, 1841-1865.* London: J. Cape, 1955.

——— introd. *The Heart of Charles Dickens: As Revealed in His Letters to Angela Burdett-Coutts*. New York: Duell, Sloan and Pearce, 1952.

———. *Charles Dickens: His Tragedy and Triumph*. 2 vols. New York: Simon and Schuster, 1952.

———. *Charles Dickens: His Tragedy and Triumph*. London: Victor Gollancz, 1953.

Johnson, Spencer. *The Value of Imagination: The Story of Charles Dickens*. La Jolla, CA: Value Communications, 1977.

Johnson, Wendell S., ed. *Charles Dickens: New Perspectives*. Englewood Cliffs, NJ: Prentice-Hall, 1982.

Johnstone, F.D. *Dickens in Our Commonwealth*. Melbourne, 1909.

Jones, C.H. *A Short Life of Charles Dickens*. New York, 1880.

Jones, Richard. *Walking Dickensian London: Twenty-five Original Walks Through London's Victorian Quarters*. London: New Holland, 2004.

Jordan, John O. *The Cambridge Companion to Charles Dickens*. Cambridge: Cambridge UP, 2001.

Kaplan, Fred. *Charles Dickens' Book of Memoranda*. New York: New York Public Library, 1981.

———. *Dickens and Mesmerism: The Hidden Springs of Fiction*. Princeton, NJ: Princeton UP, 1975.

———. *Dickens: A Biography*. London: Hodder and Stoughton, 1989.

———. *Dickens: A Biography*. New York: William Morrow, 1988.

Kent, Charles. *Charles Dickens as a Reader*. London: Chapman, 1872.

Kent, W. *With Charles Dickens in the Borough*. London, 1926.

Kent, William. *Dickens and Religion*. London: Watts, 1930.

———. *London for Dickens Lovers*. London: Methuen, 1935.

Kincaid, James R. *Dickens and the Rhetoric of Laughter.* Oxford: Clarendon, 1971.

King, R.W. *England from Wordsworth to Dickens.* London: Methuen, 1928.

Kingsmill, Hugh. *The Sentimental Journey: A Life of Charles Dickens.* London: Wishart, 1934.

Kitton, F.G., ed. *The Poems and Verses of Charles Dickens.* New York: Harper, 1903.

Kitton, Fred. G., comp. *Dickensiana: A Bibliography of the Literature Relating to Charles Dickens and His Writings.* London: George Redway, 1886.

Kitton, Frederic G. *Charles Dickens by Pen and Pencil: Including Anecdotes and Reminiscences Collected from His Friends and Contemporaries.* 3 vols. London: Sabin, 1890.

———. *Charles Dickens: His Life, Writings and Personality.* London: Blackwood, 1900.

———. *Dickens and His Illustrators: Cruikshank, Seymour, Buss, "Phiz", Cattermole, Leech, Doyle, Stanfield, Maclise, Tenniel, Frank Stone, Landseer, Palmer, Topham, Marcus Stone, and Luke Fildes.* London: George Redway, 1899.

———. *The Dickens Country.* London: Adam and Charles Black, 1905.

———. *The Minor Writings of Charles Dickens: A Bibliography and Sketch.* London: Stock, 1897.

Klein, Shelley. *Wicked Wit of Charles Dickens.* London: Michael O'Mara, 2003.

Knezevic, Borislav. *Figures of Finance Capitalism: Writing, Class, and Capital in the Age of Dickens.* New York: Routledge, 2003.

Kosky, Jules. *Mutual Friends: Charles Dickens and Great Ormond Street Children's Hospital.* London: Weidenfeld and Nicolson, 1989.

Kotera, Risa. *Another Side to Charles Dickens: From Dombey and Son to Our Mutual Friend.* Tokyo: Eihosha, 1994.

Kotzin, Michael. *Dickens and the Fairy Tale*. Bowling Green, OH: Bowling Green UP, 1972.

Kucich, John. *Excess and Restraint in the Novels of Charles Dickens*. Athens, GA: U of Georgia P, 1981.

———. *Repression in Victorian Fiction: Charlotte Bronte, George Eliot, and Charles Dickens*. Berkeley: U of California P, 1987.

Lambert, Mark. *Dickens and the Suspended Quotation*. New Haven, CT: Yale UP, 1981.

Lang, Andrew. *The Puzzle of Dickens's Last Plot*. London: Chapman and Hall, 1905.

Langton, Robert. *Charles Dickens and Rochester*. London: Chapman and Hall, 1880.

Langton, Robert. *The Childhood and Youth of Charles Dickens: With Retrospective Notes, and Elucidations, from His Books and Letters*. Manchester: Albert Chambers, 1883.

Larson, Janet L. *Dickens and the Broken Scripture*. Athens, GA: U of Georgia P, 1985.

Lary, N.M., *Dostoevsky and Dickens: A Study of Literary Influence*. London: Routledge and Kegan Paul, 1973.

Laurence, Dan H. and Martin Quinn, ed. *Shaw on Dickens*. New York: Frederick Ungar, 1985.

———. ed. *Shaw on Dickens*. New York: Frederick Ungar, 1987.

Leacock, Stephen. *Charles Dickens: His Life and Work*. London: P. Davies, 1933.

Leavis, F.R. and Q.D. *Dickens: The Novelist*. London: Chatto and Windus, 1970.

Ledger, Sally. *Dickens and the Popular Radical Imagination*. Cambridge, UK: Cambridge UP, 2007.

Lehmann, R.C., ed. *Charles Dickens as Editor: Being Letters Written by Him to William Henry Wills, His Sub-Editor*. London: Smith and Elder, 1912.

Lenard, Mary. *Preaching Pity: Dickens, Gaskell, and Sentimentalism in Victorian Culture.* New York: Peter Lang, 1999.

Lester, Valerie Browne. *Phiz: The Man Who Drew Dickens.* London: Pimlico, 2006.

Lettis, Richard. *Dickens on Literature: A Continuing Study of His Aesthetic.* New York: AMS, 1990.

———. *The Dickens Aesthetic.* New York: AMS, 1989.

Levit, Fred. *A Dickens Glossary for American Readers.* Wilmett, IL: Hall Design, 1996.

Ley, J.W.T. *The Dickens Circle: A Narrative of the Novelist's Friendships.* New York: E.P. Dutton, 1919.

Lightwood, James T. *Charles Dickens and Music.* London: Charles H. Kelly, 1912.

Lindsay, Jack. *Charles Dickens: A Biographical and Critical Study.* London: Andrew Dakers, 1950.

Litvack, Leon. *Charles Dickens's Dombey and Son: An Annotated Bibliography.* New York: AMS, 1999.

Livingston, Flora V., ed. *Charles Dickens's Letters to Charles Lever.* Cambridge, MA: Harvard UP, 1933.

Loewen, Nancy. *Charles Dickens.* Mankato, MN: Creative Education, 2000.

Lougy, Robert E. *Martin Chuzzlewitt: An Annotated Bibliography.* The Garland Dickens Bibliographies. New York: Garland, 1990.

Lubitz, Rita. *Marital Power in Dickens' Fiction.* New York: Peter Lang, 1996.

Lucas, John. *Charles Dickens: The Major Novels.* Harmondsworth: Penguin, 1992.

———. *The Melancholy Man: A Study of Dickens's_Novels.* London: Methuen, 1970.

Lupton, Edward B. *Dickens the Immortal.* Kansas City, MO: A. Fowler, 1923.

Lynch, Tony. *Dickens's England: A Travellers' Companion.* London: B.T. Batsford, 1986.

MacKay, Carol H., ed. *Dramatic Dickens*. London: Macmillan, 1989.

MacKenzie, Norman and Jeanne. *Dickens: A Life*. Oxford: Oxford UP, 1979.

MacKenzie, R.S. *Life of Charles Dickens*. Philadelphia: T.B. Peterson, 1870.

MacPike, Loralee. *Dostoevsky's Dickens: A Study of Literary Influence*. London: George Prior, 1981.

Maglavera, Soultana. *Time Patterns in Later Dickens*. Amsterdam Rodopi, 1994.

Magnet, Myron. *Dickens and the Social Order*. Philadelphia, PA: U of Pennsylvania P, 1985.

Mankowitz, Wolf. *Dickens of London*. London: Weidenfeld and Nicolson, 1976.

Manning, John. *Dickens on Education*. Toronto: U of Toronto P, 1959.

Manning, Sylvia B. *Dickens as Satirist*. New Haven, CT: Yale UP, 1971.

Marcus, Steven. *Dickens: From Pickwick to Dombey*. London: Chatto and Windus, 1965.

Marlow, James E. *Charles Dickens: The Uses of Time*. Selinsgrove, PA: Susquehanna UP, 1994.

Marshall, Brenda. *Mr Pickwick's Plentiful Portions: The Charles Dickens' Cookbook for Today*. London: Frederick Muller, 1980.

Marzials, Frank. *Life of Charles Dickens*. London: Walter Scott, 1887.

Matz, B.W. *Dickensian Inns and Taverns*. London: Cecil Palmer, 1922.

Maurois, Andre. *Dickens*. Trans. Hamish Miles. London: John Lane the Bodley Head, 1934.

Mazzeno, Laurence W. *The Dickens Industry: Critical Perspectives 1836-2005*. Rochester, NY: Camden House, 2008.

McGovern, Timothy M. *Dickens in Galdos*. New York: Peter Lang, 2000.

McGuire, M. *Role of Women in the Novels of Charles Dickens*. London: Minerva, 1995.

McHugh, Stuart D. *Knock on the Nursery Door: Tales of the Dickens Children*. London: Joseph, 1972.

McKenzie, Charles H. *The Religious Sentiments of Charles Dickens*. London: W. Scott, 1884.

McKnight, Natalie. *Idiots, Madmen, and Other Prisoners in Dickens*. New York: St. Martin's, 1993.

McMaster, Juliet. *Dickens the Designer*. New York: Barnes and Noble, 1987.

McNulty, J.H. *Concerning Dickens and Other Literary Characters*. Keighley, West Yorkshire: Wadsworth, 1933.

McSpadden, J. Walker. *Synopses of Dickens's Novels*. London: Chapman and Hall, 1909.

Meckier, Jerome. *Dickens's Great Expectations: Misnar's Pavilion Versus Cinderella*. Lexington, KY: UP of Kentucky, 2002.

———. *Hidden Rivalries in Victorian Fiction: Dickens, Realism, and Revaluation*. Lexington, KY: UP of Kentucky, 1987.

———. *Innocent Abroad: Charles Dickens's American Engagements*. Lexington, KY: UP of Kentucky, 1990.

Meier, Stefanie. *Animation and Mechanization in the Novels of Charles Dickens*. Bern: Francke Verlag, 1982.

Mengham, Rod. *Charles Dickens*. Devon: Northcote House, 1991.

Miller, J.H. and D. Borowits. *Charles Dickens and George Cruikshank*. California, 1971.

Miller, J. Hillis. *Charles Dickens: The World of His Novels*. Cambridge, MA: Harvard UP, 1958.

Miltoun, Francis. *Dickens's London*. London, 1904.

Miyazaki, Koichi. *The Inner Structure of Charles Dickens's Later Novels*. Tokyo: Sanseido, 1974.

Monod, Sylvere. *Dickens the Novelist.* Norman, OK: U of Oklahoma P, 1968.

Moon, Sangwha. *Dickens in the Context of Victorian Culture: An Interpretation of Three of Dickens's Novels from the Viewpoint of Darwinian Nature.* Ann Arbor, MI: UMI Dess. Services, 1996.

Moreland, Arthur. *Dickens in London: Forty-Seven Drawings.* London: Palmer, 1928.

———. *Dickens Landmarks in London: Written and Illustrated by Arthur Moreland with a Foreword by Sir Henry F. Dickens.* 1931; New York: Haskell House, 1973.

Morgan, Nicholas H. *Secret Journeys: Theory and Practice in Reading Dickens.* Cranbury, NJ: Associated UP, 1992.

Morgentaler, Goldie. *Dickens and Heredity: When Like Begets Like.* New York: St. Martin's, 1999.

Morris, Pam. *Dickens's Class Consciousness: A Marginal View.* London: Macmillan, 1991.

Moss, Sidney P. and Carolyn J. Moss. *Charles Dickens and His Chicago Relatives: A Documentary Narrative.* Troy, NY: Whitston, 1994.

———. *Dickens, Trollope, Jefferson: Three Anglo-American Encounters.* Troy, NY: Whitston, 1999.

———. *The Charles Dickens-Thomas Powell Vendetta: The Story in Documents.* Troy, NY: Whitston, 1996.

Moss, Sidney P. *Charles Dickens' Quarrel with America.* New York: Whitston, 1984.

Moxham, Jeffrey. *Interfering Values in the Nineteenth-Century British Novel: Austen, Dickens, Eliot.* Palgrave, 2002.

Murray, Brain. *Charles Dickens.* New York: Continuum, 1993.

Naeff-Hinderling, Annabeth. *The Search for the Culprit; Dickens's Conflicting Self- and Object-Representation.* Bern: Francke, 1983.

Nayder, Lillian. *Unequal Partners: Charles Dickens, Wilkie Collins, and Victorian Authorship*. Ithaca, NY: Cornell UP, 2002.

Nelson, Harland S. *Charles Dickens*. Boston: Twayne Publishers, 1981.

Newcomb, Mildred. *The Imagined World of Charles Dickens*. Athens, OH: Ohio UP, 1989.

Newey, Vincent. *The Scriptures of Charles Dickens: Novels of Ideology, Novels of Self*. Aldershot, Hampshire: Ashgate, 2004.

Newlin, George, ed. *Every Thing in Dickens*. Westport, CT: Greenwood, 1995.

Newlin, George. *Every Thing in Dickens: Ideas and Subjects Discussed by Charles Dickens in His Complete Works: A Topicon*. Westport, CT: Greenwood, 1996.

Newman, S.J. *Dickens At Play*. London: Macmillan, 1981.

Newsom, Robert. *Charles Dickens Revisited*. Twayne's English Authors Series, 558. New York: Twayne, 2000.

———. *Dickens on the Romantic Side of Familiar Things: "Bleak House" and the Novel Tradition*. New York: Columbia UP, 1977.

Newton, Ruth and Naomi Lebowitz. *Dickens, Manzoni, Zola, and James: The Impossible Romance*. Columbia, MO: U of Missouri P, 1990.

Nicoll, W. Robertson. *The Problem of "Edwin Drood": A Study in the Methods of Dickens*. 1912; New York: Haskell House, 1972.

Nicoll, W. Robertson. *The Problem of 'Edwin Drood'*. London: Hodder and Stoughton, 1912.

Nicoll, William R. *Dickens's Own Story: Side-Lights on His Life and Personality*. London: Chapman and Hall, 1923.

Nisbet, Ada and Blake Nevius, ed. *Dickens Centennial Essays*. Berkeley, CA: U of California P, 1971.

Nisbet, Ada. *Dickens and Ellen Ternan*. Berkeley, CA: U of California P, 1952.

Oberhelman, David D. *Dickens in Bedham: Madness and Restraint in His Fiction*. Fredericton, NB: York, 1995.

Oppenlander, Ella A. *Dickens' All the Year Round: Descriptive Index and Contributor List*. New York: Whitston, 1984.

Orwell, George. *Dickens, Dali and Others: Studies in Popular Culture*. New York: Reynal and Hitchcock, 1946.

Osborne, Charles C., ed. *Letters of Charles Dickens to the Baroness Burdett-Coutts*. London: J. Murray, 1931.

Ostry, Elaine. *Social Dreaming: Dickens and the Fairy Tale*. New York: Routledge, 2002.

Oulton, Carolyn W. de la L. *Literature and Religion in Mid-Victorian England: From Dickens to Eliot*. Basingstoke, Hampshire: Palgrave Macmillan, 2003.

Paganoni, Maria Cristina. *The Magic Lantern: Representation of the Double in Dickens*. New York: Routledge, 2008.

Page, Norman, ed. *Charles Dickens: Family History*. 5 vols. New York: Routledge, 2000.

———. ed. *Hard Times, Great Expectations, and Our Mutual Friend: A Casebook*. Casebook Series. London: Macmillan, 1979.

———. *A Dickens Chronology*. Basingstoke: Macmillan, 1988.

———. *A Dickens Companion*. London: Macmillan, 1984.

Palmer, William J. *Dickens and New Historicism*. London: Macmillan, 1998.

Palmer, William J. *The Proverbial Charles Dickens: An Index to Proverbs in the Works of Charles Dickens*. New York: Peter Lang, 1997.

———. ed. *The Detective and Mr. Dickens: Being an Account of the Macbeth Murders and the Strange Events Surrounding Them*. New York: St. Martin's, 1990.

Parker, David. *Christmas and Charles Dickens*. Brooklyn, NY: AMS, 2005.

Parker, Michael St. John. *Charles Dickens*. London: Pitkin Pictorials, 1973.

Paroissien, David, ed. *Selected Letters of Charles Dickens*. Boston: Twayne, 1985.

———. *A Companion to Charles Dickens*. Malden, MA: Blackwell, 2008.

———. *The Companion to A Tale of Two Cities*. London: Unwin Hyman, 1988.

———. *The Companion to Oliver Twist*. Edinburgh UP, 1991.

Partlow, Robert B., Jr. *Dickens the Craftsman: Strategies of Presentation*. Carbondale, IL: Southern Illinois UP, 1970.

Patten, Robert L. *Charles Dickens and His Publishers*. Oxford: Clarendon, 1978.

Payne, E.F. and H.H. Harper. *The Romance of Charles Dickens and Maria Beadnell Winter*. Boston: P for members of the Bibliophile Society, 1929.

———. *The Charity of Charles Dickens: His Interest in the Home for Dallen Women and a History of the Strange Case of Caroline Maynard Thompson*. Boston: P for members of the Bibliophile Society, 1929.

Payne, Edward F. *Dickens's Days in Boston: A Record of Daily Events*. Boston: Houghton, 1927.

Pearson, Hesketh. *Dickens: His Character, Comedy, and Career*. London: Methuen, 1949.

Pemberton, T. Edgar. *Charles Dickens and the Stage: A Record of His Connection with the Drama as Playwright, Actor and Critic*. London: Redway, 1888.

———. *Dickens's London; or, London in the Works of Charles Dickens*. 1876; New York: Haskell House, 1972.

Perera, Suvendrini. *Reaches of Empire: The English Novel from Edgeworth to Dickens*. New York: Columbia UP, 1991.

Perkins, Donald. *Charles Dickens: A New Perspective*. Guildford, Worcester: Biling, 1982.

Peters, Peters C. *Charles Dickens (Pocket Biographies)*. Stroud, Gloucestershire: Sutton, 1998.

Philip, Alex J. and W. Laurence Gadd. *A Dickens Dictionary: The Characters and Scenes of the Novels and Miscellaneous Works Alphabetically Arranged*. London: Routledge, 1909.

Philip, Alex J. *Dickens's Honeymoon and Where He Spent It*. London: Chapman and Hall, 1912.

Philip, Alexander J. and Carl Fuchs. *Maxnotes Dickens Dictionary: A Key to the Characters and Places in the Books of Charles Dickens*. Piscataway, NJ: Research and Education Ass., 2001.

Philip, Alexander J., et al. *A Dickens Dictionary: A Key to the Characters and Places in the Books of Charles Dickens (Maxnotes)*. 1928; New York: Crescent, 1990.

Philip, Neil and Victor Neuburg. *A December Vision: Dickens's Social Journalism*. London: Collins, 1986.

Phillips, Walter C. *Dickens, Reade and Collins: Sensation Novelists*. New York: Columbia UP, 1919.

———. *Dickens, Reade, and Collins: Sensation Novelists; A Study in the Conditions and Theories of Novel Writing in Victorian England*. New York: Russell, 1962.

Pierce, Gilbert A. *The Dickens Dictionary: A Key to the Characters and Principal Incidents in the Tales of Charles Dickens*. 1878; New York: Haskell House, 1972.

———. *The Dickens Dictionary: A Key to the Plots and Characters in the Tales of Charles Dickens*. Boston: Houghton Mifflin, 1900.

Pluckrose, H. and F. Peacock. *A Dickens Anthology*. London: Mills and Boon, 1970.

Podeschi, John B. *Dickens and Dickensiana: A Catalogue of the Richard Gimbel Collection in the Yale University Library*. New Haven: Yale U Lib., 1980.

Pointer, Michael. *Charles Dickens on the Screen: The Film, Television, and Video Adaptations*. Lanham, MD: Scarecrow, 1996.

Pool, Daniel. *Dickens' Fur Coat and Charlotte's Unanswered Letters*. New York: HarperPerennial, 1997.

———. *What Jane Austen Ate and Charles Dickens Knew: From Fox Hunting to Whist.* New York: Simon and Schuster, 1993.

Pope, Norris. *Dickens and Charity.* London: Macmillan, 1978.

Pope-Hennessy, Una. *Charles Dickens: 1812-1870.* London: Chatto and Windus, 1945.

Powers, Ella M., ed. *A Dickens Reader.* Riverside Literature Series. Boston: Houghton Mifflin, 1911.

Prettejohns, Graham. *Charles Dickens and Southwark.* Southwark Libraries Dept., 1974.

Price, Martin, ed. *Dickens: A Collection of Critical Essays.* New Jersey, 1976.

———. ed. *Dickens: A Collection of Critical Essays.* Englewood, NJ: Prentice-Hall, 1967.

Priestley, J.B. *Charles Dickens, and His World.* London: Thames and Hudson, 1961.

———. *Charles Dickens: A Pictorial Biography.* London: Thames and Hudson, 1961.

Pringle, Patrick. *The Young Dickens.* London: Max Parrish, 1962.

Pritchard, R.E., ed. *Dickens's England: Life in Victorian Times.* Westport, CT: Praeger, 2003.

Pugh, Edwin. *Charles Dickens: The Apostle of the People.* London: New Age, 1908.

———. *The Charles Dickens Originals.* London: T.N. Foulis, 1912.

Pykett, Lyn. *Charles Dickens.* Basingstoke: Palgrave, 2002.

Quiller-Couch, Arthur. *Charles Dickens and Other Victorians.* Cambridge: Cambridge UP, 1925.

Quirk, Randolph. *Charles Dickens and Appropriate Language: Inaugural Lecture of the Professor of English Language Delivered in the Appleby Lecture Theatre on 26 May 1959.* Durham: Durham UP, 1959.

Rackham, Jeff. *The Rag and Bone Shop: A Novel Based on the Secret Life of Charles Dickens.* London: Penguin, 2002.

Raina, Badri N. *Charles Dickens: The Dialectic of Self.* Madison WI: U of Wisconsin-Madison P, 1976.

———. *Dickens and the Dialectic of Growth.* Madison, NJ: U of Wisconsin P, 1986.

Rainsford, Dominic. *Authorship, Ethics, and the Reader: Blake, Dickens, Joyce.* Basingstoke: Macmillan, 1997.

Rantavaara, Irma I. *Dickens in the Light of English Criticism.* Helsinki: R. West, 1944.

Reed, John R. *Dickens and Thackeray: Punishment and Forgiveness.* Athens, OH: Ohio UP, 1995.

Rees, R.J. *English Literature.* New Delhi: Macmillan, 2000.

Reid, J.C. *Charles Dickens: Little Dorrit.* Studies in English Literature. London: Edward Arnold, 1967.

———. *The Hidden World of Charles Dickens.* Auckland, NZ: U of Auckland P, 1962.

Rice, C.M. *The Story of Our Mutual Friend: Transcribed into Phonetic Notation from the Work of Charles Dickens.* Cambridge: W. Heffer, 1920.

Richards, Jeffrey. *Films and British National Identity: From Dickens to Dad's Army.* Manchester: Manchester UP, 1997.

Rimmer, Alfred. *About England with Dickens.* London: Chatto and Windus, 1883.

Romano, John. *Dickens and Reality.* New York: Columbia UP, 1978.

Ronald, Ann. *Functions of Setting in the Novel: From Mrs. Radcliffe to Charles Dickens.* New York: Arno, 1971.

Rooke, Patrick. *The Age of Dickens.* London: Wayland, 1970.

Rotkin, Charlotte. *Deception in Dickens' Little Dorrit.* New York: Peter Lang, 1989.

Russell, Corinna, ed. *Charles Dickens.* London: Pickering and Chatto, 2003.

Sadoff, Dianne F. *Monsters of Affection: Dickens, Eliot, and Bronte on Fatherhood.* Baltimore, MD: Johns Hopkins UP, 1982.

Sadrin, Anny, ed. *Dickens, Europe and the New Worlds.* Basingstoke: Macmillan, 1998.

———. *Parentage and Inheritance in the Novels of Charles Dickens.* Cambridge: Cambridge UP, 1994.

Saintsbury, George. *Dickens: The Cambridge History of English and American Literature.* Ed. A.W. Ward and A.R. Waller. 13.10. New York: Putnam, 1916.

Sala, George A. *Charles Dickens: An Essay.* London: Routledge, 1870.

Salotto, Eleanor. *Gothic Returns in Collins, Dickens, Zola, and Hitchcock.* New York: Palgrave Macmillan, 2006.

Sanders, Andrew. *Charles Dickens.* Authors in Context. Oxford: Oxford UP, 2003.

———. *Charles Dickens: Resurrectionist.* London: Macmillan, 1982.

———. *Dickens and the Spirit of the Age.* Oxford: Clarendon, 1999.

Santayana, George. *Interpretations of Poetry and Religion: Hamlet; Shelley; Dickens; Tragic Philosophy.* New York: Charles Scribner, 1936.

Sawyer, Robert. *Victorian Appropriations of Shakespeare: George Eliot, A.C. Swinburne, Robert Browning, and Charles Dickens.* Madison, NJ: Fairleigh Dickinson UP, 2003.

Schad, John. *The Reader in the Dickensian Mirrors: Some New Language.* London: Macmillan, 1992. *In the Works of Frances Trollope, Charles Dickens, and Anthony Trollope.* New York: Peter Lang, 1992.

Schilling, Bernard N. *Rain of Years: Great Expectations and the World of Dickens.* Rochester, NY: U of Rochester P, 2001.

———. *The Comic Spirit: Boccaccio to Thomas Mann: Giovanni Boccaccio, Charles Dickens, Henry Fielding, Israel Zangwill, Thomas Mann.* Detroit: Wayne State UP, 1965.

Schlicke, Paul, ed. *The Oxford Reader's Companion to Dickens.* Oxford: Oxford UP, 1999.

———. *Dickens and Popular Entertainment*. London: Allen and Unwin, 1985.

Schlicke, Priscilla and Paul. *The Old Curiosity Shop: An Annotated Bibliography*. Garland Dickens Bibliographies. New York: Garland, 1988.

Scholey, Arthur. *The Dickens Christmas Carol Show*. New Orleans, LA: Anchorage, 1979.

Schor, Hilary M. *Dickens and the Daughter of the House Cambridge Studies in Nineteenth-Century Literature and Culture*. Cambridge: Cambridge UP, 1999.

———. *Dickens and the Daughter of the House*. Cambridge: Cambridge UP, 2007.

Schwarzbach, F.S. *Dickens and the City*. London: Athlone, 1979.

Scott, P.J.M. *Reality and Comic Confidence in Charles Dickens*. London: Macmillan, 1979.

Selby, J. Keith. *How to Study a Charles Dickens Novel*. London: Macmillan, 1989.

Sell, Roger D., ed. *Great Expectations, Charles Dickens*. New Casebooks. Basingstoke: Macmillan, 1994.

Shatto, Susan. *The Companion to Bleak House*. London: Unwin Hyman, 1988.

Shattock, Joanne, ed. *Dickens and Other Victorians: Essays in Honor of Philip Collins*. New York: St. Martin's, 1988.

Shelston, Alan, ed. *Dickens: Dombey and Son, and Little Dorrit: A Casebook*. Casebook Series. London: Macmillan, 1985.

Shepherd, R.H., ed. *The Speeches of Charles Dickens*. London: Chatto and Windus, 1884.

Shipton, Paul. *Charles Dickens*. Harlow: Pearson Education, 2007.

Shore, W. Teignmouth. *Charles Dickens and His Friends*. London: Cassell, 1909.

———. *Charles Dickens*. London: Cassell, 1910.

Sicher, Efraim. *Rereading the City, Rereading Dickens: Representation, the Novel, and Urban Realism.* New York: AMS, 2003.

Sidney, P. Moss and Carolyn J. Moss. *American Episodes Involving Charles Dickens.* Troy, NY: Whitston, 1999.

Simpson, David. *Fetishism and Imagination: Dickens, Melville, Conrad.* Baltimore, MD: Johns Hopkins UP, 1982.

Sitwell, Osbert. *Dickens.* London: Chatto and Windus, 1932.

Skom, Edith. *The Charles Dickens Murders: A Beth Austin Mystery.* New York: Dell, 2000.

Slater, Michael, ed. *Dickens 1970: Centenary Essays.* London: Chapman and Hall, 1970.

———. ed. *Dickens on America and the Americans.* Hassocks, Sussex: Harvester, 1978.

———. ed. *Gone Astray and Other Papers from Household Words, 1851-59.* London: J.M. Dent, 1999.

———. ed. *The Catalogue of the Suzannet Charles Dickens Collection.* London: Sotheby Parke Bernet, 1975.

———. *An Intelligent Person's Guide to Dickens.* London: Gerald Duckworth, 1999.

———. *Dickens and Women.* London: J.M. Dent, 1983.

Smith, F. Hopkinson. *In Dickens's London.* New York: Charles Scribner, 1914.

———. *With Dickens and Thackeray in London.* New York: Charles Scribner, 1915.

Smith, Graham. *Dickens, Money, and Society.* Berkeley, CA: U of California P, 1968.

Smith, Grahame, *Charles Dickens: A Literary Life.* London: Macmillan, 1995.

———. *Charles Dickens: Bleak House.* Studies in English Literature. London: Edward Arnold, 1974.

———. *Dickens and the Dream of Cinema.* Manchester: Manchester UP, 2003. Of Dickens. New York: Routledge, 2003.

Smith, Karl Ashley. *Dickens and the Unreal City: Searching for Spiritual Significance in Nineteenth-Century London.* Basingstoke: Palgrave Macmillan, 2008.

Smith, Mabell S.C. *Studies in Dickens.* New York: Chautauqua, 1910.

Smithers, David W. *Dickens's Doctors.* Oxford: Pergamon, 1979.

Snow, C.P. *The Realists: Eight Portraits: Stendhal, Balzac, Dickens, Dostoevsky, Tolstoy, Galdos, Henry James, Proust.* New York: Scribner, 1978.

Solomon, Pearl C. *Dickens and Melville in Their Time.* New York: Columbia UP, 1975.

Sorensen, Knud. *Charles Dickens: Linguistic Innovator.* Aarhus: Arkona, 1985.

Spence, Gordon. *Charles Dickens as a Familiar Essayist.* Salzburg Studies in English Literature. Salzburg: Universitat Salzburg, 1977.

Spilka, Mark. *Dickens and Kafka: A Mutual Interpretation.* Bloomington, IN: Indiana UP, 1963.

Steig, Michael. *Dickens and Phiz.* Bloomington: Indiana UP, 1978.

Stevens, James S. *Quotations and References in Charles Dickens.* Boston: Christopher, 1929.

Stewart, Garrett. *Dickens and the Trials of Imagination.* Cambridge, MA: Harvard UP, 1974.

Stoddard, Richard H., ed. *Anecdote Biographies of Thackeray and Dickens.* New York: C. Scribner, 1874.

Stoehr, Taylor. *Dickens: The Dreamer's Stance.* Ithaca, NY: Cornell UP, 1965.

Stokes, Edward. *Hawthorne's Influence on Dickens and George Eliot.* St. Lucia: U of Queensland, 1985.

Stone, Harry, ed. *Dickens's Working Notes for His Novels.* Chicago: U of Chicago P, 1987.

———. ed. *The Uncollected Writings of Charles Dickens.* London: Allen Lane, 1969.

———. *Dickens and the Invisible World.* London: Macmillan, 1980.

———. *Dickens and the Invisible World: Fairy Tales, Fantasy, and Novel-Making.* Bloomington: Indiana UP, 1979.

———. *The Night Side of Dickens: Cannibalism, Passion, Necessity.* Columbus, OH: Ohio State UP, 1994.

Stonehouse, J.H. *Green Leaves: New Chapters in the Life of Charles Dickens.* London: Piccadilly Fountain, 1930.

———. *Green Leaves: New Chapters in the Life of Charles Dickens.* 1931; New York: Haskell House, 1973.

Storey, Gladys. *Dickens and Daughter.* London: Frederick Muller, 1939.

Storey, Graham. *Charles Dickens, Bleak House.* Landmarks of World Literature. Cambridge: Cambridge UP, 1987.

Straus, Ralph. *A Portrait of Dickens.* London: J.M. Dent, 1938.

———. *Charles Dickens: A Biography from New Sources.* New York: Cosmopolitan Book, 1928.

———. *Dickens: A Portrait in Pencil.* London: Victor Gollancz, 1928.

———. *Dickens: The Man and the Book.* London: Thomas Nelson, 1936.

Suchoff, David. *Critical Theory and the Novel: Mass Society and Cultural Criticism in Dickens, Melville, and Kafka.* Madison, NJ: U of Wisconsin P, 1994.

Sucksmith, Harvey P. *The Narrative Art of Charles Dickens: The Rhetoric of Sympathy and Irony in His Novels.* Oxford: Clarendon, 1970.

Swinburne, A.C. *Charles Dickens.* London: Chatto and Windus, 1913.

Swinden, Patrick. *Unofficial Selves: Character in the Novel from Dickens to the Present Day.* London: Macmillan, 1973.

Swisher, Clarice, ed. *Readings on Charles Dickens.* San Diego, CA: Greenhaven, 1997.

Symons, Julian. *Charles Dickens.* London: Arthur Barker, 1951.

Szladits, L.L. *Charles Dickens, 1812-1870: An Anthology*. New York, 1970.

Tambling, Jeremy. *Dickens, Violence and the Modern State: Dreams of the Scaffold*. London: Macmillan, 1995.

———. *Lost in the American City: Dickens, James and Kafka*. Basingstoke: Palgrave, 2001.

Thacker, John. *Edwin Drood: Antichrist in the Cathedral*. London: Vision, 1990.

Thomas, Deborah. *Dickens and the Short Story*. Philadelphia, PA: U of Pennsylvania P, 1982.

Thomas, George. *Charles Dickens: Great Expectations*. Studies in English Literature. London: Edward Arnold, 1964.

Thomson, W.R. *In Dickens Street*. London: Chapman and Hall, 1912.

Thornton, De Sara, ed. *David Copperfield de Charles Dickens*. Paris: Ed. du Temps, 1996.

Thurley, Geoffrey. *The Dickens Myth: Its Genesis and Structure*. London: Routledge and Kegan Paul, 1976.

Tomalin, Claire. *The Invisible Woman: The Story of Nelly Ternan and Charles Dickens*. Harmondsworth: Penguin, 1990.

Tomlin, F.W.F., ed. *Charles Dickens 1812-1870: A Centennial Volume*. London: Weidenfeld and Nicolson, 1969.

Trotter, David. *Circulation: Defoe, Dickens, and the Economies of the Novel*. Basingstoke: Macmillan, 1988.

Trumble, Alfred. *In Jail with Charles Dickens*. London: Suckling and Galloway, 1896.

Van Amerongen, J.B. *The Actor in Dickens: A Study of the Histrionic and Dramatic Elements in the Novelist's Life and Works*. New York: D. Appleton, 1926.

Vlock, Deborah. *Dickens, Novel Reading, and the Victorian Popular Theatre*. Cambridge: Cambridge UP, 1998.

Vlock, Edith. *The Charles Dickens Murders*. New York: Delacorte, 1998.

Vogel, Jane. *Allegory in Dickens*. Tuscaloosa: U of Alabama P, 1977.

Wagenknecht, Edward, ed. *An Introduction to Dickens*. Chicago: Scott, 1952.

———. *Dickens and the Scandalmongers: Essays in Criticism*. Norman, OK: U of Oklahoma P, 1965.

———. *The Man Charles Dickens: A Victorian Portrait*. Boston: Houghton, 1929.

———. *The Man Charles Dickens: A Victorian Portrait*. Norman, OK: U of Oklahoma P, 1966.

Walder, Dennis. *Dickens and Religion*. London: George Allen and Unwin, 1981.

Wall, Stephen, ed. *Charles Dickens: A Critical Anthology*. Harmondsworth: Penguin, 1970.

Walters, John C. *Clues to Dickens's "Mystery of Edwin Drood"*. 1905; New York: Haskell House, 1970.

———. *Phases of Dickens: The Man, His Message and His Mission*. New York: Haskell House, 1911.

Ward, Adolphus W. *Dickens*. New York: A.L. Fowle, 1882.

Ward, Henry S. *The Real Dickens Land*. London: Chapman and Hall, 1904.

Waters, Catherine. *Dickens and the Politics of the Family*. Cambridge: Cambridge UP, 1997.

Watkins, A.H. *Charles Dickens and H.G. Wells*. H.G. Wells Society, 1976.

Watkins, Gwen. *Dickens in Search of Himself: Recurrent Themes and Characters in the Work of Charles Dickens*. London: Macmillan, 1987.

Watkins, William. *Charles Dickens*. London, 1870.

Watt, Ian. *The Victorian Novel: Modern Essays in Criticism*. London: Oxford, 1971.

Watts, Alan S. *Dickens at Gad's Hill*. Reading, Berkshire: Celdric Dickens and Elvendon, 1989.

———. *Life and Times of Charles Dickens*. London: Studio Editions, 1991.

———. *The Confessions of Charles Dickens: A Very Factual Fiction*. New York: Peter Lang, 1991.

Watts, Richard J. *The Pragmalinguistic Analysis of Narrative Texts: Narrative Co-operation in Charles Dickens's 'Hard Times'*. Tubingen: G. Narr, 1981.

Waugh, Arthur. *Charles Dickens and His Illustrators*. London, 1937.

Webb, L.K. *Charles Dickens*. London: Evergreen Lives, 1983.

Weinstein, Philip M. *The Semantics of Desire: Changing Models of Identity from Dickens to Joyce*. Princeton, NJ: Princeton UP, 1984.

Welsby, Paul A. *Rochester Cathedral in the Time of Charles Dickens*. Rochester: Brewster Printing Co., 1976.

Welsh, Alexander. *From Copyright to Copperfield: The Identity of Dickens*. Cambridge, MA: Harvard UP, 1987.

———. *The City of Dickens*. Oxford: Clarendon, 1971.

Welsh, Charles. *Character Portraits from Dickens*. London: Chatto and Windus, 1908.

Westburg, Barry. *The Confessional Fictions of Charles Dickens*. Dekalb: Northern Illinois UP, 1977.

Wethered, H.N. and Charles Turley. *Dickens All the Year Round: A Dickens Anthology*. London: Seeley Service, 1933.

Whipple, Edwin P. *Charles Dickens: The Man and His Work*. Boston: Houghton Mifflin, 1912.

Wiggin, K.D. *A Child's Journey with Charles Dickens*. London, 1912.

Wilkins, William G. *Charles Dickens in America*. 1911; New York: Haskell House, 1970.

Williams, Emlyn. *Readings from Dickens*. London: Heinemann, 1954.

Williams, Mary. *The Dickens Concordance: Being a Compendium of Names and Characters and Principal Places Mentioned in all the Works of Charles Dickens*. London: F. Griffiths, 1907.

Williams, Raymond. *The English Novel: From Dickens to Lawrence*. Oxford: Oxford UP, 1970.

Wilson, Edmund. "Dickens: The Two Scrooges." *The Wound and the Bow*. London: W.H. Allen, 1941.

Wing, George. *Charles Dickens*. Edinburgh: Oliver and Boyd, 1969.

Wolfreys, Julian. *The Trace of the Urban Text from Blake to Dickens*. New York: St. Martin's, 1998.

Woollcott, Alexander. *Mr. Dickens Goes to the Play*. New York: G.P. Putnam's, 1922.

Worth, George J. *Dickensian Melodrama: A Reading of the Novels*. Lawrence: U of Kansas P, 1978.

Wright, Thomas. *The Life of Charles Dickens*. London: Herbert Jenkins, 1935.

Yamamoto, Tadao. *Growth and System in the Language of Dickens*. 1950; Hiroshima: Seisuisha, 2003.

Yancey, Diane. *Life in Charles Dickens's England*. San Diego, CA: Lucent, 1999.

Yoon, Hye-Joon. *Physiognomy of Capital in Charles Dickens: An Essay in Dialectical Criticism*. San Francisco: Intl. Scholars, 1998.

Zambrano, A.L. *Dickens and Film*. New York, 1977.

Zarifopol-Johnston, Ilinca. *To Kill a Text: The Dialogic Fiction of Hugo, Dickens, and Zola*. London: Associated P, 1995.

Zweig, Stefan. *Three Masters: Balzac, Dickens, Dostoevsky*. Trans. Eden and Cedar Paul. London: G. Allen and Unwin, 1930.

Index

E

F

G

H

I

J

K

L

M